Religion, Education and Adolescence

Religion, Education and Culture

Series Editors:
William K. Kay (University of Wales, Bangor, UK), Leslie
J. Francis (University of Wales, Bangor, UK) and Jeff Astley
(University of Durham, UK)

This series addresses issues raised by religion and education within contemporary culture. It is intended to be of benefit to those involved in professional training as ministers of religion, teachers, counsellors, psychologists, social workers and health professionals while also contributing to the theoretical development of the academic fields from which this training is drawn.

Religion, Education and Adolescence

International Empirical Perspectives

Edited by

LESLIE J. FRANCIS, MANDY ROBBINS and JEFF ASTLEY

on behalf of The International Seminar on
Religious Education and Values (ISREV)

UNIVERSITY OF WALES PRESS
CARDIFF
2005

British Library Cataloguing-in-Publication Data
A catalogue record for this book is available from the British Library.

ISBN 0-7083-1957-2

The editors and publishers wish to acknowledge the financial assistance received from the Welsh National Centre for Religious Education.

Printed in Great Britain by Cambridge Printing, Cambridge

Contents

The contributors

The Revd Professor Jeff Astley is Director of the North of England Institute for Christian Education and Honorary Professional Fellow in Practical Theology and Christian Education, University of Durham, England.

Dr Erling Birkedal is Director of the Institute for Church Education, Oslo, Norway.

Dr Judith Everington is Senior Lecturer in Religious Education in the Institute of Education, University of Warwick, England.

The Revd Professor Leslie J. Francis is Director of the Welsh National Centre for Religious Education and Professor of Practical Theology, University of Wales, Bangor, Wales.

Anna Halsall is Research Officer for the St Christopher's Educational Trust Project at the Welsh National Centre for Religious Education, University of Wales, Bangor, Wales.

Professor John M. Hull is Emeritus Professor of Religious Education, University of Birmingham, England.

The Revd Dr William K. Kay is Senior Lecturer in Religious and Theological Education, King's College, London, England.

Dr David W. Lankshear is Deputy Director of the National Society of the Church of England.

Professor Avraham Leslau is at the School of Education, Bar-Ilan University, Israel.

Professor Yisrael Rich is at the School of Education, Bar-Ilan University, Israel.

Dr Mandy Robbins is Teaching and Research Fellow, Centre for Ministry Studies, University of Wales, Bangor, Wales.

Dr Abdullah Sahin is Lecturer in Islamic Education in the School of Education, University of Birmingham, England.

Professor Heinz Streib is Professor for Religious Education and Ecumenical Theology, University of Bielefeld, Germany.

Professor Hans-Georg Ziebertz is Professor in Practical Theology, University of Würzburg, Germany.

Preface

Since its inception in 1978, the International Seminar on Religious Education and Values has become the key meeting-place for many researchers in religious education across the world. The seminar which met in Norway in 2002 took as its theme religion, education and adolescence. We are pleased in this book to be able to make some of the formative contributions to the seminar available to a wider audience.

In preparing this manuscript for publication, we are grateful to the individual authors for developing these papers and for working with us to produce a coherence of presentation and style, and to our colleagues, Diane Drayson and Susan Thomas, who have worked with us on the text.

This volume also represents the well-established collaboration that exists between the Welsh National Centre for Religious Education and the North of England Institute for Christian Education, two Church-related foundations committed to research and development in religious education in schools and churches.

Leslie J. Francis
Mandy Robbins
Jeff Astley

Foreword

JOHN M. HULL

It is significant that as religion becomes an increasingly important issue in the modern world, both for good and ill, more and more nations are introducing religious education into their school systems. Religion has never been more controversial, more dangerous or more promising as a source of values, and education into and concerning this vital area has never been more relevant. Academic research occupies a vital place in this enterprise, providing constantly renewed sources of information about how young people perceive spirituality and faith, and developing both theoretical and practical strategies for teaching and learning. The International Seminar on Religious Education and Values (ISREV) was established nearly thirty years ago to pioneer the development and dissemination of such research. Those who wish to find out more about ISREV and its work may consult the website (http://www.isrev.org).

Although individual members of ISREV have been publishing their presentations to sessions of the seminar since its first meeting in the University of Birmingham in 1978, it is only since 1998 that collections of these studies have been presented to the public in the form of full-length books. The first such volume arose from the meeting of the seminar that took place in Trinity College, Camarthen, Wales in 1998. This is entitled *The Fourth R for the Third Millennium: Education in Religion and Values for the Global Future* (Dublin, Lindisfarne Books, 2001) and is edited by Leslie J. Francis, Jeff Astley and Mandy Robbins. At the session that took place in Israel in 2000, a book in memory of the late Motti Bar Lev was presented to his widow and family under the title *Joining and Leaving Religion: Research Perspectives* (Leominster, Gracewing Books, 2000), edited by Leslie J. Francis and Yaacov Katz.

It is a pleasure to welcome the third ISREV volume, and the seminar owes a great deal to the energy and vision of Professor Francis, who is not only the Publications Officer of the seminar, but also the chair of its Academic Subcommittee. I recommend this new volume of studies not only to teachers and researchers in religion and religious education, but also to those who believe that the future of our world lies to some extent within the values and commitments of the present generation of adolescents.

John M. Hull
General Secretary
International Seminar on Religious Education and Values

Introduction

LESLIE J. FRANCIS

Religion in the twenty-first century

The confidence with which an apparently secularized western world could dismiss the continuing significance and power of religion has already been challenged, time and time again, through the first years of the twenty-first century. On an international stage the confident assumption that religion had become so thoroughly privatized as to be of no public significance was exploded by the dramatic events of 11 September 2001 (Gill, 2002).

Nearer to home, in the United Kingdom, serious attention is once again being given at the beginning of the twenty-first century to the power of religion both to unite and to divide, both to strengthen and to weaken society. For the first time the Parliament in Westminster determined that the 2001 census for England and Wales should include a question on religious identity. In Edinburgh the Scottish Parliament was even more convinced of the need for information about religious identity and drafted a more exacting census question. Far from dismissing religion as an irrelevancy or, at most, as a matter of personal idiosyncrasy, politicians are beginning to recognize religion as a matter of considerable social significance and as a concern of proper public enquiry. Religion is seen to have implications for the delivery of effective health care, for the structuring of appropriate educational systems, for the anticipation of social coherence and of social disruption, for the understanding of disadvantage, discrimination and social exclusion. Religion is for real.

If religion remains for real in the twenty-first century, then the task of religious education needs to be taken seriously as well. In a world where religion remains powerful, but not properly understood, there are at least three major reasons why religious educators need to reflect deeply about their task, and why religious education needs to be properly promoted and resourced within the educational system.

The first reason concerns the self-evident need for every educated citizen, living within a global, multicultural and multi-faith society, to be well informed about the beliefs and practices of different religious traditions. Here education holds a major key to breaking down prejudices which keep groups apart, misunderstanding, mistrust and exclusion. In a multi-faith society religious diversity cannot be ignored in the school and in the workplace. Religious diversity affects the supermarket and the factory as much as it does the hospital and the social services. Educated citizens need to be informed about such matters.

The second reason concerns the need for young people who are themselves growing up within a faith community to be able to reflect rationally on their faith and to perceive their faith as appreciated and valued within the school. Faith which is not discussed within the bounds of mutual respect and trust becomes separated from the main core of secular life, compartmentalized and detached. It is faith of this nature which becomes irrational and potentially dangerous to society. Educated citizens need to feel secure in their own faith.

The third reason concerns the persistent attraction of religious and spiritual systems to young people themselves. The barren futility of consumerism, the limited vision of materialism, and the purposelessness and meaninglessness of secularism leave young people tempted to explore ancient and esoteric systems which promise that there is more to life (Drane, 1999). For those uneducated about matters of religion it is impossible to make a rational choice between what constitutes healthy spirituality and what constitutes unhealthy spirituality. Few in today's society would argue that attraction to a form of vampirism which leads to ritual murder is a healthy form of spirituality, and yet high-profile cases in western Europe indicate the power of such belief systems to influence young adherents. Educated citizens need to make informed choices regarding their own spiritual quest.

Listening to adolescents

It is the contention of the present collection of essays that an informed approach to religious education needs to be grounded, not only in a deep understanding of religious traditions, but also in an informed appreciation of the ways in which these traditions are currently seen by young people themselves and of the ways in which these traditions continue to impact the lives of young people in the contemporary world. Here is a proper task for empirical enquiry.

In different cultural contexts today, religious education is located either in practical theology or in educational studies. Both disciplines have access to appropriate empirical techniques to illuminate the fundamental questions regarding the religious perceptions of the young. The present volume brings together original empirical studies conducted within both the domain of empirical theology and the domain of educational research. In their turn, both empirical theology and educational research draw on the empirical techniques refined in the social sciences, including anthropology, psychology and sociology.

Since its inception in 1978, the International Seminar on Religious Education and Values (ISREV) has convened every other year in order to bring together leading religious educationalists from across the world. Each meeting of the seminar has included some invaluable empirical input from the perspectives of empirical theology and educational research. The seminar convened in Norway in 2002 included a greater emphasis than usual on such empirical enquiry. The theme of the seminar on 'Religion, Education and Adolescence' clearly demanded listening to young people themselves. In *Religion, Education and Adolescence: International Empirical Perspectives*, the editors have invited twelve of the contributors to the seminar to re-craft their presentations and to integrate them into a connected and coherent volume. Together these essays provide the most recent and most securely grounded insights into adolescents' views of religion in the United Kingdom, in Europe and in Israel. The book is divided into two parts.

Religion and values survey

The first part of *Religion, Education and Adolescence: International and Empirical Perspectives* presents six chapters which all draw on the Religion and Values Today database, a unique source of information compiled on a sample of nearly 34,000 young people between the ages of 13 and 15, recruited from throughout England and Wales. This database was first described by Francis (2001) in a book entitled *The Values Debate: A Voice from the Pupils*. Subsequently the data have been available to help test a wide range of focused questions.

In chapter 1 Leslie J. Francis recognizes that prayer is at the heart of religion and spirituality, and raises key questions about the significance of prayer in the lives of young people. He argues that there is a growing body of empirical evidence to suggest that personal prayer is associated with positive psychological correlates among those who pray. Then he employs the Religion and Values Today database to test that thesis against one specific psychological construct (purpose in life) among two very different groups of adolescents within the database. The first group comprises 7,083 males and 5,634 females who never attend church. The second group comprises 1,738 males and 2,006 females who attend church nearly every week. In this way it is possible to separate out the respective influences of church attendance and of prayer. The data demonstrate a significant positive relationship between frequency of personal prayer and perceived purpose in life, among both the churchgoers and the non-churchgoers. This finding suggests that personal prayer is associated with positive psychological benefits for young people growing up outside the churches as well as within the churches. Here is evidence that some forms of religious practice may be good for young people.

In chapter 2 Jeff Astley recognizes that the debate between science and religion has often polarized religious opinion and has become an increasingly significant factor in the politics of education in a number of countries. Then he employs the Religion and Values Today database to examine the interface between science and religion within adolescents' attitudes and values. He develops four reliable indices from the data, which are described as measures of personal dissatisfaction, moral values, religious values and credulity. He employs these four measures to provide an account of the psychological correlates of belief in creationism among this age group. The data demonstrate that overall belief in creationism is associated with more conservative moral values and with more traditional religious values. Neither of these findings comes as a great surprise. They simply confirm that young creationists espouse a somewhat different world-view from that of their peers. The data also demonstrate that belief in creationism is associated with higher levels of personal dissatisfaction and with higher levels of credulity. Now these findings may be both more interesting and more disturbing, since they suggest that young creationists may enjoy a lower level of psychological health, in comparison with their peers. Here is evidence to suggest that some forms of religious belief may not be so good for young people.

In chapter 3 David W. Lankshear recognizes the educational and political controversy generated by 'faith schools' and identifies the lack of empirical knowledge about the influence of these schools on their pupils. Then he employs the Religion and Values Today database to examine the influence of Anglican secondary schools on adolescents' personal, moral and religious values. He develops three reliable indices from the data, which are described as measures of personal dissatisfaction, moral values and religious values. He employs these three measures to compare the values of 957 pupils attending Anglican voluntary aided schools with the values of 24,027 pupils attending non-denominational schools within the state-maintained sector. The ratio between the two samples reflects the comparative strengths of the two systems of schools. In this analysis further comparisons are made between boys and girls and between three religious groups: non-affiliates, Anglicans and those affiliated with other Christian denominations. The data demonstrate that Anglicans attending Anglican schools recorded higher levels of religious values, comparable levels of moral values and higher levels of personal dissatisfaction, in comparison with Anglicans attending non-denominational schools. Non-affiliates attending Anglican schools recorded higher levels of personal dissatisfaction, lower levels of moral values and comparable levels of religious values, in comparison with non-affiliates attending non-denominational schools. Here is evidence to suggest that attending a church school does have a measurable influence on pupil values, but that this influence may not always be in the direction that the churches would hope for it to be.

In chapter 4 Anna Halsall raises questions about the significance of denominational identity for young people, and in particular about nominalism among those who claim to belong but do not practise. Then she employs the Religion and Values Today database to profile the world-view of young Anglicans in comparison with that of non-affiliates. In this sample 46% of the young people identified themselves as having no religious affiliation and 32% identified themselves as Anglicans. The analysis forms part of the continuing debate concerning the potential importance of self-assigned religious affiliation as a socially significant indicator. She tests this thesis against six value areas included in the database, using individual value items rather than cumulative scale scores. The value areas are defined as religious beliefs, worries, school, law and order, substance use, and societal and world concerns. Two main conclusions emerge from the analyses. First, the data confirm that young Anglicans project a distinctive values profile and a distinctive identity, when compared with young people who profess no religious affiliation. Here is further evidence that the kind of basic information collected by the census (concerning religious affiliation, rather than practice or belief) provides information of social significance. Second, when the data are interpreted in the light of gender-orientation theory, the value profile associated with Anglican affiliation, among both young males and young females, emerges as distinctively feminine. This finding is consistent with the view that the Anglican Church has become a highly feminized environment, much more attractive to men and women who espouse a feminine values system. This finding also helps to explain why so many young men fail to feel at home in the Anglican Church today.

In chapter 5 Mandy Robbins addresses the current concern about the levels of smoking among young people, especially among girls, in spite of the efforts of health education campaigns. Then she employs the Religion and Values Today database to examine the relationship between religiosity and smoking among female adolescents. The analysis is undertaken against the reported growth of smoking among young women and the concerns of health educators to identify the psychosocial predictors of such behaviour. Although from a theoretical perspective religiosity is likely to affect a range of health-related issues, research into the predictors of smoking has tended to overlook the potential significance of individual differences in religiosity. In this analysis, Robbins constructs a regression model to take into account the influence of a range of factors before examining the impact of religiosity on attitude toward smoking. The data demonstrate that, even after controlling for age, social class, personality and parental marital status, religiosity is a significant predictor of a more negative attitude toward smoking. Among the three indices of religiosity employed in the model (belief in God, personal prayer and church attendance), it is belief in God which is the strongest inhibitor against smoking. Here is evidence to suggest that belief in God may in fact help to promote a more healthy lifestyle among young people.

In chapter 6 William K. Kay builds on the contemporary interest in spirituality and the growing willingness to take religious experience seriously. He then employs the Religion and Values Today database, first to examine the incidence of religious experience among adolescents and then to explore the implications of religious experience for individual differences in attitude toward religious education, toward religious assemblies held in school, toward social morality, toward sexual morality and toward discussion of problems with parents. The analysis is undertaken by dividing the sample into four groups, according to their religious affiliation and their reporting of religious experience. In this way it is possible to compare the profiles of adolescents who have had no religious experience and have no religious affiliation, those who have had no religious experience but have religious affiliation, those who have had religious experience but have no religious affiliation, and those who have had religious experience and have religious affiliation. The data demonstrate that religious experience is linked with social morality and with sexual morality, as well as with greater acceptance of religious education and religious assemblies in schools. These findings are discussed from the perspectives of psychology, pedagogy and spirituality. Here is evidence to suggest that religious experience has social and personal implications, even for young people who do not consider themselves to have any religious affiliation.

Quantitative and qualitative perspectives

The second part of *Religion, Education and Adolescence: International and Empirical Perspectives* presents six chapters which illustrate significant empirical research traditions concerned with investigating religion during adolescence in Europe and in Israel. These chapters open up the world-views of adolescents and illustrate the impact of religious education programmes on them. Such studies are of considerable significance for politicians, educationalists, teachers and leaders of faith communities.

In chapter 7 Heinz Streib provides fascinating insights into the religious world-views of adolescents growing up in Germany after the unification between East and West. Drawing on quantitative data from the Shell youth surveys conducted in Germany (see Fischer, 1997), Streib argues that religiosity among German adolescents has more stability and continuity than has been deduced from the decline of church membership and church participation. German adolescents, he argues, have not turned away from religion but have transformed the way in which their religiosity is expressed. Religion has become a matter of individual practice and preference. Because of its retreat from the public sphere, the religion of adolescents has become more invisible. Nonetheless, religious orientation, belief and practice continue to be a dimension of some importance in adolescents' lives and self-understanding. Drawing on both quantitative and qualitative data, Streib then identifies the notion of 'spiritual quest' as key to understanding the changing nature of adolescents' religiosity. Here is evidence to suggest that Europe is far from heading for a thoroughly secular future.

In chapter 8 Abdullah Sahin explores the religious life-world of Muslim young people in Britain, by investigating the construction of religious identity and attitudes toward Islam among Muslim adolescents attending three sixth-form colleges in Birmingham. The research employs two complementary research techniques. First, a quantitative questionnaire study was conducted among 383 students in order to measure frequency of religious practice, level of attitude toward Islam and the way in which adolescents conceptualized their own religious perspective, in relation to the religious perspective of their parents. The data demonstrate that the majority of Muslim young people did not pray regularly, but retained a generally very positive attitude toward Islam. Just over half (54%) of Muslim young people took the view that their understanding of Islam was the same as that of their parents. Second, a qualitative interview study was conducted among 15 randomly selected students, using the *Modes of Muslim Subjectivity Interview Schedule*. The analysis identified a fourfold typology of religious subjectivity, in which the four modes are characterized as 'foreclosed commitment', 'achieved commitment', 'diffused commitment' and 'moratorium non-commitment'. Each of these modes is richly illustrated from the interview data. Here is evidence to illuminate the changing identity of the Islamic community in Britain.

In chapter 9 Yisrael Rich and Avraham Leslau report on an important component of a comprehensive study of the religious and educational world-views of students completing their last year of study in public religious Israeli high schools. Two relatively large cohorts of students completed a questionnaire survey. The first cohort comprised students who graduated from high school in 1990 (see Leslau and Bar-Lev, 1993) and the second cohort comprised students who graduated from high school in 1999. Similarity of sampling procedures and in the contents of the questionnaires to which the students responded facilitated comparison of the two cohorts, generating valuable insights into the changes occurring among these young people in some key aspects of their religious behaviour and beliefs over the last decade of the twentieth century. This was an especially tumultuous period in Israel's political, religious and cultural life and had the potential to spawn significant change in the religious behaviour and beliefs of young people. The data demonstrated relatively little overall change in the state of religious practice and belief of students in public religious Israeli high schools from 1990 to 1999. At the same time, however, this overall picture disguised some significant movements toward greater religiosity among certain groups of Israeli adolescents and toward lesser religiosity among other groups of Israeli adolescents. Here is evidence to support the real value of careful and systematic replication of research concerning adolescent religiosity at regular intervals in order to highlight changing patterns of beliefs, practices and attitudes.

In chapter 10 Hans-Georg Ziebertz explores the ways in which adolescents in Germany understand and how they feel about religious education. In his conceptual analysis Ziebertz distinguishes between three different understandings of religious education, which he characterizes as 'mono-religious', 'multi-religious' and 'inter-religious'. The objective of the mono-religious model is to discern religious truth. The objective of the multi-religious model is to compare different religious traditions. The objective of the inter-religious model is the pursuit of mutual understanding, tolerance, respect and appropriate self-criticism. In his empirical analysis Ziebertz examined the views of around 3,000 pupils regarding these three models. The data demonstrate that, overall, pupils judge the mono-religious model negatively, and that they value the multi-religious model more highly than the inter-religious model. Ziebertz concludes that the 'zoo perspective' of the multi-religion model appears to be more attractive to adolescents. In the religious zoo adolescents may look around and marvel, but in that zoo they experience no need to commit themselves to any particular religious perspective. Here is evidence to support the value of listening to the pupils' understanding and expectation of religious education. While students may not themselves be setting the agenda in the religious education classroom, their sympathy for and cooperation with that agenda are crucial factors in effective learning.

In chapter 11 Erling Birkedal describes an empirical study conducted among 13-year-olds in the central eastern part of Norway. The study employs both quantitative and qualitative methods. The quantitative survey demonstrates a low level of conventional religious practice. Over half (55%) never attend church, 41% attend sometimes and only 4% often attend church. Regarding personal religious practice, 53% never say evening prayer, 12% seldom say evening prayer, 23% sometimes say evening prayer and 7% often say evening prayer. At the same time, however, the quantitative study clearly shows that faith in God among the 13-year-olds is much more than a conventional faith maintained by the church. In this analysis of the adolescents three forms of faith are identified. First, there is conventional faith (a faith in accordance with what the church teaches). Second, there is enquiring faith (critical, but related to conventional faith). Third, there is movement away from conventional faith (which may also mean an alternative kind of faith). The qualitative study, based on thirty in-depth interviews, provides illuminating case-histories which illustrate each of these three forms of faith. Here is further evidence to support the view that adolescent faith is not disappearing throughout Europe so much as changing in its form and expression.

In chapter 12 Judith Everington draws on data from a life-history study conducted among four cohorts of trainee secondary religious education teachers undergoing a one-year postgraduate initial teacher-education course. The study, begun in 1997, followed the trainees through the course into their first year in a teaching post. Everington identifies five key themes, running through the life-history studies, which appear to be common to all four cohorts. These themes are described as: ideals and aspirations, difficulties and dilemmas, negative perceptions of and attitudes toward religion, pupils' views that minority ethnic communities 'have nothing to do with them' and pupils' views that minority ethnic communities are a threat to 'British people'. Each of these themes is illustrated by the voices of the trainee teachers. Here is evidence from religious educators themselves concerning what they perceive to be going on in the classroom and in the world-view of their pupils. Such data may be crucial to shaping an approach to religious education relevant to pupils in the twenty-first century.

Conclusion

Eight key conclusions emerge from this focused collection of contributions:

- Europe and Israel are not heading toward rapid secularization in the way that some have predicted.
- Religion remains a significant factor in the lives of young Europeans at the beginning of the twenty-first century.
- Religion retains the power to shape young lives – for better or for worse – and for this reason is properly a matter for public interest and scrutiny.
- Young people across Europe are involved in a process of redefining their religious traditions for themselves.
- The way in which young people express their spirituality and their religiosity is changing and becoming less visible to the public gaze, but no less real.
- Today young people's concern with religion is often focused more on personal quest than on an allegiance to religious institutions.
- The task of the religious educator is enriched and enabled by the discipline of empirical enquiry which listens to young people themselves.
- The churches need to listen to young people engaged in their own spiritual and religious quest.

The International Seminar on Religious Education and Values will continue to act as an advocate for such enquiry. The Seminar will also continue to enhance the quality of research in religious education by bringing together leading researchers from a range of countries and by providing opportunities for them to exchange insights and to benefit from peer review and critique.

References

Drane, J. (1999), *What the New Age is Still Saying to the Church* (Grand Rapids, Mich., Zondervan).

Fischer, A. (1997), *Jugend '97. Zukunftsperspektiven, Gesellschaftliches Engagement, Politische Orientierungen, Shell Jugendstudie, 12* (Opladen, Leske and Budrich).

Francis, L. J. (2001), *The Values Debate: A Voice from the Pupils* (London, Woburn Press).

Gill, R. (2002), *Changing Worlds: Can the Church Respond?* (Edinburgh, T. and T. Clark).

Leslau, A. and Bar-Lev, M. (1993), *The Religious World of Graduates of Public Religious Education* (Ramat Gan, Bar Ilan University, Israel Sociological Institute for the Study of Communities) (in Hebrew).

I

Religion and Values Survey

1

Prayer, personality and purpose in life among churchgoing and non-churchgoing adolescents

LESLIE J. FRANCIS

Summary

There is growing empirical evidence that personal prayer is associated with positive psychological correlates among those who pray. In this chapter the relationship between personal prayer and one specific positive psychological construct (purpose in life) is explored among two samples of 13- to 15-year-olds. The first sample comprises 7,083 males and 5,634 females who never attend church. The second sample comprises 1,738 males and 2,006 females who attend church nearly every week. The data demonstrate a significant positive relationship between frequency of personal prayer and perceived purpose in life among both the churchgoers and the non-churchgoers. This finding suggests that personal prayer is correlated with positive psychological benefits for young people growing up outside the churches as well as within the churches.

Introduction

Historical roots

Interest in the empirically established correlates of prayer can be traced back at least to the pioneering statistical enquiries of Sir Francis Galton (1869, 1872, 1883). Writing in the *Fortnightly Review*, Galton (1872: 125) stated his case clearly, if somewhat crudely, as follows:

> The efficacy of prayer seems to me a simple, as it is a perfectly appropriate and legitimate subject of scientific enquiry. Whether prayer is efficacious or not, in any given sense, is a matter of fact on which each

man must form an opinion for himself. His decision will be based upon data more or less justly handled, according to his educational habits. An unscientific reasoner will be guided by a confused recollection of crude experience. A scientific reasoner will scrutinise each separate experience before he admits it as evidence, and will compare all the cases he has selected on a methodological system.

In his initial attempts to subject such a broad question to statistical investigation, Galton made two particularly important contributions to the debate. First, he proposed the index of longevity as a readily available and objective indicator of the efficacy of prayer. Second, he distinguished between analyses of the objective effects of prayer (the longevity of those for whom others pray) and analyses of the subjective effects of prayer (the longevity of those who pray for themselves).

As a test for the objective benefits of prayer, Galton (1872) selected royalty. He observed that the formal state prayers offered throughout the Church of England made the petition on behalf of the Queen 'Grant her in health long to live'. He then argued that 'the public prayer for the sovereign of every state, Protestant and Catholic, is and has been in the spirit of our own'. Surely, he reasoned, if petitionary prayer is effective, then royalty should live longer than comparable groups.

To test this question empirically, Galton examined the mean age attained by males of various classes who had survived their thirtieth year, from 1758 to 1843, excluding deaths by accident or violence. The data comprised 1,632 gentry, 1,179 English aristocracy, 945 clergy, 569 officers of the army, 513 men in trade and commerce, 395 men in English literature and science, 366 officers of the royal navy, 294 lawyers, 244 men in medical professions, 239 men in fine arts and 97 members of royal houses. The highest mean age was among the gentry, 70.22 years. The lowest mean age was among members of royal houses, 64.04 years. Galton concluded as follows:

> The sovereigns are literally the shortest lived of all who have the advantage of influence. The prayer has, therefore, no efficacy, unless the very questionable hypothesis be raised, that the conditions of royal life may naturally be yet more fatal, and that their influence is partly, though incompletely, neutralised by the effects of public prayers.

As a test for the subjective benefits of prayer, Galton (1872) selected the clergy. In his first enquiry Galton found that a sample of 945 clergy had a mean life value of 69.49 years, compared with a mean life value of 68.14 years among a sample of 294 lawyers and 67.31 years among a sample of 244 medical men. He argued that: 'we are justified in considering the clergy to be a far more prayerful class than either of the other two. It is their profession to pray.'

While on the face of it these statistics suggest at least a positive correlation between prayer and higher life-expectancy, Galton rejected the conclusion that such data provide evidence for the efficacy of prayer, on two grounds. First, he argued that the comparative longevity of the clergy might be more readily accounted for by their 'easy country life and family repose'. Second, he found that the difference in longevity between the professional groups was reversed when the comparison was made between *distinguished* members of the three classes, that is, persons who had their lives recorded in a biographical dictionary. According to this category, the average length of life among clergy, lawyers and medical men was 66.42, 66.51 and 67.04 years respectively, the clergy being the shortest lived of the three professional groups. On the basis of this finding Galton concluded as follows: 'Hence the prayers of the clergy for protection against the perils and dangers of the night, for protection during the day, and for recovery from sickness, appear to be futile in result.' In a second attempt to assess the influence of a prayerful life on the constitution of the clergy, Galton (1869) reviewed the lives of 192 divines recorded in Middleton's *Biographia Evangelica* of 1786. The four volumes of this work set out to provide 'an historical account of the lives and deaths of the most eminent and evangelical authors or preachers, both British and foreign'. They included figures like John Calvin, John Donne, Martin Luther and John Wyclif. On the basis of these biographies Galton concluded that divines are not founders of notably influential families, whether on the basis of wealth, social position or abilities; that they tend to have fewer children than average; that they are less long-lived than other eminent men; and that they tend to have poor constitutions.

Objective correlates of prayer

Considerable progress has been made in statistical enquiries regarding the objective efficacy of prayer since Galton's pioneering work. Some particularly impressive good quality medical-style studies have been reported, for example on the objective correlates of prayer in the context of coronary care. Byrd (1988) reported in the *Southern Medical Journal* a study conducted over a ten-month period, during which 393 patients admitted to the coronary care unit at San Francisco General Hospital were randomized to an intercessory prayer group or to a control group. The patients, staff, doctors and Byrd himself were all unaware which patients had been targeted for prayer. The prayer treatment was supplied by 'born again' Christians who prayed outside the hospital. Each interviewer was asked to pray daily for rapid recovery and for prevention of complications and death, in addition to other areas of prayer they believed to be beneficial to the named patients. At entry to the coronary care unit there was no significant statistical difference between the two groups. After admission, however, the intercessory prayer group had a statistically significant lower severity score than the control group.

Byrd's pioneering study was developed and extended by Harris, Gowda, Kolb, Strychacz, Vacek, Jones, Forker, O'Keefe and McCallister (1999), as reported in the *Archives of Internal Medicine*. Over a period of nearly a year 1,013 patients admitted to the coronary care unit at the Mid American Heart Institute, Kansas City, were randomized at the time of admission to receive remote intercessory prayer (prayer group) or not (usual care group). The first names of the patients in the prayer group were given to a team of outside intercessors, who prayed for them daily for four weeks. Patients were unaware that they were being prayed for, and the intercessors did not know and never met the patients. In this study the medical course, from the time of admission to hospital to the time of discharge from hospital, was summarized in a 'coronary care unit course score', derived from blinded, retrospective chart review. The data demonstrated that, compared with the usual care group, the prayer group experienced a statistically significant better outcome.

Subjective correlates of prayer

Concern with the subjective correlates of prayer stood at the heart of the emerging discipline of the psychology of religion at the beginning of the twentieth century. For example, William James (1902), in his classic study, *The Varieties of Religious Experience*, claimed that prayer 'is the very soul and essence of religion'. Then, in his work, *The Psychology of Religion*, Coe (1916) wrote that 'a history and psychology of prayer would be almost equivalent to a history and psychology of religion'. The case was put even more strongly by Hodge (1931), in his study, *Prayer and its Psychology*, that 'prayer is the centre and soul of all religion, and upon the question of its validity depends the trustworthiness of religious experience in general'. Then, for some reason or another, psychologists largely lost interest in religion in general and in prayer in particular. In their review of the field in the mid-1980s, Finney and Malony (1985: 104) concluded as follows: 'Nowhere is the long-standing breach between psychology and religion more evident than in the lack of research on prayer. Only a few studies of prayer exist in spite of the fact that prayer is of central religious importance.' Similar points were made during the following decade in reviews by Hood, Morris and Watson (1987, 1989), by Poloma and Pendleton (1989), by Janssen, de Hart and den Draak (1989) and by McCullough (1995). Renewed interest in the field from the early 1990s has been signalled, for example by Brown's *The Human Side of Prayer: The Psychology of Praying* (1994) and by Francis and Astley's *Psychological Perspectives on Prayer: A Reader* (2001).

Two strands of research in the United Kingdom began in the 1990s to explore the psychological correlates of prayer during childhood and adolescence. The first strand focused on the relationship between personal prayer and school-related attitudes. An initial study by Francis (1992) drew attention to the somewhat surprising finding that frequency of personal prayer was a significant predictor of school-related attitudes among a sample of 3,762 11-year-old pupils in England. The pupils completed six semantic differential scales of attitudes toward school and toward lessons in English, music, mathematics, sports and religious education. After controlling for the potential influences of sex and social class, frequency of personal prayer was a significant predictor of a more positive attitude toward school and toward lessons in English, music, mathematics and religious education, but not in sports.

A replication of this original study was reported by Montgomery and Francis (1996) among a sample of 392 11- to 16-year-old girls attending a state-maintained single-sex Catholic secondary school in England. The pupils completed the same set of six semantic differential scales. After controlling for the potential influence of age and social class, frequency of personal prayer was a significant predictor of a more positive attitude toward school and toward lessons in music, religion and English, but not in mathematics and sports.

The second, more significant, strand focused on the relationship between personal prayer and purpose in life. Purpose in life is a particularly rich concept, explored both by theology (Tillich, 1952) and by psychology (Frankl, 1978). Purpose in life is understood to be central to the meaning-making process, which counters meaninglessness. As such, purpose in life is a central component of psychological well-being. It is purpose in life which makes living worthwhile and which stands between despair and suicide. Moreover, it is precisely to this construct that religious traditions speak. Substantive analyses of religion point to the beliefs, teaching and rituals which explicitly address the fundamental questions concerning the meaning and purpose of life. Functional analyses of religion point to the meaning-making process as central to the *raison d'être* of religious and para-religious systems. There are clear grounds, therefore, for hypothesizing a positive relationship between religiosity and purpose in life.

In an initial study, Francis and Burton (1994) explored the relationship between personal prayer and perceived purpose in life among a sample of 674 12- to 16-year-olds attending a Catholic school and identifying themselves as members of the Catholic Church. Two main conclusions emerged from these data. First, the data demonstrated a significant positive relationship between frequency of personal prayer and perceived purpose in life, even after controlling for individual differences in frequency of church attendance. Second, personal prayer was shown to be a stronger predictor of perceived purpose in life than church attendance.

Building on this initial study, Francis and Evans (1996) strengthened the research design in two ways. They obtained a larger sample of pupils from across a wider range of schools. Then they ensured that church attendance was not a contaminating variable, in explaining the correlation between prayer and purpose in life, by conducting their analyses on two discrete subsets of their data. One subset comprised 914 males and 726 females who *never* attended church. The other subset comprised 232 males and 437 females who attended church in *most weeks*. The data demonstrated a significant positive relationship between frequency of personal prayer and perceived purpose in life, both among those pupils who attended church in most weeks and among those pupils who never attended church.

These simple and basic findings are consistent with the following psychological theory, which links prayer with purpose in life. The theory suggests that young people who pray are, consciously or unconsciously, acknowledging and relating to a transcendence beyond themselves. Acknowledging such a transcendence and relating to that transcendence through prayer places the whole of life into a wider context of meaning and purpose. The significance of the findings of the two studies by Francis and Burton (1994) and Francis and Evans (1996) for understanding the beneficial nature of prayer in the lives of adolescence is such that these studies deserve further replication and extension.

Against this background, the present study builds on the work of Francis and Burton (1994) and Francis and Evans (1996) by addressing two of the criticisms to which the earlier studies remain vulnerable. The first criticism concerns the unrepresentative nature of the samples used. Francis and Burton (1994) drew on the responses of pupils from just one Roman Catholic voluntary aided school. Francis and Evans (1996) drew on questionnaires completed by pupils who had watched a school's television series. The present study addresses this first criticism by drawing on a database of almost 34,000 13- to 15-year-olds throughout England and Wales and reported fully by Francis (2001) in his book, *The Values Debate: A Voice from the Pupils.*

The second criticism concerns the lack of control variables employed in the two studies reported by Francis and Burton (1994) and by Francis and Evans (1996). In particular, these studies overlooked the potentially contaminating influence of personality. A number of recent studies have demonstrated, for example, that Eysenck's three-dimensional model of personality (Eysenck and Eysenck, 1991) is able to predict individual differences in prayer.

These include studies among school pupils (Francis and Wilcox, 1994, 1996; Smith, 1996), students (Maltby, 1995; Lewis and Maltby, 1996; Francis, 1997a), school teachers (Francis and Johnson, 1999), senior citizens (Francis and Bolger, 1997) and the general adult population (Kaldor, Francis and Fisher, 2002). Another set of recent studies have demonstrated that Eysenck's three-dimensional model of personality is able to predict individual differences over a range of areas concerned with subjective well-being, in general (Francis, Brown, Lester and Philipchalk, 1998; Francis, 1999; Hills and Argyle, 2001) and with purpose in life, in particular (Addad, 1987; Moomal, 1999). The present study addresses this second criticism by drawing on a database which includes a reliable measure of the Eysenckian dimensional model of personality.

Method

Sample
The Religion and Values Today survey, described in detail by Francis (2001), was completed by a total of 33,982 pupils attending year nine and year ten classes throughout England and Wales. This database was constructed to be thoroughly representative of young people in this age group (13- to 15-year-olds) being educated within both the state-maintained sector and the independent sector of schools. Data were provided from 163 schools, stretching from Pembrokeshire in the west to Norfolk in the east, and from Cornwall in the south to Northumberland in the north. A proper mix of rural and urban areas was included, as was a proper mix of independent and state-maintained schools. Within the state-maintained sector proper attention was given to the balance between Roman Catholic voluntary schools, Anglican voluntary schools and non-denominational schools. Of the total respondents, 51% were male and 49% were female; 53% were in year nine and 47% were in year ten. Of those educated within the state-maintained sector, 86% were in non-denominational schools, 9% in Roman Catholic schools and 5% in Anglican schools. Of the total sample of pupils, 10% were being educated outside the state-maintained sector.

Procedure

Participating schools were asked to follow a standard procedure. The questionnaires were administered in normal class groups to all year nine and year ten pupils throughout the school. Pupils were asked not to write their names on the booklet and to complete the inventory under examination-like conditions. Although pupils were given the choice not to participate, very few declined to do so. They were assured of confidentiality and anonymity. They were informed that their responses would not be read by anyone in the school, and that the questionnaires would be despatched to the University of Wales for analysis.

Measures

In addition to basic information about sex and school year, the present analysis draws on the following measures included in the survey:

Church attendance was measured by the item, 'Do you go to church or other place of worship?', rated on a five-point scale, ranging from *never* through *once or twice a year*, *sometimes* and *at least once a week* to *nearly every week*.

Personal prayer was measured by the item, 'Do you pray by yourself?', rated on a five-point scale, ranging from *never* through *occasionally*, *at least once a month* and *at least once a week* to *nearly every day*.

Religious affiliation was assessed by the question, 'Do you belong to a religious group?', followed by a multiple-choice grid, beginning with *no* and then listing the major world faiths and Christian denominations.

Purpose in life was measured by the item, 'I feel my life has a sense of purpose', rated on a five-point Likert-type scale (Likert, 1932), ranging from *agree strongly* through *agree*, *not certain* and *disagree* to *disagree strongly*.

Personality was assessed by the short-form Junior Eysenck Personality Questionnaire (Francis and Pearson, 1988). This instrument proposes four six-item indices of extraversion, neuroticism, psychoticism and a lie scale. Each item is rated on a two-point scale: *yes* and *no*.

Analysis

The present analysis is conducted on two subsets of the data. The first subset comprises the 12,717 pupils who reported that they never attended church and who did not identify themselves as affiliated to a non-Christian religious group. This subset included 7,083 males and 5,634 females, 6,440 year nine pupils and 6,277 year ten pupils. The second subset comprised the 3,744 pupils who reported that they attended a Christian church nearly every week. This subset included 1,738 males and 2,006 females, 2,052 year nine pupils and 1,692 year ten pupils. The composition of this subset reflects the general finding that girls are more regular in church attendance than are boys (Francis, 1997b) and that church attendance declines during the years of secondary schooling (Kay and Francis, 1996). The data were analysed by means of the SPSS statistical package (SPSS Inc., 1988).

Results and discussion

Table 1.1 presents the frequency with which personal prayer is reported by the two groups of young people, those who never attend church and those who attend church nearly every week. These data demonstrate that 28.5% of the young people who never attend church nonetheless pray at least occasionally. This figure is very close to the figure of 33.2% reported in the earlier study of Francis and Evans (1996) among non-churchgoers, and confirms the point that personal prayer is not entirely outside the experience of young people growing up outside the churches. These data also demonstrate that 12.2% of the young people who attend church nearly every week never pray, outside their participation in church services. Once again, this figure is very close to the figure of 12.6% reported in the earlier study of Francis and Evans (1996) among weekly churchgoers, and confirms the point that the diligent practice of personal prayer cannot be assumed among churchgoing young people.

Table 1.1 Frequency of personal prayer by church attendance

Frequency of prayer	Non-churchgoers %	Churchgoers %
Never	71.5	12.2
Occasionally	22.8	30.3
At least once a month	1.2	4.5
At least once a week	1.5	17.2
Nearly every day	2.9	35.8

Table 1.2 presents the perceived purpose in life reported by the two groups of young people, those who never attend church and those who attend church nearly every week. These data demonstrate that 49.2% of the young people who never attend church feel that their lives have a sense of purpose, compared with 70.0% of those who attend church nearly every week. The earlier study of Francis and Evans (1996) found a similar marked contrast between the two groups, with 42.5% of the non-churchgoers and 69.1% of the weekly churchgoers recording a perceived purpose in life. These data confirm the point that churchgoing is associated with a much higher sense of purpose in life.

Table 1.2 Purpose in life by church attendance

Purpose in life	Non-churchgoers %	Churchgoers %
Agree	49.2	70.0
Not certain	38.2	24.5
Disagree	12.5	5.5

Table 1.3 employs the simple device of cross-tabulation to display the different levels of perceived purpose in life associated with different frequencies of personal prayer among churchgoers and non-churchgoers separately. Among non-churchgoers, 61.4% of those who pray nearly every day feel that their life has a sense of purpose, compared with 46.4% of those who never pray. Among weekly churchgoers, 81.3% of those who pray nearly every day feel that their life has a sense of purpose, compared with 52% of those who never pray. It may also be interesting to note that churchgoers

who never pray are not much more likely to feel a sense of purpose in life than are non-churchgoers who never pray.

Table 1.3 Purpose in life by frequency of personal prayer by church attendance

Frequency of prayer	Non-churchgoers %	Churchgoers %
Never	46.4	52.0
Occasionally	55.1	63.5
At least once a month or once a week	60.4	70.5
Nearly every day	61.4	81.3

The statistical evidence presented so far has illustrated trends without testing their statistical significance. Table 1.4 advances the debate further by examining the psychometric properties of the Eysenckian personality indices among churchgoers and non-churchgoers separately. For short scales of only six items each, the extraversion and the neuroticism scales record satisfactory levels of internal consistency reliability (alpha). The psychoticism and lie scales are less satisfactory but adequate.

Table 1.4 Personality measures: scale properties

Personality scales	alpha	Male mean	sd	Female mean	sd	t	P<
Churchgoers							
Extraversion	0.6768	4.2	1.7	4.5	1.5	6.3	.001
Neuroticism	0.6968	3.1	1.9	3.8	1.7	11.9	.001
Psychoticism	0.6202	1.8	1.4	0.9	1.1	20.6	.001
Lie scale	0.5736	2.4	1.5	2.7	1.6	6.4	.001
Non-churchgoers							
Extraversion	0.6840	4.5	1.6	4.8	1.4	11.6	.001
Neuroticism	0.6861	2.8	1.8	3.8	1.8	30.5	.001
Psychoticism	0.5797	2.2	1.6	1.3	1.3	37.2	.001
Lie scale	0.5594	1.9	1.5	2.2	1.6	9.7	.001

Eysenck's neuroticism scales measure emotional lability and overreactivity, and identify the underlying personality traits which, at one extreme, define neurotic mental disorders. The opposite of neuroticism is emotional stability. The high scorers on the neuroticism scale are characterized by Eysenck and Eysenck (1975) in the test manual as anxious, worrying individuals, who are moody and frequently depressed, likely to sleep badly and likely to suffer from various psychosomatic disorders. There is considerable evidence from a wide range of international studies to indicate that females record significantly higher scores on the Eysenckian neuroticism scale than males (Francis, 1993). Table 1.4 demonstrates that this anticipated finding has been found among both churchgoers and non-churchgoers.

Eysenck's psychoticism scales identify the underlying personality traits which, at one extreme, define psychotic mental disorder. The opposite of psychoticism is normal personality. The high scorers on the psychoticism scale are characterized by Eysenck and Eysenck (1976), in their study of psychoticism as a dimension of personality, as being cold, impersonal, hostile, lacking in sympathy, unfriendly, untrustful, odd, unemotional, unhelpful, lacking in insight, strange and with paranoid ideas that people were against them. There is considerable evidence to indicate that males record significantly higher scores on the Eysenckian psychoticism scale than females (Eysenck and Eysenck, 1976). Table 1.4 demonstrates that this anticipated finding has been found among both churchgoers and non-churchgoers.

Eysenck's extraversion scales measure sociability and impulsivity. The opposite of extraversion is introversion. The high scorers on the extraversion scale are characterized by Eysenck and Eysenck (1975) in the test manual as sociable individuals, who like parties, have many friends, need to have people to talk to and prefer meeting people to reading or studying alone. The typical extraverts crave excitement, take chances, act on the spur of the moment and are carefree and easygoing. Although in the 1960s and 1970s males were generally found to record higher scores on the Eysenckian extraversion scale than females, by the mid-1980s the normative data were reporting higher extraversion scores among females than among males (Eysenck, Eysenck and Barrett, 1985). Table 1.4 demonstrates that this anticipated finding has been found among both churchgoers and non-churchgoers.

The lie scales were originally introduced into personality measures to detect the tendency of some respondents to 'fake good' and so to distort the resultant personality scores (O'Donovan, 1969). The notion of the lie scale has not, however, remained as simple as that, and the continued use of lie scales has resulted in them being interpreted as a personality measure in their own right (McCrae and Costa, 1983; Furnham, 1986). According to one prominent account, the lie scale measures social acquiescence or social conformity (Finlayson, 1972; Massey, 1980). The general finding from a number of studies is that females record higher scores on the Eysenckian lie scales than males (Pearson and Francis, 1989). Table 1.4 demonstrates that this anticipated finding has been found among both churchgoers and non-churchgoers.

The foregoing analyses have provided confidence for employing the Eysenckian personality indices in the present study. Tables 1.5 and 1.6, therefore, present the Pearson correlation matrix between extraversion, neuroticism, psychoticism, lie scale, age, sex, prayer and purpose in life, for non-churchgoers and for churchgoers respectively. In view of the number of correlations being tested simultaneously the probability level has been set at .01. Two main conclusions emerge from these correlation matrices. The first conclusion is that frequency of prayer and perceived purpose in life are significantly correlated, both among churchgoers and among non-churchgoers. The second conclusion is that personality is significantly correlated with frequency of prayer and with perceived purpose in life, both among churchgoers and among non-churchgoers, suggesting that personality may be a contaminant in the relationship between prayer and purpose in life.

Tables 1.7 and 1.8, therefore, present the multiple regression significance tests, among non-churchgoers and among churchgoers respectively, which control for the influence of sex, school year and personality, before examining the influence of frequency of prayer on perceived purpose in life. These data continue to find a significant relationship between frequency of prayer and perceived purpose in life, both among churchgoers and among non-churchgoers.

Table 1.5 Correlation matrix: non-churchgoers

	Purpose in life	Lie scale	Psychoticism	Neuroticism	Extraversion	School year	Sex
Prayer	+0.1088 .001	+0.1184 .001	-0.1053 .001	+0.1352 .001	+0.0106 NS	-0.0100 NS	+0.1417 .001
Sex	+0.0000 NS	+0.0858 .001	-0.3133 .001	+0.2612 .001	+0.1023 .001	+0.0190 NS	
School year	+0.0004 NS	-0.1024 .001	+0.0274 .01	-0.0024 NS	+0.0308 .001		
Extraversion	+0.1649 .001	-0.1387 .001	+0.1204 .001	-0.1226 .001			
Neuroticism	-0.1810 .001	-0.0327 .001	-0.0764 .001				
Psychoticism	-0.1080 .001	-0.4208 .001					
Lie scale	+0.1324 .001						

Table 1.6 Correlation matrix: churchgoers

	Purpose in life	Lie scale	Psychoticism	Neuroticism	Extraversion	School year	Sex
Prayer	+0.2786 .001	+0.1745 .001	-0.1540 .001	-0.0312 NS	-0.0132 NS	+0.0046 NS	+0.1320 .001
Sex	+0.0157 NS	+0.1036 .001	-0.3188 .001	+0.1912 .001	+0.1031 .001	-0.0243 NS	
School year	+0.0290 NS	-0.0834 .001	+0.0560 .001	-0.0290 NS	+0.0025 NS		
Extraversion	+0.1422 .001	-0.0837 .001	+0.1155 .001	-0.1122 .001			
Neuroticism	-0.2449 .001	-0.1012 .001	-0.0169 NS				
Psychoticism	-0.1270 .001	-0.4157 .001					
Lie scale	+0.1766 .001						

Table 1.7 Multiple regression significance tests: non-churchgoers

Predictor variables	R^2	Increase R^2	Increase F	Increase P<	Beta	t	P<
Sex	0.0000	0.0000	0.0	NS	−0.0283	−3.0	.01
School year	0.0000	0.0000	0.0	NS	+0.0090	+1.1	NS
Extraversion	0.0277	0.0277	361.6	.001	+0.1714	+19.6	.001
Neuroticism	0.0545	0.0268	359.8	.001	−0.1721	−19.2	.001
Psychoticism	0.0734	0.0189	258.2	.001	−0.0966	−9.8	.001
Lie scale	0.0835	0.0101	140.3	.001	+0.1004	+10.6	.001
Prayer	0.0955	0.0120	168.9	.001	+0.1122	+13.0	.001

Table 1.8 Multiple regression significance tests: churchgoers

Predictor variables	R^2	Increase R^2	Increase F	Increase P<	Beta	t	P<
Sex	0.0002	0.0002	0.0	NS	−0.0265	−1.6	NS
School year	0.0011	0.0009	3.2	NS	+0.0334	+2.2	NS
Extraversion	0.0210	0.0199	76.2	.001	+0.1422	+9.2	.001
Neuroticism	0.0763	0.0552	223.6	.001	−0.2067	−13.3	.001
Psychoticism	0.0954	0.0191	78.8	.001	−0.0787	−4.5	.001
Lie scale	0.1091	0.0137	57.5	.001	+0.0971	+5.8	.001
Prayer	0.1677	0.0587	263.3	.001	+0.2483	+16.2	.001

Conclusion

The present study has built on the two earlier studies reported by Francis and Burton (1994) and by Francis and Evans (1996) to test the hypothesis that there is a positive correlation between frequency of prayer and perceived purpose in life among 13- to 15-year-old adolescents. The study has drawn on a unique database of 34,000 pupils, representative of the school population across England and Wales. In exploring the relationship between prayer and perceived purpose in life, care has been taken to control for the potentially contaminating influences of church attendance, sex, school year and individual differences in personality. These data demonstrate a clear relationship between frequency of prayer and perceived purpose in life. The relationship holds good both among young people who never attend church and among young people who attend church in most weeks.

This finding is of particular significance in light of the renewed interest among psychologists in the significance of purpose in life for psychological development. Early research in this area, as reviewed by Yalom (1980), focused largely on the relation between purpose in life and psychopathology. Some more recent studies have maintained this focus. For example, Newcomb and Harlow (1986) found, in two different samples, that perceived loss of control and meaninglessness in life mediated the relation between uncontrollable stress and substance use. Harlow, Newcomb and Bentler (1986) found meaninglessness to mediate between depression and self-derogation and subsequent drug use, for women, and suicidal ideation, for men. Coleman, Kaplan and Downing (1986) reported that drug addicts were less likely than non-addicts to have a well-defined meaning in life. Schlesinger, Susman and Koenigsberg (1990) found lower purpose-in-life scores among alcoholic men and women than among non-alcoholics. Newcomb (1986) found meaning and purpose in life to be associated with lessened nuclear fear. Rappaport, Fossler, Bross and Gilden (1993) found purpose in life to be associated with lower death anxiety. However, another set of more recent studies has focused much more on the perspective of positive psychology. For example, Zika and Chamberlain (1987) found meaning in life to be a strong and consistent predictor of psychological well-being. Zika and Chamberlain (1992) examined the relationship between purpose in life and indices both of positive well-being and of negative well-being in two independent samples, a sample of 194 mothers of young children and a sample of 150 elderly people aged 60 or over. Their data found purpose in life to relate consistently more strongly to the positive dimensions of well-being than to the negative dimensions.

The present findings, based on a cross-sectional correlation study, have demonstrated that prayer and purpose in life are associated in a positive direction. The more plausible causal hypothesis is that prayer influences purpose in life, rather than that purpose in life influences prayer. The following psychological mechanism, for example, proposes one causal model according to which prayer may influence purpose in life. The practice of prayer implies both a cognitive and an affective component. The cognitive component assumes, at least, the possibility of a transcendent power. Such a belief system is likely to support a purposive view of the nature of the universe. The affective component assumes, at least, the possibility of that transcendent power being aware of and taking an interest in the individual engaged in prayer. Such an affective system is likely to support a sense of value for the individual.

If the practice and experience of prayer is of value in promoting a sense of purpose in life among adolescents, and if a sense of purpose in life is, in turn, of value in promoting psychological well-being during adolescence, then there may be important implications from the present research both for the churches and for the secular educational system.

Three aspects of these data should be of particular significance to the churches. First, these data remind the churches just how many young people in England and Wales are growing up without ever crossing the threshold into church services. A significant number of these young people, growing up outside the churches, nonetheless retain a basic instinct to turn to prayer. If young people outside the churches are interested in prayer, then the churches may well have here a way of accessing their attention and interest.

Second, these data provide hard evidence that prayer and purpose in life go hand in hand. Young people are themselves interested in the search for meaning and purpose. Here is real evidence that the churches possess something for which young people are themselves seeking.

Third, these data remind the churches that significant numbers of their active young participants are not engaging in the practice of personal prayer. Moreover, young churchgoers who do not pray have almost as low a level of purpose in life as young non-churchgoers who do not pray. Churches may well be advised to reconsider the emphasis which they give to teaching on prayer and to the priority given to the practice of prayer in programmes of spiritual formation shaped for young people.

The secular education system in England and Wales continues to provide for a daily statutory act of collective worship in all state-maintained schools, as reaffirmed by the 1988 Education Reform Act (Cox and Cairns, 1989). Since it is difficult to conceive of worship without prayer, schools in England and Wales have not only the opportunity, but also the legal right, to introduce young people to the activity of prayer. The present data suggest that this very provision could be of positive benefit to the pupils' psychological development.

Acknowledgement

The analysis reported in this chapter was sponsored by a grant from the John Templeton Foundation. The opinions expressed herein are those of the author and do not necessarily reflect the views of the John Templeton Foundation.

References

Addad, M. (1987), 'Neuroticism, extraversion and meaning of life: a comparative study of criminals and non-criminals', *Personality and Individual Differences*, 8, 879–83.

Brown, L. B. (1994), *The Human Side of Prayer: The Psychology of Praying* (Birmingham, Ala., Religious Education Press).

Byrd, R. C. (1988), 'Positive therapeutic effects of intercessory prayer in a coronary care unit population', *Southern Medical Journal*, 81, 826–9.

Coe, G. A. (1916), *The Psychology of Religion* (Chicago, Ill., University of Chicago Press).

Coleman, S., Kaplan, J. and Downing, R. (1986), 'Life cycle and loss: the spiritual vacuum of heroin addiction', *Family Process*, 25, 5–23.

Cox, E. and Cairns, J. M. (1989), *Reforming Religious Education: The Religious Clauses of the 1988 Education Reform Act* (London, Kogan Page).

Eysenck, H. J. and Eysenck, S. B. G. (1975), *Manual of the Eysenck Personality Questionnaire (Adult and Junior)* (London, Hodder and Stoughton).

Eysenck, H. J. and Eysenck, S. B. G. (1976), *Psychoticism as a Dimension of Personality* (London, Hodder and Stoughton).

Eysenck, H. J. and Eysenck, S. B. G. (1991), *Manual of the Eysenck Personality Scales* (London, Hodder and Stoughton).

Eysenck, S. B. G., Eysenck, H. J. and Barrett, P. (1985), 'A revised version of the psychoticism scale', *Personality and Individual Differences*, 6, 21–9.

Finlayson, D. S. (1972), 'Towards the interpretation of children's lie scale scores', *British Journal of Educational Psychology*, 42, 290–3.

Finney, J. R. and Malony, H. N. (1985), 'Empirical studies of Christian prayer: a review of the literature', *Journal of Psychology and Theology*, 13, 104–15.

Francis, L. J. (1992), 'The influence of religion, gender and social class on attitudes toward school among eleven-year-olds in England', *Journal of Experimental Education*, 60, 339–48.

Francis, L. J. (1993), 'The dual nature of the Eysenckian neuroticism scales: a question of sex differences?', *Personality and Individual Differences*, 15, 43–59.

Francis, L. J. (1997a), 'Personality, prayer, and church attendance among undergraduate students', *International Journal for the Psychology of Religion*, 7, 127–32.

Francis, L. J. (1997b), 'The psychology of gender differences in religion: a review of empirical research', *Religion*, 27, 81–96.

Francis, L. J. (1999), 'Happiness is a thing called stable extraversion: a further examination of the relationship between the Oxford Happiness Inventory and Eysenck's dimensional model of personality and gender', *Personality and Individual Differences*, 26, 5–11.

Francis, L. J. (2001), *The Values Debate: A Voice from the Pupils* (London, Woburn Press).

Francis, L. J. and Astley, J. (2001), *Psychological Perspectives on Prayer: A Reader* (Leominster, Gracewing).

Francis, L. J. and Bolger, J. (1997), 'Personality, prayer and church attendance in later life', *Social Behaviour and Personality*, 25, 335–8.

Francis, L. J., Brown, L. B., Lester, D. and Philipchalk, R. (1998), 'Happiness as stable extraversion: a cross-cultural examination of the reliability and validity of the Oxford Happiness Inventory among students in the UK, USA, Australia and Canada', *Personality and Individual Differences*, 24, 167–71.

Francis, L. J. and Burton, L. (1994), 'The influence of personal prayer on purpose in life among Catholic adolescents', *Journal of Beliefs and Values*, 15, 2, 6–9.

Francis, L. J. and Evans, T. E. (1996), 'The relationship between personal prayer and purpose in life among churchgoing and non-churchgoing 12–15-year-olds in the UK', *Religious Education*, 91, 9–21.

Francis, L. J. and Johnson, P. (1999), 'Mental health, prayer and church attendance among primary school teachers', *Mental Health, Religion and Culture*, 2, 153–8.

Francis, L. J. and Pearson, P. R. (1988), 'The development of a short form of the JEPQ (JEPQ-S): its use in measuring personality and religion', *Personality and Individual Differences*, 9, 911–16.

Francis, L. J. and Wilcox, C. (1994), 'Personality, prayer and church attendance among 16- to 18-year-old girls in England', *Journal of Social Psychology*, 134, 243–6.

Francis, L. J. and Wilcox, C. (1996), 'Prayer, church attendance and personality revisited: a study among 16- to 19-year-old girls', *Psychological Reports*, 79, 1265–6.

Frankl, V. E. (1978), *The Unheard Cry for Meaning: Psychotherapy and Humanism* (New York, Simon and Schuster).

Furnham, A. (1986), 'Response bias, social desirability and dissimulation', *Personality and Individual Differences*, 7, 385–400.

Galton, F. (1869), *Hereditary Genius: An Inquiry into its Laws and Consequences* (London, Macmillan and Co.).

Galton, F. (1872), 'Statistical inquiries into the efficacy of prayer', *Fortnightly Review*, 12, 125–35.

Galton, F. (1883), *Inquiries into Human Faculty and its Development* (London, Macmillan).

Harlow, L. L., Newcomb, M. D. and Bentler, P. M. (1986), 'Depression, self-derogation, substance use, and suicide ideation: lack of purpose in life as a mediational factor', *Journal of Clinical Psychology*, 42, 5–21.

Harris, W. S., Gowda, M., Kolb, J. W., Strychacz, C. P., Vacek, J. L., Jones, P. G., Forker, A., O'Keefe, J. H. and McCallister, B. D. (1999), 'A randomised, controlled trial of the effects of remote, intercessory prayer on outcomes in patients admitted to the coronary care unit', *Archives of Internal Medicine*, 159, 2273–8.

Hills, P. and Argyle, M. (2001), 'Happiness, introversion–extraversion and happy introverts', *Personality and Individual Differences*, 30, 595–608.

Hodge, A. (1931), *Prayer and its Psychology* (London, SPCK).

Hood, R. W., Morris, R. J. and Watson, P. J. (1987), 'Religious orientation and prayer experience', *Psychological Reports*, 60, 1201–2.

Hood, R. W., Morris, R. J. and Watson, P. J. (1989), 'Prayer experience and religious orientation', *Review of Religious Research*, 31, 39–45.

James, W. (1902), *The Varieties of Religious Experience* (New York, Longmans Green).

Janssen, J., Hart, J. de and Draak, C. den (1989), 'Praying practices', *Journal of Empirical Theology*, 2(2), 28–39.

Kaldor, P., Francis, L. J. and Fisher, J. W. (2002), 'Personality and spirituality: Christian prayer and Eastern meditation are not the same', *Pastoral Psychology*, 50, 165–72.

Kay, W. K. and Francis, L. J. (1996), *Drift from the Churches: Attitude toward Christianity during Childhood and Adolescence* (Cardiff, University of Wales Press).

Lewis, C. A. and Maltby, J. (1996), 'Personality, prayer, and church attendance in a sample of male college students in the USA', *Psychological Reports*, 78, 976–8.

Likert, R. (1932), 'A technique for the measurement of attitudes', *Archives of Psychology*, 140, 1–55.

McCrae, R. R. and Costa, P. T. (1983), 'Social desirability scales: more substance than style', *Journal of Consulting and Clinical Psychology*, 51, 882–8.

McCullough, M. E. (1995), 'Prayer and health: conceptual issues, research review, and research agenda', *Journal of Psychology and Theology*, 23, 15–29.

Maltby, J. (1995), 'Personality, prayer and church attendance among US female adults', *Journal of Social Psychology*, 135, 529–31.

Massey, A. (1980), 'The Eysenck Personality Inventory lie scale: lack of insight or . . . ?', *Irish Journal of Psychology*, 4, 172–4.

Montgomery, A. and Francis, L. J. (1996), 'Relationship between personal prayer and school-related attitudes among 11–16 year old girls', *Psychological Reports*, 78, 787–93.

Moomal, Z. (1999), 'The relationship between meaning in life and mental well-being', *South African Journal of Psychology*, 29, 36–41.

Newcomb, M. D. (1986), 'Nuclear attitudes and reactions: associations with depression, drug use, and quality of life', *Journal of Personality and Social Psychology*, 50, 906–20.

Newcomb, M. D. and Harlow, L. L. (1986), 'Life events and substance use among adolescents: mediating effects of perceived loss of control and meaninglessness in life', *Journal of Personality and Social Psychology*, 51, 564–77.

O'Donovan, D. (1969), 'An historical review of the lie scale: with particular reference to the Maudsley Personality Inventory', *Papers in Psychology*, 3, 13–19.

Pearson, P. R. and Francis, L. J. (1989), 'The dual nature of the Eysenckian lie scales: are religious adolescents more truthful?', *Personality and Individual Differences*, 10, 1041–8.

Poloma, M. M. and Pendleton, B. F. (1989), 'Exploring types of prayer and quality of life: a research note', *Review of Religious Research*, 31, 46–53.

Rappaport, H., Fossler, R. J., Bross, L. S. and Gilden, D. (1993), 'Future time, death anxiety, and life purpose among older adults', *Death Studies*, 17, 369–79.

Schlesinger, S., Susman, M. and Koenigsberg, J. (1990), 'Self-esteem and purpose in life: a comparative study of women alcoholics', *Journal of Alcohol and Drug Education*, 36, 127–41.

Smith, D. L. (1996), 'Private prayer, public worship and personality among 11–15-year-old adolescents', *Personality and Individual Differences*, 21, 1063–5.

SPSS Inc. (1988), *SPSSX User's Guide* (New York, McGraw-Hill).

Tillich, P. (1952), *The Courage to Be* (New Haven, Conn., Yale University Press).

Yalom, I. D. (1980), *Existential Psychotherapy* (New York, Basic Books).

Zika, S. and Chamberlain, K. (1987), 'Relations of hassles and personality to subjective well-being', *Journal of Personality and Social Psychology*, 53, 155–62.

Zika, S. and Chamberlain, K. (1992), 'On the relation between meaning in life and psychological well-being', *British Journal of Psychology*, 83, 133–45.

2

The science and religion interface within young people's attitudes and beliefs

JEFF ASTLEY

Summary

Previous research has shown the significance of the science and religion debate for the complexity of religious beliefs and stances for living held by adolescents. This chapter focuses the debate around the issue of creationism, which has been identified as a matter of key interest by much of the previous research in this area. Using the data from the Religion and Values Today database, some of the wider relationships between creationist belief and other variables are explored in the lives of young people, together with their social and personal implications.

Introduction

Creation versus evolution?

The so-called 'warfare' between science and religion appears most intense and difficult to resolve when theories proposed by science clash directly with particular claims of religion or theology. This can happen when the latter are presented as operating at the same level of explanation as the scientific perspective. When the doctrine of creation is treated as an ultimate, metaphysical explanation of the dependent ontological status of created reality, scientific beliefs and beliefs about creation cannot conflict. As theologians from the time of St Thomas have insisted, the doctrine of creation makes its claim primarily about God's continuous preservation of the world and of life, a claim that is independent of questions about origins (see Temple, 1953: 37). As a consequence, to put it at its mildest, 'it is not at all certain that belief in God as the Creator and Providential Ruler of all of life necessarily involves a belief that the world is only 6,000 years old and that all present species were named by Adam in the first days' (Gilkey, 1968: 167). 'Theistic evolutionism' is a position that is both scientifically and theologically defensible (Devine, 1996; Pigliucci, 2002: 42–3; see also Ruse, 2001; Alexander, 2001: chapters 9 and 10).

But the view that there was a 'special creation' (an independent, separate creation) by God of each of the present-day species is clearly a direct challenge to the theory of a descent-with-modification that has led to the evolution of those species from earlier forms over many millions of years. This is particularly the case if creation is said to have taken place over a period of days or to have occurred only a few thousand years ago. Under such circumstances, conflict is unavoidable. 'Theology can often solve such problems, but only by shifting the level at which it operates' (Astley, 2001: 29, cf. Astley, 2000: 5; Barbour, 1990: 179); this is how most theology has dealt with the creation versus evolution debate.

But not everyone is willing to call a truce in this way. The year 2002 saw the resurgence in Britain of the long-dormant debate concerning evolution, a debate that many had assumed was now limited to the more exotic educational and religious landscapes of the United States (see Barker, 1985). In north-east England a state-maintained secondary school, the Emmanuel City Technology College in Gateshead, was reported to be teaching creationism as well as evolution in its biology curriculum. Both views, the college maintained, were 'faith positions'. This accords with the creationist claim that 'children should be informed that there are *two conflicting views on origins*: *some* scientists believe in evolution, others in special creation. The arguments on *both* sides should be presented, and children should be *free to choose* between them' (Watson, 1976: 103).

The matter was raised in the British Parliament and a group that included the present Bishop of Oxford (the successor, ironically, of Bishop Samuel Wilberforce, who opposed Darwinism in the famous 1860 British Association for the Advancement of Science Debate), as well as the evolutionary biologist and atheist Richard Dawkins, called on the Prime Minister to monitor 'faith schools' strictly, 'in order that the respective disciplines of science and religious studies are properly respected'. Bishop Richard Harries wrote:

An intellectual battle that was fought and resolved . . . seems to have opened up again on the basis of a misunderstanding of both science and the Bible . . . The faith position of the Bible is that however the world has come into being and however it has developed, over whatever period of time, there is an ultimate purpose behind it that is wise and loving. (Harries, 2002: 25)

Mainstream theology, like mainstream science, rejects creationism; indeed, only twenty-five years after the publication of Darwin's *The Origin of Species*, his champion T. H. Huxley wrote that 'even the theologians have almost ceased to pit the plain meaning of Genesis against the no less plain meaning of Nature' (Darwin, 1887: 181). By contrast, creationism advocates an adherence to the biblical stories, bolstered by a 'creation science' that seeks to support this interpretation using scientific data. It holds that all living species have arisen from separate, supernatural origins and have not descended by modification from other species.

Scientific creationists typically include in their list of theological com-mitments the following: (1) the creation of the world out of nothing; (2) the insufficiency of mutation and natural selection to explain the process of evolution; (3) the stability of existing species and the impossibility of one species evolving out of another; (4) separate ancestry for apes and humans; (5) catastrophism to explain certain geological formations, for example, the flood explains why sea fossils appear on mountains; and (6) the relatively recent formation of the earth about six to ten thousand years ago. (Peters, 1998: 16)

Despite its claim to scientific status, the movement is largely pri-marily motivated by a biblical fundamentalism that asserts the inerrancy of scripture. According to the overwhelming majority of biologists:

creation 'science' is not a promising rival to evolutionary theory. It is not integrated with the rest of science, but is a hodgepodge of doctrines, lacking independent support. It offers no startling predictions, no advance in knowledge. We cannot commend it for any ability to shed light on questions that orthodox theories are unable to answer . . . [It] has no evidence that speaks in its favor. (Kitcher, 1983: 171)

Philip Kitcher concludes, 'It is educationally irresponsible to pretend that an idea that is scientifically worthless deserves scientific discussion' (p. 174; but cf. Weeks, 1985).

Adolescent creationists

The extent and nature of creationist belief is clearly a significant concern for both scientific and religious education in schools today.

Empirical studies routinely show that adopting a creationist position is detrimental to young people's interest in science, whereas interest in science is usually unconnected either with attitude to Christianity or with churchgoing (Kay and Francis, 1996: 110). In one of their Northern Ireland studies, however, Francis and Greer (2001) used multiple regression analysis so as to control for both creationism and 'scientism' (the view that absolute truth may be obtained through science, and only through science). Using this technique, they were able to demonstrate that there was a significant underlying positive relationship between the attitude of these pupils toward Christianity and their attitude toward science. Such a relationship is at least parallel to the theoretical claims that are sometimes made about an interdependence or common cause between science and religion, for example, that a proper (that is, non-fundamentalist) education in or about religion should assist learners in their understanding of the nature of science, that science and religion (or theology) show a kinship in the attitudes to nature that they encourage, or even that they are 'intellectual cousins under the skin' (Polkinghorne, 1994: 47; cf. Astley, 2001).

Further work has been done on the extent to which adolescents believe that creationism is a necessary part of Christianity (for example, Fulljames and Francis, 1987, 1988; Francis, Gibson and Fulljames, 1990). Interestingly, while creationism per se correlates positively with both churchgoing and prayer (Francis and Greer, 2001), the data indicate that those teenagers who believe that creationism is an essential part of Christianity tend to have a negative attitude to Christianity as they get older, or when creationist belief itself has been controlled for (Francis, Gibson and Fulljames, 1990; Fulljames, Gibson and Francis, 1991; Fulljames, 1996). This fact illuminates one of the dangers of allowing young people –

especially religiously uncommitted young people – to adopt the assumption that a creationist position is necessarily implied by the Christian belief-system. Leslie Francis's study of nearly 34,000 young people in England and Wales between the ages of 13 and 15 years (Francis, 2001) reveals that only 20% of the whole sample agreed or strongly agreed with the creationist claim 'that God made the world in six days and rested on the seventh', whereas 40% disagreed with this statement (the remaining 40% expressing themselves uncertain about it). Exploring the data further, Francis found that the younger teenagers were significantly more likely to endorse creationism than were the older ones, and that female students were more likely to do so than male students, and regular church attenders than occasional attenders or non-attenders.

The present chapter explores these data in more depth in an attempt to assess the relationship between creationist belief and a number of other areas of adolescent beliefs and values. The areas chosen are: personal dissatisfaction (a measure of perceived well-being), traditional Christian beliefs and values, a conservative stance on individual and social morality, and the adolescents' 'credulity'.

The most controversial of these areas is undoubtedly this last one. While educational rhetoric occasionally expresses the absurd position that 'belief' as such is a good thing, most teachers and parents recognize a distinction between the beliefs of a mainstream religious tradition and a range of other, arguably more suspect, transempirical claims that are often associated with religious belief in the popular mind. The psychological literature includes studies of 'irrational belief' focused on measures of rational responses to frustration, value judgements and so on (cf. Shorkey and Whiteman, 1977). There is also a considerable literature on 'paranormal beliefs' such as ESP, communication with the dead and astrology (for example, Orenstein, 2002), as well as on some broader measures of paranormal believing that include, among other species of belief, the acceptance of witchcraft, superstition, spiritualism and the existence of extraordinary life-forms (for example, Tobacyk and Milford, 1983). Such beliefs are fairly widespread. In the Conventional Religion and Common Religion in Leeds project, some 36% of adults expressed a belief that 'such things as ghosts or poltergeists or anything like that' exist, while 61% accepted telepathy, 54% clairvoyance and 26% communication with the dead; but only 13% confessed to having a lucky mascot and 19% to being 'a superstitious person' (Krarup, n.d.). More recent studies on a wider canvas in Britain reveal that 26% of the adult population hold to a belief in horoscopes, 47% in foretelling the future, 18% in lucky charms, 10% in black magic, 32% in ghosts and 14% in exchanging messages with the dead (Gill, 1999: 70).

Furnham and Gunter's study of 2,000 British adolescents found that 26% of young people aged between 10 and 14, but only 16% of 15- to 16-year-olds, described themselves as superstitious. The figures in this survey for belief in ghosts or poltergeists ranged from 21% (aged 10–14) to 19% (aged 15–16), and for believing in newspaper horoscopes from 35% (10–14) to 25% (15–16) (Furnham and Gunter, 1989: 134–5). The statistics for such beliefs in the present database of 13- to 15-year-olds are: horoscopes 35%, ghosts 40%, black magic 20%, fortune-telling 20%, contact with spirits 31% (Francis, 2001: 40).

According to the dictionary, to be 'credulous' is to have 'too great a readiness to believe things'. While drawing on some of the studies detailed above, the index of credulity utilized in this chapter does not attempt to measure the rationality of a subject's responses to life events and operates with a notion of credulity that is in principle wider than paranormal belief. Judgements of which beliefs go 'too far' and strain 'normal' credulity will inevitably involve some contentious evaluations. In this case it has seemed appropriate to sin boldly. Five items have therefore been adopted from the questionnaire that reflect something of this construct of credulity. They are: 'I believe in the Devil', 'I believe in black magic', 'I believe that it is possible to contact the spirits of the dead', 'I believe in my horoscope' and 'I believe in ghosts'.

The decision to include belief in the Devil in a credulity scale is, of course, open to the challenge that it belongs in the company of traditional religious beliefs, rather than sharing a cognitive bed with horoscopes and ghosts. It is indeed one of the 'traditional beliefs' or 'indicators of orthodox belief' adopted by the European Values Study, although less than 25% of adults are reported as assenting to it (see Harding, Phillips and Fogarty, 1986: 48; Barker, Halman and Vloet, 1992: 48; Gill, 1999: 70). Nevertheless, one may argue that it is worth separating belief in the existence of the Devil from traditional religious concerns centred on God, Jesus and the Church, thus allowing us to test whether it does in fact tend to cohere with the more usual measures of superstition and paranormal beliefs as another 'weird' belief that rather strains common sense.

Method

Sample

As part of the Religion and Values Today project (Francis, 2001), a detailed questionnaire was administered to all year nine and year ten classes within 163 schools throughout England and Wales. The sample had a proper mix of rural and urban areas, and of independent and state-maintained schools. Within the state-maintained sector, attention was given to the balance between Roman Catholic voluntary schools, Anglican voluntary schools and non-denominational community schools.

Participating schools were asked to follow a standard procedure, with the questionnaires being completed anonymously in normal class groups under examination-like conditions. Although pupils were given the choice not to participate, very few declined to do so. Thoroughly completed questionnaires were processed for 33,982 pupils.

Instrument

The questionnaire used in this study is a revision of the Centymca Attitude Inventory, previously employed by Francis (1982a, 1982b, 1984a, 1984b) and Francis and Kay (1995). The instrument was designed to profile values over a number of areas, from which four have been selected for examination in the present analysis, namely *personal dissatisfaction, moral values, religious values,* and *credulity.* These four areas were each assessed by scales designed for Likert scaling (see Likert, 1932). Pupils were required to grade their agreement with each statement on a five-point scale anchored by *strongly agree, agree, not certain, disagree* and *disagree strongly.*

Church attendance was assessed on a five-point scale: *never, once or twice a year, sometimes, at least once a month* and *nearly every week.*

Belief in God was assessed by the item 'I believe in God' rated on the five-point scale: *agree strongly, agree, not certain, disagree* and *disagree strongly. Belief in creationism* was assessed on the same scale by the item 'I believe that God made the world in six days and rested on the seventh'.

Personality was assessed by the short-form Junior Eysenck Personality Questionnaire (Francis and Pearson, 1988). This instrument proposes three six-item measures of extraversion, neuroticism and psychoticism, together with a six-item lie scale. Each item is assessed on a dichotomous scale as *yes* and *no*.

Results

Tables 2.1, 2.2, 2.3 and 2.4 present the items for the scale of personal dissatisfaction, the scale of moral values, the scale of religious values and the scale of credulity, together with the item rest of test correlations and the alpha coefficients. These statistics confirm the basic internal reliability and item homogeneity for all four scales.

Table 2.1 Scale of personal dissatisfaction: reliability

Item	r
I find life really worth living*	0.3581
I often worry about my school work	0.3343
I often feel depressed	0.5114
I have sometimes considered taking my own life	0.3580
I am worried about how I get on with other people	0.4270
I am worried about my sex life	0.3357
I am worried about my exams at school	0.3231
I tend to be a lonely person	0.4064
I feel I am not worth much as a person	0.4966
alpha	0.7183

Note: *This item is reverse coded.

Table 2.5 presents the bivariate correlations of personal dissatisfaction, moral values, religious values and credulity with sex, age, extraversion, neuroticism, psychoticism, lie scale, church attendance,

Table 2.2 Scale of moral values: reliability

Item	r
Abortion is wrong	0.2684
There is too much violence on television	0.4039
It is wrong to have sexual intercourse outside marriage	0.4842
It is wrong to become drunk	0.5102
Divorce is wrong	0.3203
It is wrong to smoke cigarettes	0.4007
Pornography is too readily available	0.3285
It is wrong to use heroin	0.3116
It is wrong to have sexual intercourse under the legal age	0.5477
alpha	0.7211

Table 2.3 Scale of religious values: reliability

Item	r
I believe in God	0.7194
I believe Jesus really rose from the dead	0.7599
I believe in life after death	0.3626
I believe Jesus Christ is the Son of God	0.7493
The church seems irrelevant to life today*	0.4099
I want my children baptised in church	0.5578
I want to get married in church	0.4050
Church is boring*	0.4809
Ministers and priests do a good job	0.5696
alpha	0.8437

Note: *These items are reverse coded.

belief in God and belief in creationism. These data demonstrate that belief in creationism is associated with significantly higher levels of personal dissatisfaction (that is to say lower well-being), higher levels of commitment to conservative moral values, higher levels of commitment to traditional religious values and higher levels of credulity. These data also demonstrate that other variables are significant predictors of individual differences in personal dissatisfaction, moral values, religious values and credulity.

Table 2.4 Scale of credulity: reliability

Item	r
I believe in the Devil	0.3772
I believe in black magic	0.5482
I believe that it is possible to contact the spirits of the dead	0.5810
I believe in my horoscope	0.2787
I believe in ghosts	0.5602
alpha	0.7081

Table 2.5 Correlations

	Personal dissatisfaction	Moral values	Religious values	Credulity
Sex	+0.1727***	+0.1233***	+0.1458***	+0.1239***
Age	+0.0006	−0.0952***	−0.0453***	+0.0098
Extraversion	−0.2276***	−0.1676***	+0.0034	+0.1334***
Neuroticism	+0.6155***	+0.0197**	+0.0665***	+0.1508***
Psychoticism	−0.0828***	−0.3567***	−0.2409***	+0.1446***
Lie scale	+0.0108	+0.3925***	+0.2764***	−0.1351***
Church attendance	+0.0535***	+0.2500***	+0.4926***	−0.0550***
Belief in God	+0.0811***	+0.3311***	+0.8023***	+0.0791***
Creationism	+0.0854***	+0.3474***	+0.6216***	+0.0741***

Note: * = P<.05; ** = P<.01; *** = P<.001.

Higher levels of personal dissatisfaction are associated with being female, introversion, neuroticism, tendermindedness, church attendance and belief in God. Higher levels of commitment to conservative moral values are associated with being female, being younger, introversion, neuroticism, tendermindedness, social conformity, church attendance, and belief in God. Higher levels of commitment to traditional religious values are associated with being female, being younger, neuroticism, tendermindedness, social conformity, church attendance and belief in God. Higher levels of credulity are associated with being female, extraversion, stability, toughmindedness, social non-conformity, non-attendance at church and belief in God.

In view of the complexity of interaction between the variables,

Table 2.6 employs multiple regression analysis to control for the influence of sex, age, personality, church attendance and belief in God, before exploring the influence of belief in creationism on personal dissatisfaction, moral values, religious values and credulity. These data demonstrate that, after controlling for these variables, belief in creationism remains predictive of higher levels of personal dissatisfaction, higher levels of commitment to conservative moral values, higher levels of commitment to traditional religious values and higher levels of credulity.

Discussion

One might have anticipated a close association between both moral and religious conservatism, on the one hand, and belief in creationism, on the other. At least in its full-blown adult redactions, religious fundamentalism presents itself as something of a package-deal which meshes traditional theological claims with conservative instincts in morality (and politics). And, on one criterion, creationists are extreme fundamentalists. Thus, according to the biblical scholar James Barr (1981: 42), 'it is now only very extreme fundamentalists who assert that a literal interpretation of the six days of creation is obligatory, or even desirable'. Creationists not only affirm an inerrancy view of scripture; those whom Kitcher surveyed also accept that the Genesis narratives record 'a series of straightforward historical facts', which are to be taken literally (Kitcher, 1983: 7). If adolescent creationists mirror such a Christian fundamentalism, we might expect them to show a similar conservatism.

However, the fact that belief in creationism is predictive of higher levels of personal dissatisfaction is more surprising. Creationists and fundamentalists might be expected to argue that a firm belief in the word of God, plainly understood, should tend to an easing of the human spirit. But it does not appear to work like that. A non-creationist might explain this lack of psychological solace in terms of the cognitive dissonance between creationist belief and the adolescent's wider understanding of scientific, particularly biological, matters, as well as her recognition that creationism is a minority option within society.

Table 2.6 Regression

Predictor variables	R^2	Change R^2	F	P<	B	t	P<
Personal dissatisfaction							
Sex	0.0263	0.0263	646.5	.001	+0.0272	4.9	.001
Age	0.0263	0.0000	1.1	NS	+0.0148	3.0	.01
Extraversion	0.0866	0.0603	1581.2	.001	−0.1560	30.3	.001
Neuroticism	0.4055	0.3190	12860.8	.001	+0.5904	113.1	.001
Psychoticism	0.4058	0.0003	10.6	.001	−0.0041	0.7	NS
Lie scale	0.4063	0.0005	19.0	.001	+0.0160	2.8	.01
Church attendance	0.4063	0.0001	2.3	NS	−0.0102	1.8	NS
Belief in God	0.4071	0.0008	31.7	.001	+0.0104	1.6	.001
Creationism	0.4082	0.0011	45.2	.001	+0.0418	6.7	.001
Moral values							
Sex	0.0160	0.0160	390.0	.001	+0.0293	4.9	.001
Age	0.0248	0.0088	215.1	.001	−0.0460	8.4	.001
Extraversion	0.0568	0.0320	813.2	.001	−0.1161	20.6	.001
Neuroticism	0.0584	0.0016	40.9	.001	−0.0156	2.7	.01
Psychoticism	0.1494	0.0910	2564.0	.001	−0.1777	27.7	.001
Lie scale	0.2136	0.0642	1956.7	.001	+0.2252	36.4	.001
Church attendance	0.2427	0.0291	919.5	.001	+0.0735	11.8	.001
Belief in God	0.2685	0.0259	848.1	.001	+0.0823	11.3	.001
Creationism	0.2937	0.0251	852.6	.001	+0.1983	29.2	.001
Religious values							
Sex	0.0215	0.0215	527.0	.001	+0.0194	5.2	.001
Age	0.0236	0.0021	51.7	.001	−0.0016	0.5	NS
Extraversion	0.0237	0.0001	1.7	NS	+0.0335	10.2	.001
Neuroticism	0.0246	0.0009	21.7	.001	+0.0193	5.5	.001
Psychoticism	0.0665	0.0419	1076.0	.001	−0.0374	9.4	.001
Lie scale	0.1075	0.0410	1100.2	.001	+0.0622	16.2	.001
Church attendance	0.3124	0.2049	7143.1	.001	+0.1191	30.9	.001
Belief in God	0.6944	0.3820	29955.2	.001	+0.6000	132.4	.001
Creationism	0.7279	0.0335	2948.7	.001	+0.2289	54.3	.001
Credulity							
Sex	0.0166	0.0166	404.7	.001	+0.1375	19.6	.001
Age	0.0166	0.0001	1.4	NS	−0.0070	1.1	NS

Table 2.6 contd

Predictor variables	R^2	Change			B	t	P<
		R^2	F	P<			
Extraversion	0.0320	0.0153	379.9	.001	+0.1068	16.9	.001
Neuroticism	0.0523	0.0203	514.7	.001	+0.1332	20.8	.001
Psychoticism	0.0798	0.0275	716.8	.001	+0.1639	22.7	.001
Lie scale	0.0822	0.0025	64.8	.001	–0.0757	10.9	.001
Church attendance	0.0843	0.0020	53.1	.001	–0.1187	16.9	.001
Belief in God	0.1017	0.0174	465.0	.001	+0.1252	15.2	.001
Creationism	0.1035	0.0019	50.3	.001	+0.0542	7.1	.001

What should we make of the credulity data? It would appear that creationist adolescents are more credulous in general, tending to adopt a range of other 'unusual' beliefs. The relationship between credulity and creationist belief may be a direct causal relation, with the one predisposing to the other. But in which direction? Perhaps the credulous tend toward adopting creationism, or perhaps a creationist position opens the floodgates to all sorts of other beliefs, about which many would (and should?) be cautious. Defenders of creationism are unlikely to welcome either hypothesis.

So one conclusion may be a form of 'Bad News for the Creationist Party'. Adolescent creationists are more likely to be willing believers in general – even believing in horoscopes and black magic, which are not exactly biblical credos. They also tend to feel more worried, worthless, lonely and even desperate than do their evolutionist peers. Creationism is scientifically mistaken, most would insist, and therefore bad for the brain. Arguably, it is also theologically misled and misleading. And now, it would appear, we should recognize that it is not even good for the heart and soul.

The other conclusion, as usual, is that further research is needed to provide a more nuanced account of the nature of adolescent creationism.

References

Alexander, D. (2001), *Rebuilding the Matrix: Science and Faith in the 21st century* (Oxford, Lion).

Astley, J. (2000), *God's World* (London, Darton, Longman and Todd).

Astley, J. (2001), 'From religion to science: the positive contribution of religious education to scientific understanding', in L. J. Francis, J. Astley and M. Robbins (eds), *The Fourth R for the Third Millennium: Education in Religion and Values for the Global Future* (Dublin, Veritas), pp. 17–45.

Barbour, I. G. (1990), *Religion in an Age of Science* (London, SCM).

Barker, D., Halman, L. and Vloet, A. (1992), *The European Values Study 1981–1990: Summary Report* (London, Gordon Cook Foundation).

Barker, E. (1985), 'Let there be light: scientific creationism in the twentieth century', in J. Durant (ed.), *Darwinism and Divinity: Essays on Evolution and Religious Belief* (Oxford, Blackwell), pp. 181–204.

Barr, J. (1981), *Fundamentalism* (London, SCM).

Darwin, F. (ed.) (1887), *The Life and Letters of Charles Darwin*, vol. 2 (London, Murray).

Devine, P. E. (1996), 'Creation and evolution', *Religious Studies*, 32, 325–37.

Francis, L. J. (1982a), *Youth in Transit: A Profile of 16–25-Year-Olds* (Aldershot, Gower).

Francis, L. J. (1982b), *Experience of Adulthood: A Profile of 26–39-Year-Olds* (Aldershot, Gower).

Francis, L. J. (1984a), *Young and Unemployed* (Tunbridge Wells, Costello).

Francis, L. J. (1984b), *Teenagers and the Church: A Profile of Church-going Youth in the 1980s* (London, Collins Liturgical Publications).

Francis, L. J. (2001), *The Values Debate: A Voice from the Pupils* (London, Woburn).

Francis, L. J., Gibson, H. M. and Fulljames, P. (1990), 'Attitude towards Christianity, creationism, scientism and interest in science among 11–15-year-olds', *British Journal of Religious Education*, 13, 4–17.

Francis, L. J. and Greer, J. E. (2001), 'Shaping adolescents' attitudes towards science and religion in Northern Ireland: the role of scientism, creationism and denominational schools', *Research in Science and Technological Education*, 19, 1, 39–53.

Francis, L. J. and Kay, W. K. (1995), *Teenage Religion and Values* (Leominster, Gracewing).

Francis, L. J. and Pearson, P. R. (1988), 'The development of a short form of the JEPQ (JEPQ-S): its use in measuring personality and religion', *Personality and Individual Differences*, 9, 911–16.

Fulljames, P. (1996), 'Science, creation and Christianity: a further look', in L. J. Francis, W. K. Kay and W. S. Campbell (eds), *Research in Religious Education* (Leominster, Gracewing Fowler Wright), pp. 257–66.

Fulljames, P. and Francis, L. J. (1987), 'Creationism and student attitudes towards science and Christianity', *Journal of Christian Education*, papers 90, 51–5.

Fulljames, P. and Francis, L. J. (1988), 'The influence of creationism and scientism on attitudes towards Christianity among Kenyan secondary school students', *Educational Studies*, 14, 77–96.

Fulljames, P., Gibson, H. M. and Francis, L. J. (1991), 'Creationism, scientism, Christianity and science: a study in adolescent attitudes', *British Educational Research Journal*, 17, 171–90.

Furnham, A. and Gunter, B. (1989), *The Anatomy of Adolescence: Young People's Social Attitudes in Britain* (London, Routledge).

Gilkey, L. (1968), 'Evolution and the doctrine of creation', in I. G. Barbour (ed.), *Science and Religion: New Perspectives on the Dialogue* (London, SCM), pp. 159–81.

Gill, R. (1999), *Churchgoing and Christian Ethics* (Cambridge, Cambridge University Press).

Harding, S. and Phillips, D., with M. Fogarty (1986), *Contrasting Values in Western Europe: Unity, Diversity and Change* (London, Macmillan).

Harries, R. (2002), 'So God took his time. So what?', *Times Higher Education Supplement*, 22 March, 25.

Kay, W. K. and Francis, L. J. (1996), *Drift from the Churches: Attitude toward Christianity during Childhood and Adolescence* (Cardiff, University of Wales Press).

Kitcher, P. (1983), *Abusing Science: The Case Against Creationism* (Milton Keynes, Open University Press).

Krarup, H. (n.d.), '*Conventional Religion and Common Religion in*

Leeds' Interview Schedule: Basic Frequencies by Question (Leeds, Department of Sociology, University of Leeds).

Likert, R. (1932), 'A technique for the measurement of attitudes', *Archives of Psychology*, 140, 1–55.

Orenstein, A. (2002), 'Religion and paranormal belief', *Journal for the Scientific Study of Religion*, 41, 2, 301–11.

Peters, T. (1998), 'Science and theology: towards consonance', in T. Peters (ed.), *Science and Theology: The New Consonance* (Boulder, Col., Westview), pp. 11–39.

Pigliucci, M. (2002), *Denying Evolution: Creationism, Scientism, and the Nature of Science* (Sunderland, Mass., Sinauer).

Polkinghorne, J. (1994), *Science and Christian Belief* (London, SPCK).

Ruse, M. (2001), *Can a Darwinian be a Christian? The Relationship between Science and Religion* (Cambridge, Cambridge University Press).

Shorkey, C. T. and Whiteman, V. L. (1977), 'Development of the Rational Belief Inventory: initial validity and reliability', *Educational and Psychological Measurement*, 37, 527–34.

Temple, W. (1953), *Nature, Man and God* (London, Macmillan).

Tobacyk, J. and Milford, G. (1983), 'Belief in paranormal phenomena: assessment instrument development and implications for personality functioning', *Journal of Personality and Social Psychology*, 44, 5, 1029–37.

Watson, D. C. C. (1976), *The Great Brain Robbery* (Chicago, Ill., Moody).

Weeks, N. (1985), 'Can the creation/evolution debate be educational? A review article', *Journal of Christian Education*, Papers 82, 27–46.

3

The influence of Anglican secondary schools on personal, moral and religious values

DAVID W. LANKSHEAR

Summary

This chapter compares the personal, moral and religious values of 957 pupils attending Anglican voluntary aided secondary schools with the values of 24,027 pupils attending non-denominational schools. In this analysis further comparisons are made between boys and girls and between three religious groups: non-affiliates, Anglicans and those affiliated with other Christian denominations. The data demonstrated that Anglicans attending Anglican schools recorded higher levels of personal dissatisfaction, higher levels of religious values and comparable levels of moral values, in comparison with Anglicans attending non-denominational schools. Non-affiliates attending Anglican schools recorded higher levels of personal dissatisfaction, lower levels of moral values and comparable levels of religious values, in comparison with non-affiliates attending non-denominational schools.

Introduction

In September 1999 there were 189 Anglican secondary schools within the state-maintained system in England and Wales (this includes middle schools that are deemed to be secondary). In order to understand the way in which these schools fit into the total system, it is important to trace the development of schooling within England and Wales, from the beginnings of provision of schools for the 'poor and manufacturing classes' through to the separation of the school system into two phases, primary and secondary, following the 1944 Education Act. The Church of England and the Church in Wales were active in the early stages for the provision of education for the poor and manufacturing classes within England and Wales, working through the National Society. Between 1811, when the National Society was founded, and 1870, when the state first made provision for education for all, the National Society, along with the British and Foreign Schools Society, received government grant aid in order to promote the provision of schools throughout the country. Only when it became apparent that the churches were unable to provide education for all did the government of the day intervene directly in the provision of schooling by the creation of school boards, to be replaced in 1902 by local education authorities.

From 1870 to 1944 board schools and local education authority schools developed alongside church schools. Most of these schools provided an elementary education for children between the ages of 5 and 14. In 1944 this dual system was encapsulated within a new law of education, which provided for a partnership in the provision of schooling between the church authorities and the state. From the implementation of the 1944 Education Act schooling was to be divided into a primary phase, usually from 5 to 11, and a secondary phase, usually from 11 to at least 15 (subsequently raised to 16 in 1972). The Anglican Church, following the 1944 Education Act, faced a considerable challenge in the provision of schools, and individual schools had to make a decision as to whether they would opt for primary or secondary status. In the event the vast majority of Anglican schools opted for status as primary schools, which led directly to the current imbalance of provision. In September 1999, almost 25% of maintained primary schools were Anglican, compared with 5.6% of maintained secondary schools.

In some areas of the country the Anglican secondary schools are in great demand from church-affiliated families and are heavily over-subscribed. In other areas of the country, as a result of the historic location of these schools, they continue to serve the local community, regardless of the faith position of individual parents, and reflect their original trust deeds, which usually define their purpose as the provision of education for the children of the poor and manufacturing classes. This imbalance in provision between the primary and secondary sectors, combined with the historic commitment to serving the local community, means that the current position with regard to Anglican secondary schools in England and Wales is complex and quite distinct from schools run by other faiths or denominations. The Anglican Church, in its own writings and reports, encapsulates this complexity by referring to a dynamic tension that exists in all its secondary and some of its primary schools, between the task of providing an Anglican education for the children of Anglican parents and the task of providing an education for all children from the community immediately around the school. This has been a subject of continuing discussion and development of thinking over the last thirty years and is encapsulated in *The Fourth R* (Ramsey, 1970), *A Future in Partnership* (Waddington, 1984) and, most recently, in *The Way Ahead* (Dearing, 2001).

In seeking to establish the implications for the Church of England of the attitudes of pupils in church schools on matters of personal, moral and religious values, it is very important to bear in mind this dynamic tension in diversity within the admissions and to understand as far as possible how this might impact on the views of pupils within an individual school.

Given the tradition of opening a proportion of the places in Anglican schools to pupils who are being brought up in homes affiliated to a variety of faiths or to none, it is important to understand how the Anglican Church expects its schools to respond to the situation while being true to their foundation. All Anglican schools within the state-maintained sector must include within their Instrument of Government an ethos statement which provides the basis from which school policy and strategy are developed. In 1999 the Anglican Church adopted the following model ethos statement for its schools, which was in turn adopted by most Anglican schools without variation.

Recognising its historic foundation, the school will preserve and develop its religious character in accordance with the principles of the Church of England/Church in Wales and in partnership with the churches at parish and diocesan level.

The school aims to serve its community by providing an education of the highest quality within the context of Christian belief and practice. It encourages an understanding of the meaning and significance of faith, and promotes Christian values through the experience it offers to all its pupils. (Brown and Lankshear, 2000)

During the 1990s a number of publications have sought to help Anglican schools develop, explore and understand their nature as

Christian communities involved in education (see, for example, Brown and Lankshear, 2000). In seeking to understand the results revealed by the survey it is important to bear in mind that Anglican schools are attempting to be Christian communities, providing an education for the pupils who attend which is explicitly Christian, but also respectful of and sensitive to the beliefs in which pupils are being nurtured in their homes and, in some cases, within their religious communities. Developing ideas of religious belief and morality amongst this age group are therefore going to reflect not only the impact of the school but also the impact of home and, for some, their religious community. Some of the differences between the groups identified within this chapter may be accounted for in this way.

Method

Sample

As part of the Religion and Values Today project (Francis, 2001), a detailed questionnaire was administered throughout all year nine and year ten classes within 163 schools throughout England and Wales, from Pembrokeshire to Norfolk, and from Cornwall to Northumberland. A proper mix of rural and urban areas was included, as was a proper mix of independent and state-maintained schools. Within the state-maintained sector attention was given to the balance between Roman Catholic voluntary schools, Anglican voluntary schools and non-denominational schools. This latter group of schools have almost all been known as 'community schools' since 1998. In the remainder of this chapter this title will be used for them.

Participating schools were asked to follow a standard procedure. The questionnaires were administered in normal class groups. Pupils were asked not to write their name on the booklet and to complete the inventory under examination-like conditions. Although pupils were given the choice not to participate, very few declined to do so. They were assured of confidentiality and anonymity. As a consequence of this process thoroughly completed questionnaires were processed for 33,982 pupils. For the purposes of this study pupils attending independent schools or Roman Catholic schools have been excluded, in order that those attending

Anglican schools can be compared directly with those attending community schools; this reduces the total number of pupils in the sample to 24,984.

Instrument

The questionnaire used in this study is a revision of the Centymca Attitude Inventory, previously employed by Francis (1982a, 1982b, 1984a, 1984b) and Francis and Kay (1995). The instrument was designed to profile values over a number of areas, from which three have been selected for examination in the present analysis, namely personal dissatisfaction, moral values and religious values. These three areas are each assessed by nine-item scales designed for Likert scaling (see Likert, 1932). Pupils were required to grade their agreement with each statement on a five-point scale anchored by *strongly agree, agree, not certain, disagree* and *disagree strongly*.

Analysis

Of the 24,984 pupils in the group 3.8% attended Anglican schools. Three subsets of pupils in the overall group were selected for separate analyses:

Non-affiliates: The first subset comprised 14,546 pupils who described themselves as belonging to no religious group: 14,089 attending non-denominational schools and 457 (3.1% of the total) attending Anglican voluntary aided schools. Of this subset, 54.7% were male and 45.3% were female.

Anglicans: The second subset comprised 7,078 pupils who described themselves as belonging to the Anglican Church (Church of England, Church in Wales, Episcopalian and so on): 6,683 attending non-denominational schools and 395 (5.6% of the total) attending Anglican voluntary aided schools. Of this subset, 44.2% were male and 55.8% were female.

Other Christians: The third subset comprised 3,360 pupils who described themselves as belonging to other Christian denominations (Roman Catholic, Baptist, Methodist, and so on): 3,255 attending non-denominational schools and 105 (3.1% of the total) attending Anglican voluntary aided schools. Of this subset, 44.9% were male and 55.1% were female.

Results

Tables 3.1, 3.2 and 3.3 present the items for the scale of personal dissatisfaction, scale of moral values and scale of religious values, together with the item rest of test correlations and the alpha coefficient. These statistics confirm the basic internal reliability and item homogeneity for the three scales.

Table 3.1 Scale of personal dissatisfaction: reliability

Item	r
I find life really worth living*	0.3440
I often worry about my school work	0.3282
I often feel depressed	0.5002
I have sometimes considered taking my own life	0.3502
I am worried about how I get on with other people	0.4350
I am worried about my sex life	0.3398
I am worried about my exams at school	0.3222
I tend to be a lonely person	0.4044
I feel I am not worth much as a person	0.5006
alpha	0.7153

Note: *This item is reverse coded.

Table 3.2 Scale of moral values: reliability

Item	r
Abortion is wrong	0.2318
There is too much violence on television	0.3711
It is wrong to have sexual intercourse outside marriage	0.4021
It is wrong to become drunk	0.4700
Divorce is wrong	0.2771
It is wrong to smoke cigarettes	0.3868
Pornography is too readily available	0.2998
It is wrong to use heroin	0.3104
It is wrong to have sexual intercourse under the legal age	0.4932
alpha	0.6831

Table 3.3 Scale of religious values: reliability

Item	r
I believe in God	0.6932
I believe Jesus really rose from the dead	0.7067
I believe in life after death	0.3259
I believe Jesus Christ is the Son of God	0.7035
The church seems irrelevant to life today*	0.3109
I want my children baptised in church	0.5047
I want to get married in church	0.3797
Church is boring*	0.3716
Ministers and priests do a good job	0.5107
alpha	0.8062

Note: *These items are reverse coded.

Tables 3.4, 3.5, 3.6 and 3.7 present the mean scale scores on the scales of personal dissatisfaction, moral values and religious values for male and female pupils according to religious affiliation and the type of school attended. Table 3.7 presents the two-way analyses of variance significance tests designed to assess the relationship between both sex and school type and the three value domains. Separate analyses of variance were calculated for each of the three groups constituted by religious affiliation. Two main conclusions emerge from these data.

The first conclusion concerns the relationship between sex and values. In all three groups constituted by religious affiliation, females recorded a significantly higher level of personal dissatisfaction. In all three groups constituted by religious affiliation, females recorded a significantly higher level of religious values. Among the non-affiliates and among the Anglicans, females recorded a significantly more conservative position regarding moral values, although no significant differences were recorded by other Christian males and females in respect of moral values.

Table 3.4 Mean scale scores of personal dissatisfaction by religious affiliation, sex and type of school

	Male		Female	
	mean	sd	mean	sd
Non-affiliates				
Community schools	24.0	5.8	26.2	5.6
Church of England aided schools	25.2	6.3	26.9	5.7
Anglicans				
Community schools	24.6	5.7	26.2	5.5
Church of England aided schools	25.6	6.3	27.5	6.1
Other Christians				
Community schools	24.6	5.9	26.5	5.7
Church of England aided schools	25.4	6.0	28.6	5.9

Table 3.5 Mean scale scores of moral values by religious affiliation, sex and type of school

	Male		Female	
	mean	sd	mean	sd
Non-affiliates				
Community schools	23.2	6.0	24.6	5.6
Church of England schools	21.9	6.7	22.9	5.8
Anglicans				
Community schools	24.4	5.9	25.8	5.8
Church of England schools	24.3	6.2	26.0	5.8
Other Christians				
Community schools	26.3	7.1	27.5	6.6
Church of England schools	26.0	7.0	26.9	7.4

The second conclusion concerns the relationship between attendance at an Anglican voluntary aided secondary school and values. The relationship between school type and values is less clear-cut than the relationship between sex and values. In respect of personal dissatisfaction, the non-affiliates and the Anglicans who attended an Anglican voluntary aided school record a significantly higher level of personal dissatisfaction, in comparison with their peers who attend community schools. On the other hand, the members of other Christian denominations who attend an Anglican voluntary aided school do not significantly differ in their level of personal dissatisfaction from their peers who attend community schools. In respect of moral values, there are no significant differences, either among the Anglicans or among those affiliated to other Christian denominations, between those who attend community schools and those who attend Anglican voluntary aided schools. On the other hand, among the pupils who belong to no religious group, those who attend Anglican voluntary aided schools display a significantly more liberal set of moral values compared with those who attend community schools. In respect of religious values, there is no significant difference, either among the non-affiliates or among the affiliates to other Christian denominations, between those who attend community schools and those who attend Anglican voluntary aided schools. On the other hand, among the Anglicans, those who attend Anglican voluntary aided schools display a significantly more positive view of religion.

Table 3.6 Mean scale scores of religious values by religious affiliation, sex and type of school

	Male		Female	
	mean	sd	mean	sd
Non-affiliates				
Community schools	25.3	6.7	27.5	6.0
Church of England schools	25.2	7.1	26.8	6.2
Anglicans				
Community schools	30.4	6.7	31.7	5.7
Church of England schools	31.2	7.4	32.7	5.9
Other Christians				
Community schools	32.5	7.1	34.1	5.8
Church of England schools	33.0	7.3	34.5	6.3

Table 3.7 Analysis of variance significance tests

	Sex		School		Interaction	
	F	P<	F	P<	F	P<
Personal dissatisfaction						
Non-affiliates	49.8	.001	8.9	.01	0.4	NS
Anglicans	36.1	.001	14.0	.001	0.4	NS
Other Christians	18.3	.001	3.2	NS	1.4	NS
Moral values						
Non-affiliates	13.5	.001	28.2	.001	1.0	NS
Anglicans	25.6	.001	0.0	NS	0.1	NS
Other Christians	1.7	NS	0.1	NS	0.1	NS
Religious values						
Non-affiliates	34.8	.001	0.3	NS	0.6	NS
Anglicans	19.0	.001	8.6	.01	0.1	NS
Other Christians	6.6	.01	0.2	NS	0.0	NS

Discussion

The first issue to note derives from the way in which the respondents to this survey have been grouped. It has been possible to identify respondents from three distinct categories, both in Anglican secondary schools and in community schools: 457 of the respondents attending Anglican voluntary schools were identified as having no religious affiliation; 395 of the respondents attending Anglican schools were identified as Anglican; and 105 of the respondents attending Anglican schools were identified as other Christians. This reflects strongly the Anglican tradition of offering places in its schools to pupils living in the locality of the school regardless of their religious affiliation, alongside an offer of places to members of the Church of England and other Christian denominations. This approach was recently reinforced in the Church of England report *The Way Ahead* (Dearing, 2001). This should be compared with the approach to admissions to Roman Catholic secondary schools, reflected in an article using data from the same overall survey, where Francis (2002) reports the results for respondents attending Roman Catholic secondary schools. Francis was able to divide these respondents into four groups: practising Catholics (31%), sliding Catholics (30%), lapsed Catholics (6%) and non-Catholics (32%). Thus, while 67% of the pupils attending Roman Catholic schools identify themselves in relation to the Roman Catholic Church, only 41.3% of pupils attending Anglican schools identify themselves as Anglican.

It cannot be assumed, however, that this proportion of Anglican pupils is represented in all Anglican schools in the sample. Without a school-by-school analysis of the way in which their admissions policy impacts on their intake of pupils it is not possible to explore the ways in which the different Anglican schools in the sample vary in this respect. One of the ways in which this issue could be tackled in greater depth in an investigation of this nature would be to include sufficient Anglican schools to be able to subdivide them by the ways in which their admission policies operate. This would enable differences to be explored between those Anglican schools admitting mostly pupils being nurtured within Anglican homes (using similar criteria to that proposed by Francis (2002) for Catholic schools) and those schools admitting pupils simply on the basis of proximity to the school.

I will now turn to three further issues which are derived directly from the model ethos statement for Anglican schools quoted above (p. 57). The statement commits the school to serve its community by providing an education of the highest quality within the context of Christian belief and practice. This appears to set the work of Anglican schools firmly within both the traditions of mainstream education as a whole and the Christian tradition of service to the wider community. In attempting to understand the results of this survey in terms of personal satisfaction, religious and moral values, it is important to reflect on how far the Church of England should expect the results of a high-quality education set in the context of service to produce pupils whose views and self perceptions reflect closely those of the Church itself. This, of course, assumes that the Anglican Church has a single coherent set of views and values, given that the Anglican Church also prides itself on containing a broad spectrum of views.

Given the variety of faith backgrounds represented in many Anglican secondary schools, it must be expected that there will be a range of views and opinions among the pupils. It could be claimed that the variety of opinion and differences of attitude revealed in this survey demonstrate that Anglican schools are achieving their aim of service to the community, with the provision of high-quality education, in so far as they are sustaining diverse opinions within their schools. If well managed, this provides a good preparation for living in a diverse community and also produces an educational institution in which there is lively debate. Given the increased levels of personal dissatisfaction among pupils in Anglican schools who are either non-affiliates or Anglicans, compared with those in community schools, it is important to consider the possible reasons for this. It might be that the parental option for their children to attend an Anglican school, which in some areas will require a significant effort on behalf of parents, represents a drive for educational success for their children, over and above that expressed by most parents.

If this drive were to result in excessive pressure on the pupils, this could account for the higher levels of personal dissatisfaction expressed by two of the three groups of pupils in the study. Alternative explanations would imply concerns about the pastoral systems in place in the schools, or about the existence of undue academic pressure within the schools. There is no evidence within the data to justify such implied criticisms of the schools.

The ethos statement also includes the intention to encourage an understanding of the meaning and significance of faith. The survey instrument that was used for this work focuses on only one of the two aspects of this particular aim. The aim itself is to be understood within the context of the meaning and significance of faith both for the individual and for others within the community. In focusing on statements about personal belief, the survey instrument can address only the first of these two issues. In this context it is not surprising that those pupils being nurtured within the Anglican community find their attitude toward religion strengthened and supported by the experience of attending an Anglican school. This will be reassuring, however, to members of the Anglican Church.

Anglican schools set out to provide education within the context of Christian belief and practice, and faith issues will, therefore, be explicit within the school context. This will provide an atmosphere in which the issues are likely to be discussed and differing religious views and practices and their importance to individuals explored. This seems likely to promote the development amongst pupils of an understanding of the importance of faith to others, so although the survey instrument does not address this issue explicitly, it is clear from the range of pupils that attend Anglican schools that there is likely to be some growth in this area.

The ethos statement also commits the school to promote Christian values through the experience it offers to all pupils. This aim is likely to impact most on the scales for religious and moral values, although it might also be expected to have some reference to the scale on personal dissatisfaction. The wording of this objective is significant because it talks about emerging Christian values and the experience the school offers pupils. The school is not setting out to produce pupils who all accept the values and teaching of the Anglican Church without question. It is setting out to provide an experience of those values in practice and to challenge pupils to respond to that experience in the ways in which they develop their own views. The degree to which Anglican schools that were part of this survey are being effective in this is difficult to measure. Is it reasonable to suggest that, where Christian values are promoted through experience, pupils will become more liberal in their moral views and will have a significantly higher level of religious values than their peers? The survey seems to suggest that, for some groups at least, this has been the result of education within Anglican schools.

Conclusion

This study has shown that, in all three groups constituted by religious affiliation, females recorded a significantly higher level of personal dissatisfaction. In all three groups constituted by religious affiliation, females also recorded a significantly higher level of religious values. Among the non-affiliates and among the Anglicans, females recorded a significantly more conservative position regarding moral values, although no significant differences were recorded by other Christian males and females in respect of moral values.

This study has also demonstrated the relationship between attendance at an Anglican voluntary aided secondary school and values. The relationship between school type and values is less clear-cut than the relationship between sex and values. In respect of personal dissatisfaction, the non-affiliates and the Anglicans who attended an Anglican voluntary aided school record a significantly higher level of personal dissatisfaction, in comparison with their peers who attend community schools. On the other hand, the members of other Christian denominations who attend an Anglican voluntary aided school do not differ significantly in their level of personal dissatisfaction from their peers who attend community schools. In respect of moral values, there are no significant differences, either among the Anglicans or among those affiliated to other Christian denominations, between those who attend community schools and those who attend Anglican voluntary aided schools. On the other hand, among the pupils who belong to no religious group, those who attend Anglican voluntary aided schools display a significantly more liberal set of moral values than that of those who attend community schools. In respect of religious values, there is no significant difference, either among the non-affiliates or among the affiliates to other Christian denominations, between those who attend community schools and those who attend Anglican voluntary aided schools. On the other hand, among the Anglicans, those who attend Anglican voluntary aided schools display a significantly more positive view of religion.

Attention has been drawn to the difficulty of interpreting results. This difficuty, it has been argued, is created by two distinct factors. One is the diversity of Anglican schools themselves within the state provision, at secondary level, and the second is the diversity of pupils they serve, and the interplay between the experience of these pupils outside school and the experience that they have within it. The survey raises some challenging issues for Anglican schools, which need to be addressed within the setting of the Anglican Church's work in education, but it also draws attention to the need for much wider research in this area, with a sufficiently large number of Anglican schools involved to be able to include within the analysis some allowance for the variety of approach, particularly on admissions, which marks out Anglican education at secondary level in England and Wales.

References

Brown, A. S. and Lankshear, D. W. (2000), *The National Society's Handbook for Inspection under Section 23* (3rd edn) (London, National Society and Church House Publishing).

Dearing, R. (2001), *The Way Ahead* (London, Church House Publishing).

Francis, L. J. (1982a), *Youth in Transit: A Profile of 16–25-Year-Olds* (Aldershot, Gower).

Francis, L. J. (1982b), *Experience of Adulthood: A Profile of 26–39-Year-Olds* (Aldershot, Gower).

Francis, L. J. (1984a), *Young and Unemployed* (Tunbridge Wells, Costello).

Francis, L. J. (1984b), *Teenagers and the Church: A Profile of Church-going Youth in the 1980s* (London, Collins Liturgical Publications).

Francis, L. J. (2001), *The Values Debate: A Voice from the Pupils* (London, Woburn Press).

Francis, L. J. (2002), 'Catholic schools and Catholic values: a study of moral and religious values among 13–15-year-old pupils attending non-denominational and Catholic schools in England and Wales', *International Journal of Education and Religion*, 3, 69–84.

Francis, L. J. and Kay, W. K. (1995), *Teenage Religion and Values* (Leominster, Gracewing).

Likert, R. (1932), 'A technique for the measurement of attitudes', *Archives of Psychology*, 140, 1–55.

Ramsey, I. (1970), *The Fourth R* (London, National Society and SPCK).

Waddington, R. (1984), *A Future in Partnership* (London, National Society).

4

The identity of young Anglicans: the feminization of the Anglican Church

ANNA HALSALL

Summary

This chapter investigates the identity of young Anglicans and forms part of the continuing debate concerning the potential importance of self-assigned religious affiliation as a socially significant indicator. The study demonstrates that, in the case of young Anglicans, self-assigned religious affiliation is a socially significant indicator of values. The identity of young Anglicans is investigated through an exploration of their values, in comparison with the values of young people of no religious affiliation, and analysed with relation to gender orientation theory. The data concerning young Anglicans are taken from a database of 33,982 young people. The study shows that young Anglicans have a distinct values profile and identity when compared with young people of no religious affiliation, and that, overall, affiliation with the Anglican Church tends to be associated with a more feminine values profile.

Introduction

Recently there has been debate over whether self-assigned religious affiliation is a socially significant indicator. For example, does self-assigned religious affiliation function as a significant predictor of differences in values and attitudes? Many studies concerned with young people's values and attitudes over the past twenty years have ignored the potential importance of religious affiliation as a socially significant indicator (see, for example, Department of Education and Science, 1983; Furnham and Stacey, 1991; Balding, 1993, 1997, 1998, 1999; Hendry, Shucksmith, Love and Glendinning, 1993; Woodroffe, Glickman, Barker and Power, 1993;

Roberts and Sachdev, 1996; Kremer, Trew and Ogle, 1997).

However, this assumption is being increasingly challenged, and studies such as Francis and Kay (1995), Fane (1999), Gill (1999) and Francis (2001) are arguing that self-assigned religious affiliation makes a significant difference to the values of affiliates and should, therefore, be taken into consideration.

With this in mind, the present study aims to investigate whether being Anglican makes a difference to the values of the young people who affiliate themselves with the Anglican Church in England and Wales. Anglicanism can be said to be different from other religious affiliations due to the large proportion of nominal, rather than practising, affiliates with the Anglican Church. However, self-assigned religious affiliation with the Anglican Church has been shown to make a difference to the values of affiliates in recent studies, including research among adult Anglicans in Canada (Bibby, 1986) and the United Kingdom (Gill, 1999), and teenage Anglicans in the United Kingdom (Francis, 1984; Francis and Kay, 1995).

Bibby (1986) investigates the values of 'active' and 'inactive' adult Anglicans in the Canadian diocese of Toronto. These groups of Anglicans are frequently compared with Canadians as a whole group. It is evident from Bibby's analysis that both groups of Anglicans are distinct from each other, and also from the Canadian population as a whole. For example, in examining what personally concerns Anglicans, Bibby (1986) demonstrates that 33% of Canadians overall, 28% of 'inactive' Anglicans and 20% of 'active' Anglicans are concerned about money.

The difference between Anglicans and the Canadian population in general is especially evident in Bibby (1986) with relation to one issue, regarding drugs. Bibby (1986) demonstrates that smaller proportions of both groups of Anglicans (13% of 'active' Anglicans and 16% of 'inactive' Anglicans) than of Canadians generally (29%) agree that marijuana should be legalized. On issues of law and order the picture changes slightly, in that the proportion of 'inactive' Anglicans is closer to that of Canadians overall than is that of 'active' Anglicans. Thus, 86% of 'inactive' Anglicans, in comparison with 85% of Canadians and 75% of 'active' Anglicans, agree that the death penalty should be exercised in some instances. However, it is apparent from the adult Anglicans' values demonstrated in Bibby (1986) that there are definite differences between the values expressed by Anglicans and those expressed by the population overall. Bibby (1986) therefore shows that affiliation with the Anglican Church makes a difference to adults' values. Adult Anglicans' values in the United Kingdom are explored to a certain extent in Gill (1999). Gill portrays data from a variety of differing sources in his investigation of the effects of churchgoing on values. In analysing the religious beliefs of United Kingdom adult Anglicans, Gill utilizes data from Gallup polls and compares Anglicans' beliefs with those of the general population. For example, Gill (1999) demonstrates that in 1996, 53% of Anglican churchgoers stated belief in the Virgin Birth, in comparison with 27% of the general United Kingdom population. Additionally, 35% of Anglican churchgoers in 1996 agreed that the Bible had 'absolute divine authority', in comparison with 16% of the general population. In 1985, 94% of Anglicans and 74% of the general population stated that they took part in personal prayer. Gill (1999) also examines the moral values of adult Anglicans in the United Kingdom. For example, in looking at attitudes to abortion, Gill shows that 92% of Anglican weekly churchgoers and 65% of Roman Catholic weekly churchgoers agree that abortion should be allowed if the woman's health is endangered. Furthermore, 82% of Anglican weekly churchgoers and 43% of Roman Catholic weekly churchgoers agree that abortion should be allowed on the grounds of a 'defective embryo'. On the issue of pornography, Gill (1999) shows that 66% of Anglicans and 57% of Roman Catholics agree that pornography should be banned altogether. Gill (1999) therefore again demonstrates differences between Anglican-affiliated adults and adults in the general population, or other Christian denominations.

Two main studies concerning the values of teenage Anglicans will be considered here. First, Francis (1984) examines the values of 'active' churchgoers and compares data provided by young Anglicans, young Roman Catholics and young Free Church members, aged between 13 and 20, who were present in church on a particular Sunday. From this study, clear differences between young Anglicans and young people of different denominations are apparent. For example, when asked questions concerning what they worry about, 70% of the older (aged 16–20) Anglican teenagers, 82% of older Catholic teenagers and 90% of older Free Church teenagers are not worried about their sex lives. Additionally, of the whole group (all 13- to 20-year-olds), 21% of both Anglicans and Roman Catholics and 10% of Free Church members are worried about their health; and 18% of Anglicans, 21% of Roman Catholics and 14% of Free Church teenagers are worried that they cannot cope.

When questioned about their religious beliefs, the differences between the young people of differing denominations are again evident. For example, 67% of Anglican young people, 85% of Roman Catholic young people and 81% of the Free Church young people believe that Jesus really rose from the dead; and 53% of Anglicans, 64% of Roman Catholics and 61% of Free Church members believe in life after death. There are clear and consistent differences expressed between the young people of different denominations here in their religious beliefs.

On issues of societal and world concern, Francis (1984) demonstrates that 70% of young Anglicans, 73% of young Roman Catholics and 62% of young Free Church members are concerned about the threat of nuclear war; and 48% of Anglicans, 58% of Roman Catholics and 64% of Free Church members are concerned about the availability of pornography.

Francis (1984) also looks at the moral values of the churchgoing young people. Questions concerning attitudes to sexuality were only asked of the older group (16- to 20-year-olds). Of these, 86% of Anglicans, 69% of Roman Catholics and 80% of Free Church members reject the suggestion that contraception is wrong. Moreover, 28% of Anglicans, 32% of Roman Catholics and 55% of Free Church members claim that it is wrong to have sex outside marriage; and 40% of both Anglicans and Roman Catholics and 54% of Free Church members agree that homosexuality is wrong.

From this review of some of the attitudes expressed by young Anglicans, Roman Catholics and members of the Free Churches, according to Francis (1984), it is clear that religious affiliation with the Anglican Church makes a difference to the values of young people.

The second study of teenage Anglicans to be examined here was conducted by Francis and Kay (1995). The data analysed in Francis and Kay (1995) constitute a profile of over 13,000 young people between the ages of 13 and 15 in state-maintained schools. The young Anglicans presented in Francis and Kay (1995) are consistently compared with young Roman Catholics and with young members of the Free Churches.

In investigating what the young people see as worrying, Francis and Kay (1995) portray that 41% of young Anglicans, in comparison with 31% of young Roman Catholics and 40% of young members of the Free Churches, are worried about going out alone at night in their area. Similarly, 30% of Anglicans, 29% of Roman Catholics and 34% of Free Church members are worried about being bullied at school.

Francis and Kay (1995) also present data regarding young Anglicans' religious beliefs. For example, 87% of young Anglicans, in comparison with 88% of young Roman Catholics and 85% of young Free Church members, believe in God. On moral issues, Francis and Kay (1995) demonstrate that 24% of young Anglicans, in comparison with 30% of young Roman Catholics and 27% of young Free Church members, agree that divorce is wrong. Furthermore, 38% of Anglicans, 66% of Roman Catholics and 47% of Free Church members agree that abortion is wrong; and 30% of Anglicans, 35% of Roman Catholics and 38% of Free Church members agree that homosexuality is wrong.

These studies (Bibby, 1986; Gill, 1999; Francis, 1984; Francis and Kay, 1995), therefore, clearly demonstrate that affiliation with the Anglican Church makes a difference to the values of affiliates, in comparison with affiliates of other denominations, those of no religious affiliation and the population in general.

Another strand of research has attempted to interpret the values profile of religious people in terms of gender orientation theory. Gender orientation theory, broadly conceived, maintains that there are psychological preferences which tend to be associated with being either female or male, but that these preferences can be present to greater or lesser degrees in both women and men. One classic account of this theory is provided by the Bem Sex Role Inventory (Bem, 1981).

Bem's account makes two important points. The first is that the psychological characteristics of femininity and masculinity can be established empirically by comparing the stereotypes associated with being female or being male. The second is that femininity and masculinity are not opposite ends of one continuum but two independent continua. In this sense both women and men may record four distinctive positions: high on femininity and low on masculinity (feminine profile), high on masculinity and low on femininity (masculine profile), high on femininity and high on masculinity (androgynous profile), and low on femininity and low on masculinity (undifferentiated profile). Studies like Thompson (1991) and Francis and Wilcox (1996, 1998a) have demonstrated that high scores on Bem's construct of femininity are core to being religious.

Another approach to discussing psychological gender orientation is by means of recognizing the clear sex differences recorded in standard personality tests. For example, Eysenck's three-dimensional model of personality consistently finds that being female is associated with high neuroticism scores and low psychoticism scores (Eysenck and Eysenck, 1985). Studies like Francis (1992a) and Francis, Lewis, Brown, Philipchalk and Lester (1995) have demonstrated that low scores on Eysenck's construct of psychoticism are core to being religious. Moreover, a close relationship has been demonstrated between Bem's model of gender orientation and Eysenck's model of personality (Francis and Wilcox, 1998b).

Against this background, the present study will investigate in detail whether young people who are affiliated in some way with the Anglican Church have a distinct identity. If they do, the nature of this identity will be explored.

Method

Sample

The sample which forms the focus for this study is taken from a database of 33,982 young people. Data were collected in schools throughout England and Wales, including a proper mix of urban and rural, and of independent and state-maintained schools. Within the state-maintained sector, a correct balance between non-denominational, Anglican voluntary and Roman Catholic voluntary schools was included. Girls and boys aged between 13 and 15 were included in the sample. Originally, pupils from many different ethnic and religious backgrounds were included. However, because the focus of this study is on young Anglicans, all pupils belonging to non-Christian faith communities were not included in the current re-analysis. After screening out non-Christian faith communities, the sample for this study comprised 30,564 young people. Of these 30,564 young people, 46% identified themselves as of no religious affiliation, and 32% identified themselves as affiliated with the Anglican Church.

Instrument

The young people were given a twenty-four-page questionnaire which they were asked to complete in school time under examination conditions. They were assured of complete confidentiality and anonymity. In addition to a number of background questions, the questionnaire included a range of easily understood statements, to which the pupils responded on a five-point Likert-type scale (Likert, 1932): *agree strongly, agree, not certain, disagree* and *disagree strongly*. The questionnaire covered fifteen value areas.

Analysis

The data are analysed here to profile the identity of young Anglicans through investigation of their values over six areas from the questionnaire: religious beliefs, my worries, school, law and order, substance use, and societal and world concerns. The analysis is conducted in three steps. First, a comparison is made between all the girls and all the boys surveyed. Second, Anglican girls are compared with girls affiliated with no religious group, and third, Anglican boys are compared with boys affiliated with no religious group. The *agree strongly* and *agree* categories have been collapsed into one for the purposes of this study, and the tables present the proportions of each group who agree with each statement.

Results

Religious beliefs

Tables 4.1, 4.2 and 4.3 examine the responses of the young people in the sample to statements concerning their religious beliefs. Table 4.1 compares the responses of all the girls and all the boys in the sample. All of the statements in Table 4.1 generate differences of high statistical significance (.001). From Table 4.1 it is evident that more of the girls agree with each statement of religious belief than of the boys. For example, 45% of the girls state that they believe in God, in comparison with 37% of the boys; and 32% of the girls state that they believe that Jesus really rose from the dead, in comparison with 29% of the boys.

Table 4.1 Religious beliefs by sex

	Girls %	Boys %	X²	P<
I believe in God	45	37	161.1	.001
I believe that Jesus really rose from the dead	32	29	39.7	.001
I believe in life after death	46	43	17.1	.001

Table 4.2 compares the responses of Anglican girls and girls of no religious affiliation to statements concerning their religious beliefs. The data in this table portray that more of the Anglican girls than of the girls of no religious affiliation agree with each statement of religious belief. For example, 50% of the Anglican girls and 27% of the girls of no religious affiliation state that they believe in God; and 36% of the Anglican girls and 18% of the girls of no religious affiliation state that they believe Jesus really rose from the dead. All of the statements in Table 4.2 generate differences of high statistical significance (.001).

Table 4.2 Religious beliefs by Anglican girls and girls of no religious affiliation

	Anglicans %	No religion %	X²	P<
I believe in God	50	27	623.4	.001
I believe that Jesus really rose from the dead	36	18	515.5	.001
I believe in life after death	46	41	31.0	.001

Table 4.3 compares the responses of Anglican boys and boys of no religious affiliation to statements concerning religious belief. Once again, all of the statements in the table generate differences of high statistical significance (.001). More of the Anglican boys than of the boys of no religious affiliation agree with each statement of religious belief. For example, 47% of the Anglican boys and just 22% of the boys of no religious affiliation believe in God; and 36% of the Anglican boys and 17% of the boys of no religious affiliation believe that Jesus really rose from the dead.

Table 4.3 Religious beliefs by Anglican boys and boys of no religious affiliation

	Anglicans %	No religion %	X^2	P<
I believe in God	47	22	817.0	.001
I believe that Jesus really rose from the dead	36	17	615.3	.001
I believe in life after death	46	37	95.2	.001

Worries

Tables 4.4, 4.5 and 4.6 examine the responses of the young people in the sample to statements concerning issues about which they may worry. Table 4.4 compares the responses of all the girls and all the boys in the sample. From the table it is evident that more of the girls than of the boys agree that they are worried about all the issues listed. For example, 44% of the girls, in comparison with only 18% of the boys, are worried about going out alone at night in their area; and 40% of the girls and 30% of the boys are worried about their attractiveness to the opposite sex. All of the statements in Table 4.4 generate differences of high statistical significance (.001).

Table 4.4 Worries by sex

	Girls %	Boys %	X^2	P<
I am worried about my attractiveness to the opposite sex	40	30	379.2	.001
I am worried about how I get on with other people	56	49	160.2	.001
I am worried about going out alone at night in my area	44	18	2437.6	.001

Table 4.5 compares the responses of Anglican girls and girls of no religious affiliation to issues about which they may worry. Although not all of the differences in Table 4.5 are of statistical significance, a clear pattern is evident from the table. This is, that for each of the suggested issues, more of the Anglican girls than of the girls of no religious affiliation demonstrate worry. For example, 46% of the Anglican girls and 41% of the girls of no religious affiliation

are worried about going out alone at night in their area; and 41% of the Anglican girls and 39% of the girls of no religious affiliation are worried about their attractiveness to the opposite sex.

Table 4.5 Worries by Anglican girls and girls of no religious affiliation

	Anglicans %	No religion %	X^2	P<
I am worried about my attractiveness to the opposite sex	41	39	7.1	.01
I am worried about how I get on with other people	56	54	3.5	NS
I am worried about going out alone at night in my area	46	41	23.2	.001

Table 4.6 compares the responses of Anglican boys and boys of no religious affiliation to issues about which they may worry. All of the statements in Table 4.6 generate differences of high statistical significance (.001). Once again, a clear pattern is evident from the table, in that more of the Anglican boys than of the boys of no religious affiliation are worried about all of the suggested issues. For example, 54% of the Anglican boys, in comparison with 45% of the boys of no religious affiliation, are worried about how they get on with other people; and 33% of the Anglican boys, in comparison with 27% of the boys of no religious affiliation, are worried about their attractiveness to the opposite sex.

Table 4.6 Worries by Anglican boys and boys of no religious affiliation

	Anglicans %	No religion %	X^2	P<
I am worried about my attractiveness to the opposite sex	33	27	41.1	.001
I am worried about how I get on with other people	54	45	89.0	.001
I am worried about going out alone at night in my area	19	16	16.9	.001

School

Tables 4.7, 4.8 and 4.9 examine the responses of the young people in the sample to issues regarding school. Table 4.7 compares the responses of all the girls and all the boys in the sample. From this table it is apparent that the girls are more positive than the boys concerning school, yet also are more worried than the boys about issues connected with school. For example, 73% of the girls, in comparison with 70% of the boys, are happy in their school, while 81% of the girls and 68% of the boys are worried about their exams at school. All of the statements in the table generate differences of high statistical significance (.001).

Table 4.7 School by sex

	Girls %	Boys %	X^2	P<
I am happy in my school	73	70	24.7	.001
I am worried about my exams at school	81	68	619.3	.001
I am worried about being bullied at school	31	25	132.8	.001

Table 4.8 compares the responses of Anglican girls and girls of no religious affiliation to statements regarding school. From this table it is apparent that the Anglican girls are more positive than the girls of no religious affiliation on school issues, yet also that the Anglican girls are more worried than the girls of no religious affiliation concerning school issues. For example, 77% of the Anglican girls and 70% of the girls of no religious affiliation are happy in their school; but 82% of the Anglican girls and 78% of the girls of no religious affiliation are worried about their exams at school. The statements in Table 4.8 all generate differences of statistical significance.

Table 4.9 compares the responses of Anglican boys and boys of no religious affiliation to statements concerning school. From this table it is apparent that the Anglican boys are more positive than the boys of no religious affiliation on issues concerning school, yet also that the Anglican boys are more worried than the boys of no religious affiliation concerning school issues. For example, 76% of the Anglican boys and 67% of the boys of no religious affiliation are happy in their school, while 71% of the Anglican boys and

65% of the boys of no religious affiliation are worried about their exams at school. All of the statements in Table 4.9 generate differences of high statistical significance (.001).

Table 4.8 School by Anglican girls and girls of no religious affiliation

	Anglicans %	No religion %	X^2	P<
I am happy in my school	77	70	71.4	.001
I am worried about my exams at school	82	78	24.4	.001
I am worried about being bullied at school	31	29	5.4	.05

Table 4.9 School by Anglican boys and boys of no religious affiliation

	Anglicans %	No religion %	X^2	P<
I am happy in my school	76	67	117.8	.001
I am worried about my exams at school	71	65	40.3	.001
I am worried about being bullied at school	27	23	22.7	.001

Law and order

Tables 4.10, 4.11 and 4.12 examine the responses of the young people in the sample to statements concerning law and order. Table 4.10 compares the responses of all the girls and all the boys. From the table it is apparent that the girls have a more positive approach to issues of law and order than the boys. For example, more of the boys (45%) than of the girls (38%) agree that there is nothing wrong in buying alcoholic drinks under the legal age; and more of the girls (58%) than of the boys (53%) agree that the police do a good job. All of the statements in Table 4.10 generate differences of high statistical significance (.001).

Table 4.11 compares the responses of Anglican girls and girls of no religious affiliation to statements concerning law and order.

From this table it is apparent that the Anglican girls have a more positive approach to law and order than the girls of no religious affiliation. For example, more of the girls of no religious affiliation (42%) than of the Anglican girls (35%) agree that there is nothing wrong in buying alcoholic drinks under the legal age; and more of the Anglican girls (63%) than of the girls of no religious affiliation (53%) agree that the police do a good job. All of the statements in Table 4.11 generate differences of high statistical significance (.001).

Table 4.10 Law and order by sex

	Girls %	Boys %	X^2	P<
There is nothing wrong in shoplifting	5	10	256.7	.001
There is nothing wrong in buying alcoholic drinks under the legal age (18)	38	45	152.4	.001
The police do a good job	58	53	65.4	.001

Table 4.11 Law and order by Anglican girls and girls of no religious affiliation

	Anglicans %	No religion %	X^2	P<
There is nothing wrong in shoplifting	3	6	51.2	.001
There is nothing wrong in buying alcoholic drinks under the legal age (18)	35	42	59.3	.001
The police do a good job	63	53	98.5	.001

Table 4.12 compares the responses of Anglican boys and boys of no religious affiliation to statements concerning law and order. From the table it is evident that the Anglican boys have a more positive approach to law and order than the boys of no religious affiliation. For example, more of the boys of no religious affiliation (11%) than of the Anglican boys (7%) agree that there is nothing wrong in shoplifting; and more of the Anglican boys (61%) than of

the boys of no religious affiliation (49%) agree that the police do a good job. All of the statements in Table 4.12 generate differences of high statistical significance (.001).

Table 4.12 Law and order by Anglican boys and boys of no religious affiliation

	Anglicans %	No religion %	X^2	P<
There is nothing wrong in shoplifting	7	11	69.4	.001
There is nothing wrong in buying alcoholic drinks under the legal age (18)	42	48	37.1	.001
The police do a good job	61	49	150.2	.001

Substance use

Tables 4.13, 4.14 and 4.15 examine the responses of young people in the sample to statements regarding substance use. Table 4.13 compares the responses of all the girls and all the boys. For all of the statements in this table, with the exception of one, more of the girls than of the boys agree that the use of the suggested substance is wrong. For example, 77% of the girls and 72% of the boys agree that it is wrong to use heroin. The exception concerns smoking: more boys (47%) than girls (38%) agree that it is wrong to smoke cigarettes. All of the statements in Table 4.13 generate differences of high statistical significance (.001).

Table 4.13 Substance use by sex

	Girls %	Boys %	X^2	P<
It is wrong to smoke cigarettes	38	47	235.5	.001
It is wrong to use marijuana (hash/pot)	54	50	63.5	.001
It is wrong to use heroin	77	72	113.6	.001

Table 4.14 compares the responses of Anglican girls and girls of no religious affiliation to statements concerning substance use.

From this table a clear pattern is apparent in that more of the Anglican girls than of the girls of no religious affiliation agree that it is wrong to use each of the suggested substances. For example, 59% of the Anglican girls, in comparison with 50% of the girls of no religious affiliation, agree that it is wrong to use marijuana; and 80% of the Anglican girls, in comparison with 75% of the girls of no religious affiliation, agree that it is wrong to use heroin. All of the statements in Table 4.14 generate differences of high statistical significance (.001).

Table 4.14 Substance use by Anglican girls and girls of no religious affiliation

	Anglicans %	No religion %	X^2	P<
It is wrong to smoke cigarettes	40	35	33.0	.001
It is wrong to use marijuana (hash/pot)	59	50	91.0	.001
It is wrong to use heroin	80	75	46.2	.001

Table 4.15 compares the responses of Anglican boys and boys of no religious affiliation to statements concerning substance use. The data in this table demonstrate that more of the Anglican boys than of the boys of no religious affiliation agree that it is wrong to use each of the suggested substances. For example, 55% of the Anglican boys and 46% of the boys of no religious affiliation state that it is wrong to use marijuana; and 76% of the Anglican boys and 69% of the boys of no religious affiliation agree that it is wrong to use heroin. All of the statements in Table 4.15 generate differences of high statistical significance (.001).

Table 4.15 Substance use by Anglican boys and boys of no religious affiliation

	Anglicans %	No religion %	X^2	P<
It is wrong to smoke cigarettes	49	45	24.8	.001
It is wrong to use marijuana (hash/pot)	55	46	82.2	.001
It is wrong to use heroin	76	69	74.6	.001

Societal and world concerns

Tables 4.16, 4.17 and 4.18 examine the responses of the young people in the sample to issues of societal and world concern. Table 4.16 compares the responses of all the girls and all the boys in the sample. From the table it is apparent that the girls are less apathetic and more concerned about all of the issues suggested. For example, 24% of the girls and 15% of the boys agree that there is too much violence on television; and 19% of the girls and 29% of the boys agree that there is nothing they can do to help solve the world's problems. All of the statements in the table generate differences of high statistical significance (.001).

Table 4.16 Societal and world concerns by sex

	Girls %	Boys %	X^2	P<
There is too much violence on television	24	15	366.3	.001
I am concerned about the poverty of the Third World	68	55	518.7	.001
There is nothing I can do to help solve the world's problems	19	29	417.0	.001

Table 4.17 compares the responses of Anglican girls and girls of no religious affiliation to issues of societal and world concern. A clear pattern is apparent from the table in that the Anglican girls appear less apathetic and more concerned about all of the suggested issues. For example, 73% of the Anglican girls and 61% of the girls of no religious affiliation are concerned about the poverty of the Third World; and 17% of the Anglican girls and 22% of the girls of no religious affiliation agree that there is nothing they can do to help solve the world's problems. All of the statements in Table 4.17 generate differences of high statistical significance (.001).

Table 4.18 compares the responses of Anglican boys and boys of no religious affiliation to issues of societal and world concern. From this table the pattern is evident that the Anglican boys are more concerned and less apathetic about all of the suggested issues. For example, 63% of the Anglican boys, in comparison with 48% of the boys of no religious affiliation, are concerned about the poverty of the Third World; and 25% of the Anglican boys, in comparison with 32% of the boys of no religious affiliation, agree that there is nothing they can do to help solve the world's problems. All of the statements in Table 4.18 generate differences of high statistical significance (.001).

Table 4.17 Societal and world concerns by Anglican girls and girls of no religious affiliation

	Anglicans %	No religion %	X^2	P<
There is too much violence on television	24	21	19.4	.001
I am concerned about the poverty of the Third World	73	61	9.6	.001
There is nothing I can do to help solve the world's problems	17	22	44.9	.001

Table 4.18 Societal and world concerns by Anglican boys and boys of no religious affiliation

	Anglicans %	No religion %	X^2	P<
There is too much violence on television	16	14	14.5	.001
I am concerned about the poverty of the Third World	63	48	240.5	.001
There is nothing I can do to help solve the world's problems	25	32	66.7	.001

Discussion

The data displayed in the preceding tables have established two main conclusions. The first is that there are significant differences in the values espoused by the girls and the boys across all six of the value areas in this analysis. The second is that there are significant differences in the values espoused by the Anglicans and by the young people of no religious affiliation across the six value areas. These significant differences are worth closer examination on two counts. The first is to make clear precisely how young Anglicans differ from young people of no religious affiliation. The second is to interpret the nature of this difference in the light of gender orientation theory. The six value areas will be reviewed in turn.

Religious beliefs

It is no surprise that young Anglicans display a higher level of religious belief in comparison with young people of no religious affiliation. In the present sample, both female and male young Anglicans are more inclined than young people of no religious affiliation to believe in God, to believe that Jesus really rose from the dead and to believe in life after death. It is also clear from Table 4.1 that, overall, girls are more likely to hold religious beliefs than boys. In other words, holding religious beliefs is itself associated among young people with a feminine personality profile. This point has been demonstrated in a variety of ways by a series of recent studies, including Thompson (1991) and Francis and Wilcox (1996, 1998a).

Worries

Overall, being Anglican is associated with a higher level of anxiety and worry about life. In the present sample, both female and male young Anglicans are more inclined than young people of no religious affiliation to express worry about their attractiveness to the opposite sex, and worry about going out alone at night in their area. Additionally, male young Anglicans are more inclined than young people of no religious affiliation to express worry about how they get on with other people. It is also clear from Table 4.4 that, overall, girls are more likely to worry about all these issues than boys. In other words, displaying and acknowledging worry and anxiety is itself associated among young people with a feminine personality profile. This point is consistent with the empirical model of personality established by Eysenck and his colleagues, which associates worry and anxiety with the higher order dimension of personality defined as neuroticism (Eysenck and Eysenck, 1991). The finding also concurs with the consistent finding across cultures that girls and women record higher scores of neuroticism, in comparison with boys and men (Francis, 1993).

School

Overall, being Anglican is associated with a more positive attitude toward school, combined with greater anxiety about aspects of school life. In the present sample, both female and male young Anglicans are more inclined than young people of no religious affiliation to report that they feel happy in their school. At the same time, both female and male young Anglicans are more inclined than young people of no religious affiliation to experience worry about their exams at school, and about being bullied at school. It is also clear from Table 4.7 that these differences between Anglicans and young people of no religious affiliation reflect the differences between girls and boys. In other words, both holding a positive attitude toward school and experiencing anxiety regarding aspects of school life are associated among young people with a feminine personality profile. School-related anxiety, like other areas of personal worry, is part of the more basic personality profile associated with neuroticism, and on which females generally record higher scores than males (Francis, 1993). School-related attitudes are also generally found to be more positive among girls than among boys (Fitt, 1956; Richmond, 1985; Darom and Rich, 1988; Francis, 1992b).

Law and order

Overall, being Anglican is associated with a more positive attitude toward law and order. In the present sample, both female and male young Anglicans are less inclined than young people of no religious affiliation to condone buying alcoholic drinks under the legal age, or to condone shoplifting. At the same time, both female and male young Anglicans are more inclined than young people of no religious affiliation to feel that the police do a good job. It is also clear from Table 4.10 that these differences between Anglicans and young people of no religious affiliation reflect the differences between girls and boys. In other words, holding a more positive attitude toward law and order is associated among young people with a feminine personality profile. This point is once again consistent with the empirical model of personality established by Eysenck and his colleagues, which associates law-abiding attitudes with the higher order dimension of personality defined as psychoticism (Eysenck and Eysenck, 1991), and with the consistent finding across cultures that boys and men record higher scores of psychoticism, in comparison with girls and women (Eysenck and Eysenck, 1976).

Substance use

Overall, being Anglican is associated with a more negative attitude toward substance use. In the present sample, both female and male young Anglicans display a more negative attitude than young people of no religious affiliation toward smoking cigarettes, toward using marijuana and toward using heroin. It is also clear from Table 4.13 that these differences between Anglicans and young people of no religious affiliation reflect the differences between girls and boys, in respect of gender differences in attitude toward marijuana and heroin. In other words, holding a more negative attitude toward these substances is associated among young people with a feminine personality profile. This finding is consistent with a body of previous research which has mapped gender differences in attitudes toward substances and substance use (Ben-Shlomo, Sheiham and Marmot, 1991; Francis and Kay, 1995). This general trend, however, breaks down in respect of smoking, in the sense that both the present data and a body of recent research have charted a greater openness to smoking among teenage girls than among teenage boys (National Statistics, 2000).

Societal and world concerns

Finally, being Anglican is associated with a higher level of concern regarding a range of societal and world issues. In the present sample, both female and male young Anglicans display more concern than young people of no religious affiliation about violence on television, and about the poverty of the Third World. Both female and male young Anglicans are less inclined than young people of no religious affiliation to feel helpless in facing the world's problems. It is also clear from Table 4.16 that these differences between Anglicans and young people of no religious affiliation reflect the differences between girls and boys, in respect of gender differences in societal and world concerns. In other words, being concerned about societal issues like violence on television, and being concerned about world issues like the poverty of the developing world, are associated among young people with a feminine personality profile. This finding is consistent with Eysenck's dimensional model of personality, which sees such tender-minded social attitudes as a projection of low psychoticism scores on to the social domain, and which also associates low psychoticism scores with femininity (Eysenck and Eysenck, 1976).

Conclusion

This study has investigated the identity of young Anglicans as part of the continuing debate concerning the potential importance of self-assigned religious affiliation as a socially significant indicator. The study has found that, in the case of young Anglicans, self assigned religious affiliation is a socially significant indicator of values. Young Anglicans do have a distinct values profile and identity when compared with young people of no religious affiliation.

This study has demonstrated that the distinctive values profile of young Anglicans is consistent with a broader view regarding the feminization of the Church. Several recent studies, both in the United States of America (Podles, 1999) and the United Kingdom (Brown, 2001), have drawn attention to the feminization of the churches. The present data suggest that this trend toward feminization is clearly evident among young affiliates of the Anglican Church.

The finding that young people who are affiliated with the Anglican Church are more feminine than young people of no religious affiliation is of great significance for the Church. In the face of declining attendance and involvement in the churches, particularly among young people, this research could go some way toward indicating to the Anglican Church ways in which it must change to accommodate and serve the needs of young people. The Church needs to consider such findings as it re-evaluates its place and role for the future.

Acknowledgement

This analysis was sponsored by the St Christopher's Educational Trust.

References

Balding, J. (1993), *Young People in 1992* (Exeter, Schools Health Education Unit, University of Exeter).

Balding, J. (1997), *Young People in 1996* (Exeter, Schools Health Education Unit, University of Exeter).

Balding, J. (1998), *Young People in 1997* (Exeter, Schools Health Education Unit, University of Exeter).

Balding, J. (1999), *Young People in 1998* (Exeter, Schools Health Education Unit, University of Exeter).

Bem, S. L. (1981), *Bem Sex Role Inventory: Professional Manual* (Palo Alto, Calif., Consulting Psychologists Press).

Ben-Shlomo, Y., Sheiham, A. and Marmot, M. (1991), 'Smoking and health', in R. Jowell, L. Brook and B. Taylor (eds), *British Social Attitudes: The Eighth Report* (Aldershot, Dartmouth), pp. 155–74.

Bibby, R. W. (1986), *Anglitrends: A Profile and Prognosis* (Toronto, Anglican Diocese of Toronto).

Brown, C. G. (2001), *The Death of Christian Britain* (London, Routledge).

Darom, E. and Rich, Y. (1988), 'Sex differences in attitudes towards school: student self-reports and teacher perceptions', *British Journal of Educational Psychology*, 58, 350–5.

Department of Education and Science (1983), *Young People in the 80s: A Survey* (London, Her Majesty's Stationery Office).

Eysenck, H. J. and Eysenck, M. W. (1985), *Personality and Individual Differences: A Natural Science Approach* (New York, Plenum Press).

Eysenck, H. J. and Eysenck, S. B. G. (1976), *Psychoticism as a Dimension of Personality* (London, Hodder and Stoughton).

Eysenck, H. J. and Eysenck, S. B. G. (1991), *The EPQ-R* (Sevenoaks, Hodder and Stoughton).

Fane, R. S. (1999), 'Is self-assigned religious affiliation socially significant?', in L. J. Francis (ed.), *Sociology, Theology and the Curriculum* (London, Cassell), pp. 113–24.

Fitt, A. B. (1956), 'An experimental study of children's attitudes to school in Auckland, New Zealand', *British Journal of Educational Psychology*, 26, 25–30.

Francis, L. J. (1984), *Teenagers and the Church: A Profile of*

Churchgoing Youth in the 1980s (London, Collins Liturgical Publications).

Francis, L. J. (1992a), 'Is psychoticism really a dimension of personality fundamental to religiosity?', *Personality and Individual Differences*, 13, 645–52.

Francis, L. J. (1992b), 'The influence of religion, gender, and social class on attitudes towards school among 11-year-olds in England', *Journal of Experimental Education*, 60, 339–48.

Francis, L. J. (1993), 'The dual nature of the Eysenckian neuroticism scales: a question of sex differences?', *Personality and Individual Differences*, 15, 43–9.

Francis, L. J. (2001), 'Religion and values: a quantitative perspective', in L. J. Francis, J. Astley, and M. Robbins (eds), *The Fourth R for the Third Millennium* (Dublin, Lindisfarne Books), pp. 47–78.

Francis, L. J. and Kay, W. K. (1995), *Teenage Religion and Values* (Leominster, Gracewing).

Francis, L. J., Lewis, J. M., Brown, L. B., Philipchalk, R. and Lester, D. (1995), 'Personality and religion among undergraduate students in the United Kingdom, United States, Australia and Canada', *Journal of Psychology and Christianity*, 14, 3, 250–62.

Francis, L. J. and Wilcox, C. (1996), 'Religion and gender orientation', *Personality and Individual Differences*, 20, 119–21.

Francis, L. J. and Wilcox, C. (1998a), 'Religiosity and femininity: do women really hold a more positive view toward Christianity?', *Journal for the Scientific Study of Religion*, 37, 462–9.

Francis, L. J. and Wilcox, C. (1998b), 'The relationship between Eysenck's personality dimensions and Bem's masculinity and femininity scales revisited', *Personality and Individual Differences*, 25, 683–7.

Furnham, A. and Stacey, B. (1991), *Young People's Understanding of Society* (London, Routledge).

Gill, R. (1999), *Churchgoing and Christian Ethics* (Cambridge, Cambridge University Press).

Hendry, L. B., Shucksmith, J., Love, J. G. and Glendinning, A. (1993), *Young People's Leisure and Lifestyles* (London, Routledge).

Kremer, J., Trew, K. and Ogle, S. (eds) (1997), *Young People's Involvement in Sport* (London, Routledge).

Likert, R. (1932), 'A technique for the measurement of attitudes', *Archives of Psychology*, 140, 1–55.

National Statistics (2000), 'Statistics on smoking: England, 1978 onwards', *Statistical Bulletin* (London, Department of Health).

Podles, L. J. (1999), *The Church Impotent: The Feminisation of Christianity* (Dallas, Tex., Spence Publishing Group).

Richmond, P. G. (1985), 'The relationship of grade, sex, ability and socio-economic status to parent, peer and school affiliation', *British Journal of Educational Psychology*, 55, 233–9.

Roberts, H. and Sachdev, D. (eds) (1996), *Young People's Social Attitudes: The Views of 12–19-Year-Olds* (Barkingside, Barnardos).

Thompson, E. H. (1991), 'Beneath the status characteristics: gender variations in religiousness', *Journal for the Scientific Study of Religion*, 30, 381–94.

Woodroffe, C., Glickman, M., Barker, M. and Power, C. (1993), *Children, Teenagers and Health: The Key Data* (Buckingham, Open University Press).

5

Attitude to smoking among female adolescents: is religion a significant but neglected factor?

MANDY ROBBINS

Summary

Reported growth of smoking among female adolescents has stimulated research into understanding the psychosocial predictors of such behaviour, although as yet little attention has been given to the potential role of religion. The present chapter, therefore, investigates the relationship between attitude toward cigarette smoking, personality as assessed by the abbreviated Junior Eysenck Personality Questionnaire and indices of religiosity, age, parental marital status and parental social class. The data demonstrate that a negative attitude toward cigarette smoking is positively correlated with belief in God, after controlling for age, parental social class, personality and parental marital status.

Introduction

There is an increasing awareness that female adolescents are much more likely to take up cigarette smoking than are male adolescents. Government statistics have examined the percentage of young people who smoke from the age of 11 through to the age of 15. The respondents are placed into one of five groups: regular smokers, occasional smokers, used to smoke, tried smoking and never smoked. The government statistics cover the period from 1982 to 1999 (inclusive). The statistics presented demonstrate that the percentage of female adolescent girls who are regular smokers is higher than the percentage of male adolescents who are regular smokers (National Statistics, 2000). Research which has examined this trend has put forward seven main theories which may predict why female adolescents are more likely to smoke cigarettes than are male adolescents.

First, a series of studies have examined the link between cigarette smoking and weight control. There is the view frequently expressed that smoking acts as an appetite suppressant and that female adolescents, who are concerned with their weight, perceive cigarettes as a tool for controlling their weight. For example, Charlton (1984) found that girls aged between 13 years and 16 years who smoked were significantly more likely to agree that smoking kept weight down than either girls who did not smoke or boys who did smoke. Similarly, Page, Allen, Moore and Hewitt (1993) found that, among a sample of 1,915 teenagers, smokers are much more likely to report dissatisfaction with their weight by reporting that they are fat. This is despite there being no difference found in the body weight of peers who smoke and those who do not smoke.

Second, a series of studies have examined the link between cigarette smoking and involvement with sport. It has been suggested that the number of boys smoking has been decreasing because of their active participation in sport. Girls are less likely to participate actively in sport as they enter their teens, and so concerns over the effect of smoking on health are not as strong among girls as they are among boys. For example, Michell (1997) found among a sample of thirty-six 11-year-olds and forty 13-year-olds that those considered to be the 'top' boys in the peer group were those who tended to excel in sport and consequently were less likely to smoke, whereas those considered to be 'top' girls in the peer group were those who tended to be associated with risk-taking, and that smoking was part of this image.

Third, a series of studies have examined the link between cigarette smoking and self-image and the consequent impact on self-esteem. For example, Gray, Amos and Currie (1996) found a change in image perception of smoking between two samples of pupils, one sample aged between 12 and 13 and the other sample aged between 15 and 16. The two samples were subdivided by sex. On presenting each group with the same set of photos, the younger groups consistently picked up the smoking in the pictures and consistently associated smoking with a negative image perception. In comparison, the older age-groups were less likely to mention the smoking taking place in the pictures, and if it was mentioned this tended to be in a neutral way. This negative image of smoking is carried over into research that has found smoking to be related to a low level of self-esteem. For example, Daykin (1993) conducted a survey of men and women. Daykin first surveyed a sample of thirty-five in their last year of secondary schooling and then followed this up a year later. Daykin (1993) found that those women who were engaged in secure employment were less likely to have continued to smoke, whereas those women who experienced job insecurity, domestic conflict and lack of autonomy were more likely to have continued smoking and more likely to have increased the amount smoked.

Fourth, a series of studies have examined the link between cigarette smoking and peer-group pressure which, it is thought, is exacerbated by the recent trend among advertisers to target young female adolescents (see, for example, Swan, Melia, Fitzsimons, Breeze and Murray, 1989). An examination of the link between peer group and levels of smoking was carried out by Michell (1997). Michell linked smoking with the social map held by a group of thirty-six 11-year-olds and forty 13-year-olds. The social map across the two groups was consistent. The social map was divided by the pupils into four groups: top pupils, middle status pupils, low status pupils and troublemakers. Those who were more likely to smoke were identified as top girls, low status pupils and troublemakers. The top boys were reported as being those who were keen on sport and so would tend not to smoke. The low status pupils consisted mainly of girls with low self-esteem, while the troublemakers consisted mainly of boys.

Fifth, a series of studies have examined the link between age and cigarette smoking. It is accepted that during teenage years girls mature at a faster rate than boys. It has been suggested that, as a result, girls are exhibiting smoking patterns similar to those among older boys rather than similar to boys of their own age. For example, Swan, Melia, Fitzsimons, Breeze and Murray (1989) conducted a longitudinal study among teenagers and found that between 1972 and 1986, while smoking among girls had remained consistent, smoking among boys had decreased. The reason for this suggested by Swan, Melia, Fitzsimons, Breeze and Murray (1989) is that boys' perception of smoking is different from that of girls. Girls are much more likely to report that smoking enhances social image, while boys are much more likely to be aware of the health risks and to take them into consideration. Oakly, Brannen and Dodd (1992) found that teenage smoking is consistently higher among girls. Girls link smoking to growing up and also see it as helpful in coping with stress in their lives.

Sixth, a series of studies have examined the link between cigarette smoking and personality. For example, Papakyriazi and Joseph (1998) surveyed a total of 80 students who smoked, using the Eysenck Personality Questionnaire (revised) (Eysenck, Eysenck and Barrett, 1985) together with a smoking motivation questionnaire and a self-administered nicotine-dependence scale. They found that both the smoking motivation questionnaire and the self-administered nicotine-dependence scale were correlated with personality. Introverts tended to use smoking to make them more sociable, while those who scored higher on the neuroticism scale used smoking to counteract their neurotic tendencies. This positive association between neuroticism and smoking is also supported by Stanaway and Watson (1981), who used the Eysenck Personality Inventory among a sample of 119 men and 177 women. They found that smokers recorded a higher neuroticism score than ex-smokers and non-smokers. Forgays, Bonaiuto, Kazimierz, Wrzesniewski and Forgays (1993) conducted a study among 456 women and 304 men, using the Eysenck Personality Inventory. They found that the ex-smokers recorded the highest neuroticism scores, followed by the smokers. Canals, Bladé and Doménech (1997) conducted a study among 153 young women and 137 young men aged 18 years, using the Spanish version of the Junior Eysenck Personality Questionnaire (Eysenck and Eysenck, 1984). They found that young people who recorded high scores on the neuroticism scale were more likely to smoke. This relationship between higher neuroticism scores and smoking may help to explain the greater tendency for girls to smoke, since the international research literature consistently finds that girls and women record higher scores on the neuroticism scale, in comparison with boys and men (Francis, 1993).

A seventh, and less well-developed, strand of research on cigarette smoking among teenagers has examined the relationship with religion. For example, Mullen and Francis (1995) found among a sample of 1,534 teenagers attending Protestant schools in the Netherlands that those who were 'practising believers' were significantly more likely to agree that smoking was wrong. Francis and

Kay (1995) found among a sample of 13,000 teenagers in the United Kingdom aged between 13 and 15 years that those who attend church weekly are much more likely to agree that smoking is wrong (53%), compared with those who occasionally attend church (46%) and those who never attend church (42%). In a recent study, Francis (2001) found among a sample of 33,000 teenagers between the ages of 13 and 15 that those who attended church weekly were significantly more likely to agree that it is wrong to smoke ($P<.001$).

The consistent finding that religion functions as a significant inhibitor of the tendency to smoke needs to be set alongside another consistent finding in the psychology of religion, namely that women are more religious than men. Beit-Hallahmi and Argyle (1997), for example, state that: 'The greater religiosity of women must be one of the oldest, and clearest, findings in the psychology of religion.' Kay and Francis (1996) have consistently found that girls hold a more positive image of Christianity, as defined by the Francis Scale of Attitude toward Christianity. The puzzle is that, if girls are more religious than boys and if religiosity functions as an inhibitor for smoking, it should follow that girls would be less likely to smoke than boys.

Against this background, the aim of the present study is to focus on a large sample of female adolescents in order to establish whether or not religion functions as a significant predictor of attitude toward cigarette smoking. A multivariate model of data analysis was employed, in order to control for some of the contaminating variables which are known to be predictors, not only of individual differences in smoking, but also of individual differences in religiosity, including age (Francis, 1989), social class (Gibson, Francis and Pearson, 1990), personality (Francis, 1999) and parental divorce (Francis and Evans, 1997). In view of the multidimensional nature of religiosity and the way in which different dimensions of religion have been shown to interact with substance use more generally (Francis, 1997), the present study employs three aspects of religion, namely public practice (church attendance), private practice (prayer) and personal belief (belief in God).

Method

A survey of 33,982 young people aged between 13 and 15 years of age completed a twenty-four-page questionnaire. From the total sample of 33,982 young people, responses from females only were selected, creating a subset of 13,521. It was this subset of 13,521 which was used in the following analysis:

Attitude to smoking was assessed by the response to the statement 'It is wrong to smoke cigarettes'. Participants were asked to respond to this statement on a five-point Likert-type scale (Likert, 1932): *agree strongly, agree, not certain, disagree* and *disagree strongly*.

Personality was measured using the twenty-four-item abbreviated Junior Eysenck Personality Questionnaire (Francis and Pearson, 1988). Participants were asked to respond to each item on a dichotomous scale: *yes, no*.

Prayer was measured on a five-point scale in response to the question 'Do you pray by yourself?' Participants were asked to respond in terms of frequency: *nearly every day, at least once a week, at least once a month, occasionally* and *never*.

Church attendance was measured on a five-point scale in response to the question 'Do you go to a church or other place of worship?' Participants were asked to respond in terms of frequency: *nearly every week, at least once a month, sometimes, once or twice a year* and *never*.

Belief in God was measured in response to the statement 'I believe in God' on a five-point Likert-type scale (Likert, 1932): *agree strongly, agree, not certain, disagree* and *disagree strongly*.

Parental marital status was measured on a two-point dichotomous scale (*yes, no*) in response to the question 'Have your parents ever been separated or divorced?'

Parental social class was measured by assessing each respondent's job description of their father's occupation. The assessment was made in line with the Office of Population, Censuses and Surveys (1980) classification system.

Age was measured by asking respondents to complete a question stating which year group they were in: *year nine* or *year ten*.

The data were analysed using the correlations and multiple regression routines provided by the SPSS statistical package (SPSS Inc., 1988).

Results

Table 5.1 presents the correlation matrix between attitude toward smoking, Eysenck's four dimensions of personality, age, social class, parental divorce, belief in God, church attendance and prayer. The data demonstrate that attitude toward smoking is significantly related to all four dimensions of personality. Those young people who are more likely to have a negative attitude toward smoking are introvert, stable, tenderminded and socially conforming. The data also demonstrate that attitude toward smoking is significantly related to age, social class and parental divorce. So those young people who are more likely to have a negative attitude toward smoking are younger, come from a higher social class and are from a stable family background. Finally, the data demonstrate that attitude toward smoking is significantly related to religiosity as measured by belief in God, church attendance and prayer. Those young people who hold a negative attitude toward smoking are more likely to believe in God, attend church, and pray.

Table 5.2 takes the analysis a step further by using multiple regression to calculate the cumulative impact on attitude toward smoking of age, social class, extraversion, neuroticism, psychoticism, lie scale, parental divorce, belief in God, church attendance and prayer, when the predictor variables are entered in that fixed order. These data confirm that after taking age, social class, personality and parent divorce into account, young people who believe in God are more likely to have a negative attitude toward smoking than young people who do not believe in God. However, church attendance and prayer cease to be predictors of attitude to cigarette smoking among young people after belief in God has been taken into account.

Table 5.1 Correlation matrix

	E	N	P	L	Age	Class	Divorce	God	Church attendance	Prayer
Smoking	-0.1668 .001	-0.0400 .001	-0.2262 .001	+0.2792 .001	-0.1009 .001	-0.1483 .001	-0.0832 .001	+0.1495 .001	+0.1180 .001	+0.1241 .001
Prayer	-0.0586 .001	+0.0267 .001	-0.0962 .001	+0.1618 .001	-0.0204 .001	-0.1060 .001	-0.0383 .001	+0.5822 .001	+0.57707 .001	
Church attendance	-0.0694 .001	+0.0007 NS	-0.1082 .001	+0.1420 .001	-0.0480 .001	-0.1581 .001	-0.0961 .001	+0.4926 .001		
God	-0.0475 .001	+0.0154 NS	-0.1353 .001	+0.2115 .001	-0.0319 .001	-0.0817 .001	-0.0574 .001			
Divorce	-0.0647 .001	+0.0368 .001	+0.631 .001	-0.0764 .001	+0.0156 NS	+0.0823 .001				
Class	+0.0434 .001	+0.0320 .001	+0.0294 .01	+0.0084 NS	+0.0025 NS					
Age	+0.0238 NS	+0.0220 NS	+0.0369 .001	-0.0921 .001						
L	-0.1335 .001	-0.1167 .001	-0.3966 .001							
P	+0.1392 .001	+0.0002 NS								
N	-0.1341 .001									

Table 5.2 Regression model: predicting attitude toward smoking

Predictor variables	R^2	Increase R^2	F	P<	beta	T	P<
Age	0.0107	0.0107	113.4	.001	−0.0740	−8.0	.001
Class	0.0126	0.0019	19.8	.001	−0.0229	−2.5	NS
Extraversion	0.0393	0.0267	290.0	.001	−0.1197	−12.7	.001
Neuroticism	0.0428	0.0035	38.3	.001	−0.0316	−3.4	.001
Psychoticism	0.0826	0.0398	453.3	.001	−0.1187	−11.8	.001
Lie scale	0.1161	0.0335	396.0	.001	+0.1837	+17.8	.001
Divorce	0.1187	0.0026	30.9	.001	−0.0485	−5.2	.001
God	0.1246	0.0059	70.5	.001	+0.0597	+5.0	.001
Church	0.1249	0.0002	2.6	NS	+0.0093	+0.8	NS
Prayer	0.1253	0.0004	4.9	NS	+0.0264	+2.2	NS

Conclusion

Two main conclusions emerge from this study. The first conclusion confirms findings from previous research regarding some of the personal and contextual correlates of smoking among female adolescents. The second conclusion provides new insights into the relationship between religiosity and attitude toward smoking among female adolescents.

Regarding the personal correlates of attitude toward cigarette smoking, this study confirms the importance of age and of individual differences in personality. The younger female adolescents are more likely than the older female adolescents in the sample to have a negative attitude toward cigarette smoking. Previous research had demonstrated that cigarette smoking rates increase for both female adolescents and male adolescents as they get older. The female adolescents who are introvert, stable, tenderminded and socially conforming are more likely to reject cigarette smoking. The female adolescents who are extravert, neurotic, toughminded and indifferent to social conformity are more likely to smoke. For female adolescents it is not just neuroticism that predicts attitude to smoking but each of the personality dimensions, as measured by Eysenck's model of personality.

Regarding the contextual correlates of attitude toward cigarette smoking, this study confirms the importance of social class and of intact home backgrounds. Female adolescents who come from lower social-class backgrounds are less likely to have a negative attitude toward smoking, in comparison with female adolescents who come from higher social-class backgrounds. Female adolescents from an intact family background are more likely to have a negative attitude toward cigarette smoking. Previous research has demonstrated the negative impact parental divorce has on the children. The increase in cigarette smoking among female adolescents who have experienced parental divorce is one aspect of this.

Regarding the relationship between religion and attitude toward cigarette smoking, this study both confirms that religion exercises a small but significant inhibiting effect, and provides fresh insight into the aspect of religion which exercises that influence. The correlation matrix makes it clear that, when considered independently, all three aspects of religion included in the study are significant predictors of a more negative attitude toward cigarette smoking. These three aspects of religion are public practice (church attendance), private practice (prayer) and personal belief (belief in God). The correlation matrix also makes it clear that these three aspects of religion are themselves all highly intercorrelated.

The regression analysis extends the information conveyed by the correlation matrix in two important ways. First, the regression model establishes that religion has a direct relationship with attitude toward cigarette smoking and that this relationship is not an artefact of other influences, like age, social class, home background or personality. The regression model confirms that religion conveys additional predictive power, after such factors as age, social class, parental divorce and personality have been taken into account. Second, the regression model demonstrates that of the three religion variables, the important factor is belief in God. When belief in God has been taken into account, neither prayer nor church attendance convey additional predictive power. This finding provides some insight into the psychological dynamics which may link religion with a less positive attitude toward cigarette smoking among female adolescents.

Three different theories could link religion with a more negative attitude toward cigarette smoking. The first theory concerns public religious practice as engagement with a social institution which exerts pressure to conform to certain moral standards on its adherents. This kind of social pressure is exerted through participation in church life. The regression model fails to support this theory, by demonstrating that church attendance is not the key religious predictor of attitude toward smoking. The second theory considers personal religious practice as a way of exerting control over self and over environment. Individuals who pray appear to believe that they can influence outcomes in the world. In this sense a praying individual may have less need of the psychological support generated by smoking. The regression model fails to support this theory by demonstrating that prayer is not the key religious predictor of attitude toward smoking. The third theory considers religion as a way of giving meaning and purpose to life. This theory is supported by a range of studies which show a positive correlation between religion and purpose in life among young people (Francis, 2000). In this sense, religious young people may have less need for the support which can be provided by smoking because belief in God gives their lives a greater sense of meaning. The regression model supports this theory by demonstrating that belief in God is the key religious predictor of attitude toward smoking.

Two practical implications for health education emerge from this conclusion. First, future research concerned to identify female adolescents most at risk from smoking should routinely include religion as a key variable and ensure that religious belief is part of the measure of religiosity employed. Second, health education programmes intended to discourage female adolescents from smoking might profitably explore ways in which the benefits of religious belief can be emulated among young people for whom traditional Christian concepts no longer seem attractive or relevant.

The present study has concentrated solely on the place of religion in shaping attitude toward cigarette smoking among female adolescents. Further research is necessary to establish if religion is a significant predictor of attitude toward cigarette smoking among male adolescents.

References

Beit-Hallahmi, B. and Argyle, M. (1997), *The Psychology of Religious Belief and Experience* (London, Routledge).

Canals, J., Bladé, J. and Doménech, E. (1997), 'Smoking and personality predictors in young Spanish people', *Personality and Individual Differences*, 23, 905–8.

Charlton, A. (1984), 'Smoking and weight control in teenagers', *Public Health*, 98, 277–81.

Daykin, N. (1993), 'Young women and smoking: towards a sociological account', *Health Promotion International*, 8, 95–102.

Eysenck, H. J. and Eysenck, S. B. G. (1984), *Cuestionario de Personalidad Para Niños (EPQ-J)* (Madrid, TEA).

Eysenck, S. B. G., Eysenck, H. J. and Barrett, P. (1985), 'A revised version of the psychoticism scale', *Personality and Individual Differences*, 6, 21–9.

Forgays, D. G., Bonaiuto, P., Kazimierz, M. D., Wrzesniewski, K. and Forgays, D. K. (1993), 'Personality and cigarette smoking in Italy, Poland and the United States', *International Journal of the Addictions*, 28, 399–413.

Francis, L. J. (1989), 'Monitoring changing attitudes towards Christianity among secondary school pupils between 1974 and 1986', *British Journal of Educational Psychology*, 59, 86–91.

Francis, L. J. (1993), 'The dual nature of the Eysenckian neuroticism scales: a question of sex differences?', *Personality and Individual Differences*, 15, 43–59.

Francis, L. J. (1997), 'The impact of personality and religion on attitude towards substance use among 13–15 year olds', *Drug and Alcohol Dependence*, 44, 95–103.

Francis, L. J. (1999), 'Personality and attitude toward Christianity among undergraduates', *Journal of Research on Christian Education*, 8, 179–95.

Francis, L. J. (2000), 'The relationship between Bible reading and purpose in life among 13–15-year-olds', *Mental Health, Religion and Culture*, 3, 27–36.

Francis, L. J. (2001), *The Values Debate: A Voice from the Pupils* (London, Woburn Press).

Francis, L. J. and Evans, T. E. (1997), 'The relationship between marital disruption and adolescent values: a study among 13–15-year-olds', *Journal of Divorce and Remarriage*, 26, 195–213.

Francis, L. J. and Kay, W. K. (1995), *Teenage Religion and Values* (Leominster, Gracewing).

Francis, L. J. and Pearson, P. R. (1988), 'Religiosity and the short-scale EPQ-R indices of E, N and L, compared with the JEPI, JEPQ and EPQ', *Personality and Individual Differences*, 9, 653–7.

Gibson, H. M., Francis, L. J. and Pearson, P. R. (1990), 'The relationship between social class and attitude towards Christianity among fourteen- and fifteen-year-old adolescents', *Personality and Individual Differences*, 11, 631–5.

Gray, D., Amos, A. and Currie, C. (1996), 'Exploring young people's perceptions of smoking images in youth magazines', *Health Education Research*, 11, 215–30.

Kay, W. K. and Francis, L. J. (1996), *Drift from the Churches: Attitude toward Christianity during Childhood and Adolescence* (Cardiff, University of Wales Press).

Likert, R. (1932), 'A technique for the measurement of attitudes', *Archives of Psychology*, 140, 1–55.

Michell, L. (1997), 'Loud, sad or bad: young people's perceptions of peer group and smoking', *Health Education*, 12, 1–4.

Mullen, K. and Francis, L. J. (1995), 'Religiosity and attitudes towards drug use among Dutch school-children', *Journal of Alcohol and Drug Education*, 41, 16–25.

National Statistics (2000), 'Statistics on smoking: England, 1978 onwards', *Statistical Bulletin* (London, Department of Health).

Oakley, A., Brannen, J. and Dodd, K. (1992), 'Young people, gender and smoking in the United Kingdom', *Health Promotion International*, 7, 75–88.

Office of Population Censuses and Surveys (1980), *Classification of Occupations 1980* (London, Her Majesty's Stationery Office).

Page, R. M., Allen, O., Moore, L. and Hewitt, C. (1993), 'Weight-related concerns and practices of male and female adolescent cigarette smokers and non-smokers', *Journal of Health Education*, 24, 339–46.

Papakyriazi, E. and Joseph, S. (1998), 'Individual differences in personality among smokers and their association with smoking motivation, social skills deficit, and self-efficacy to quit', *Personality and Individual Differences*, 25, 621–6.

SPSS Inc. (1988), *SPSSX User's Guide* (New York, McGraw-Hill).

Stanaway, R. G. and Watson, D. W. (1981), 'Smoking and personality: a factorial study', *British Journal of Clinical Psychology*, 20, 213–14.

Swan, A. V., Melia, R. J. W., Fitzsimons, B., Breeze, E. and Murray, M. (1989), 'Why do more girls than boys smoke cigarettes?', *Health Education Journal*, 48, 59–64.

6

Religious experience and its implications for religious education

WILLIAM K. KAY

Summary

In this chapter religious experience is examined from three angles: the psychological, the pedagogical and the spiritual. To assist empirical analysis a large sample of 13- to 15-year-olds was divided into four groups, according to their religious membership and reporting of religious experience. Results showed religious experience to be linked with social and sexual morality, and therefore with 'relational consciousness', and with greater acceptance of religious education and collective worship in schools. These findings are discussed from the perspective of psychology, pedagogy and spirituality. In terms of psychology, the consonance between the general population and the school population is of interest; in terms of pedagogy, it is arguable that experiential methods of teaching are welcome because of their affinity with progressive education; in terms of spirituality, the link between religious experience and relational consciousness calls for further research.

Introduction

By bringing empirical techniques to bear on the prevalence and nature of religious experience within a large sample of young people within England and Wales, three separate debates and traditions are being addressed. First, there is the ongoing and long-standing psychological set of issues concerned with religious experience. These revolve around the nature and frequency of religious experience, its position within a predominantly materialist account of human beings and its tendency to be found more often among women. Second, there is a long-standing debate about the place of experience within learning. Knowledge may be characterized as

static, propositional and rational, or may be thought of as stemming directly from the richness of experience, in which case
knowledge is more provisional, sensory and contextual. Third,
because the term 'spirituality' is incorporated within legislation
and subject to inspection, there is a debate specific to England and
Wales concerning the place of spirituality within the curriculum.

Psychological issues

Psychological investigations into religious experience cover such a
vast area and proceed from such different starting points that it is
impossible to introduce them comprehensively. Investigations
analysing self-reports into religious mysticism go back at least as
far as William James (1902). Subsequently mysticism has been
explored using psychometric techniques of great sophistication.
Experiments designed to elicit religious experience (cited by
Hood, Spilka, Hunsberger and Gorsuch, 1996: 266) were more
frequently successful among individuals who had previously
shown intrinsic, as opposed to extrinsic, religiosity or who were
indiscriminately pro-religious. Another experiment, more famous
and controversial, was carried out by Pahnke as part of a doctoral
dissertation (Hood, Spilka, Hunsberger and Gorsuch, 1996: 257).
Pahnke administered the drug psilocybin or a placebo in a double-
blind study of 20 volunteers. The volunteers heard a broadcast of
a Good Friday service and were then given a questionnaire to
discover whether an induced mystical experience had been interpreted religiously. Pahnke found that those who had received the
drug were far more likely than were the control group to report
that their experiences were mystical.

So far as young people at school are concerned, the relevance
of both these experiments is that they demonstrate not only that
mystical experience may be elicited in general populations, but
that these experiences may be interpreted religiously, if the right
interpretative framework is suggested (see Wilson, 1996).

These findings rest within a complex nexus of academic debate
and it should not be assumed that the psychological interpretation
of religious experience is able to offer anything more authoritative
than that which is available to theological or philosophical analysis.
In other words, one should not assume that religious experience
has no value simply because it may be cultivated through the

administration of drugs and the manipulation of response sets. An analogy associated with LSD and the perception of colour illustrates this point: perceptions fuelled by LSD are vivid and fascinating, but when artists who have extended their sensory range under the influence of LSD return to their paint, they rarely find that their work has improved as they had hoped. The life of Timothy Leary, the 1960s drug-culture hero, illustrates the point and shows that mystical experience achieved 'on the cheap' through drugs is likely to be at the cost of those other intellectual qualities through which insights in art, philosophy or religion are expressed (Marwick, 1998).

In terms of the frequency of naturally occurring religious experience Hay (1987) found that 33% of respondents in a British Gallup poll answered 'yes' to a question that enquired, 'Have you ever been aware of or influenced by a presence or power, whether you call it God or not, which is different from your everyday self?' This figure covered the whole age-range of the population. A different Gallup survey of the whole population showed that 72% believed in God or a 'life-force' in 1986 (Kay, 1997). This indicates that slightly fewer than half of those reporting a belief in God also report a religious experience.

A survey carried out by MORI in 1996 for the British Humanist Association found that 30% of 15- to 24-year-olds believed 'that God exists' (Kay, 1997). If the same proportions between belief in God and religious experience hold good for the younger population, we might expect to find about 15% have had a religious experience.

Pedagogical issues
From the sixteenth to the nineteenth centuries, and probably in the periods both before and after those eras, classrooms remained remarkably unchanged. Young people sat at their desks facing the teacher who, using the blackboard and chalk, explained, controlled and in other ways attempted to regulate the memory of the young. Excessive concentration upon handwriting, grammar, syntax, spelling, punctuation, vocabulary, lists of dates and a few simple arithmetical rules produced a system that was unimaginative, hierarchical and unsuited to the majority of young people (Petersen, 1952; Hughes, 1856/1967). Yet attempts to make the process of

learning more adapted to the minds of the young can be traced in different parts of Europe back to Comenius (1592–1670), Rousseau (1712–78), Pestalozzi (1746–1827), Herbart (1776–1841), Froebel (1782–1852) and, in Britain, to the popularization of an alternative approach by Herbert Spencer whose treatise, *Education*, was first published in 1861 and became a leading textbook. He wrote, 'while the old method of presenting truths in the abstract has been falling out of use, there has been a corresponding adoption of the new method of presenting them in the concrete' (Spencer, 1929: 59, first published in 1861).

In the twentieth century Montessori and Piaget point in the same experience-rich direction (Montessori, 1964, first published in English in 1912). Piaget's more developed theoretical position allowed him to postulate the sequences in which mental representations of the outer world were manipulated and assimilated within cognitive structures. He was able to provide a rationale for activity methods that later became pedagogically normative in the teaching of infants. Other writers took his findings and translated them into educational materials (Gruber and Vonèche, 1995).

In the United States of America Dewey, starting from philosophical pragmatism, was able to link the curriculum to the betterment of society and to incorporate within this vision a classroom environment that centred on the transmutation of unmediated experience into knowledge (Dewey, 1926). This is how progressive education came to define itself against traditional education (Rusk, 1969). So, when mass educational systems emerged in the industrialized world during the second half of the twentieth century, teaching methods loosened up and embraced direct experience. Very young children interacted with the environment to facilitate the formation of the cognitive structures whose extension, in the Piagetian paradigm, constitute learning. The methods that succeed with the young were applied to older young people. In secondary schools, young people were soon provided with pictures, visual aids, audiotapes, diagrams, films, video clips, visits and other means of making learning more than the memorizing of disconnected facts and rules.

In relation to religious education the phenomenological approach in its classroom incarnation has included an experiential dimension in the classroom. This dimension was laid out by

Ninian Smart (1968: 18) in his book, *Secular Education and the Logic of Religion*, where he writes:

> We cannot fully appreciate religion or its meaning without paying attention to the inner life of those who are involved in the life of the dimensions we have so far considered. Indeed, many of the seminal moments of religious history have involved religious experiences of a dramatic kind . . . at a humbler level there is the testimony of countless religious folk who believe themselves to have had moments of illumination, conversion, vision, a sense of presence and so on.

Smart's inclusion of experience encouraged teachers to use poetry, meditation, role-play and empathy in an attempt to gain a fully rounded picture of religion. Experience could legitimate religion in the eyes of young people and, if experience could be recreated in the classroom, then a bridge to the world of the religious believer existed over which young people might walk.

A method of mediating religious experience is also found in the 'gift to the child' approach to religious education, established after 1984. Here a religious object is presented to children and the children respond to it. The object is deliberately selected to encourage or elicit a response (Hull, 2000: 116). The response of children enables them to draw closer to a religious tradition, but it highlights the need for teachers to ensure a compensating distancing also takes place. The approach was eventually broken down into four steps: engagement, exploration, contextualization and reflection.

A more direct experiential approach to religious education was popularized by Hammond, Hay, Moxon, Netto, Raban, Straugheir and Williams (1990) in *New Methods in RE Teaching: An Experiential Approach*. This approach, making use of the research of David Hay (1987), recommended meditative practices as well as other ways of seeking unusual forms of consciousness to show young people how they might escape the tyranny of modern culture and peer-group pressure. The approach begins by asking young people to become aware of simple sensory experience and then to become aware of silence, to imagine themselves to be something else, to realize that experience differs from person to person and from body to body, and then to reflect upon the meaning of the experiences they have gathered.

Such an approach has similarities with, but also clear differences from, the concept-cracking approach advocated by Trevor and Margaret Cooling (Cooling, 1994). Here, while there is a desire to make a connection between a religion and the experience of the child, the central part of the process involves the development of concepts rather than feelings. So in the concept-cracking approach the notion is that initially alien religious concepts might be mapped on to comparable concepts spontaneously stemming from the life of the child seeking understanding.

Spirituality issues

The 1944 Education Act enshrined in law religious education and collective worship as part of the life of schools within the state-funded sector of education in England and Wales. Thereafter, the school day began with collective worship and each pupil, subject to a parental request for withdrawal on grounds of conscience, was obliged to attend.

The preamble of the Education Act passed by the British Parliament in 1944 stated that: 'It shall be the duty of the local education authority for every area, so far as their powers extend, to contribute toward the spiritual, moral, mental and physical development of the community.' The adjective 'spiritual' was preferred to the word 'religious' for the very practical reason that it engendered less argument (Priestley, 1985). Subsequently the 'spiritual' aspect of the curriculum continued as a strand within the legislative programme enacted by successive governments. In discussions in the 1970s that preceded the introduction of the national curriculum the spiritual was considered to be one of the 'areas of experience' that ought to be covered by the secondary curriculum. Spirituality was seen at that point as relating to 'those elements in existence and experience which may be defined in terms of inner feelings and beliefs . . . the way people see themselves . . . the purpose and meaning of life . . . to glimpse the transcendent' (Department of Education and Science, 1977).

The 1988 Education Reform Act, while retaining many aspects of collective worship and religious education, completely changed the educational landscape in England and Wales. Local variation was largely flattened and replaced by a pattern of provision almost completely directed centrally from London. A new curriculum was devised, 'delivered' by teachers, and school compliance was ensured by a rigorous and frequent system of inspection. Like the 1944 Education Act the 1988 Act also set out, as a central aim, that the 'school curriculum should promote the spiritual, moral, cultural, mental and physical development of pupils and society' (Department of Education, 1994: 9). Seasoned observers of educational systems around the world were not surprised to discover that the changes forced through by Conservative governments at the beginning of the 1990s had to be continued, or apparently continued, by succeeding governments controlled by the Labour party. In these circumstances it is also no surprise that terminology that expressed one set of values to Conservatives was gradually adjusted so as to fit the preferences of another set of political rulers: the law remains the same, the meaning seems to change (see Erricker and Erricker, 2000).

It is the word 'spiritual' that is most prone to alteration (Slee, 1993). For Conservatives, it appears to be a general term largely attached to religion but implying something more than the doctrinal or moral aspects of religion. For others 'there is now no longer any coherent understanding of it . . . it has become an all-things-to-all-people concept' (Grosch, 2000). This variation is evidenced by interviews carried out with 1,195 candidates for the teaching profession during the 1990s (Bainbridge, 2000). The candidates, who were predominantly young women, spoke of spirituality in terms of an 'inner aspect or personal dimension' (48.3%) that might be summarized as 'finding oneself'. Most drew a distinction between religion and spirituality; some saw religion as an impediment to spiritual development and others as an expression of it. Similarly a connection between spirituality and morality was frequently mentioned (66.9%) and an unspecified proportion believed spirituality was found in relationships. In open-ended answers the theme of transcendence was picked up, in connection sometimes with the natural world and at other times with heightened childhood perceptions and insights.

The discussion of spirituality is well summarized by Wright (1998) and may be interpreted as a struggle between different factions seeking to control the terms of the debate. There is a conflict between the realist and non-realist positions over the referent of spiritual experience. The realist position assumes that an ultimate transcendent reality is the source of spiritual experience. At the very least this position assumes that spiritual experience is a response to a value-bearing realm holding ontological status. The non-realist position assumes that spiritual experience has no referent beyond what is empirically ascertainable within the natural world. It is in some senses simply conjured up from within the psyche of the experiencer. For the non-realist spiritual experience is only a peak moment that words can hardly capture, its ineffability making it more mysterious than it really is; it is analogous to the intense joy that might be adduced by music, personal relationships or physical achievement (Maslow, 1976).

For this reason spirituality is open to a variety of religious and non-religious interpretations. Within western culture the religious interpretation of spirituality has been prevalent in the sense that spiritual experience has been seen as a consequence or correlate of doctrine. As far back as 1924 Dean Inge could write 'the centre of gravity in religion has shifted from authority and tradition to experience', and he saw this shift as being brought about by the devastating effects of the 1914–18 war on traditional religious doctrine and associated social customs (Inge, 1926: 323). Such a shift was connected in his mind, on one side, with the work of William James (1902) in *The Varieties of Religious Experience* at the beginning of the twentieth century and, on the other, with a resurgence in mysticism, and a theological revaluation of its contribution to religious life.

So spirituality was understood as growing out of religious traditions. Christianity, which most British scholars knew best, could point both to historical exemplars of mystical practice and to the experiences accompanying evangelical revivalism. The renewed place for experience identified by religious scholarship was taken up during the course of the twentieth century when religious traditions became more aware of each other's characteristics. It became feasible to argue that a common religious experience lay behind scriptural records of the divine activity within diverse cultures. The seemingly different insights of Hinduism, Buddhism, Christianity or Islam actually shared a fundamental unity. As a result commentators argued that religions were more similar than their doctrinal differences indicated and that a common core of religious experience sustained them all (Maslow, 1976: 19; Hick, 1973).

Against this pan-religious conception of spirituality, an opposing tradition has arisen. This tradition argues that spirituality is essentially a human characteristic and that the humanist, as much as the religious person, can manifest it (Newby, 1994, 1997). Indeed it may be argued that the current secularization of western culture makes it vital that spirituality now be expressed in new forms which divest themselves of religious conceptions and terms. If spirituality is to be given the place that it deserves, then religion must not be allowed to contaminate it any more. Spirituality can be reconceptualized and should now be understood as an expression of the physical, of the material. Spirituality, instead of speaking about the transcendent reality, concerns the here-and-now. 'Spirituality is about life with this body, not about a soul or spirit simply inhabiting for a while this physical frame' (Grosch, 2000).

The dispute over the nature of spiritual experience has several ramifications. It raises the issue of whether spiritual experience is universal or particular. Since religion appears to be a universal characteristic, it is reasonable to believe that spirituality is universal. Since human beings are the same species across the world, it is equally reasonable, from a humanistic perspective, to believe that spirituality is universal. On the other hand, not everybody is religious and not everybody has spiritual experiences, so is it worth asking why this should be. What particular conjunction of human capacity and culture is necessary to produce accounts of spiritual experience?

The dispute over the nature of spirituality leads to a discussion of its defining attributes. Hay and Nye have advanced a view that spirituality should be analysed in terms of 'relational consciousness' (Hay and Nye, 1998: 113). The consciousness at issue here is a special awareness of being related to other people, other things, oneself or God. In contrast, other scholars have seen spirituality in terms of a struggle between individuality and tradition (Chater, 2000). Others have seen spirituality in terms of a stress on the non-material part of human beings and assumed that spirituality and materiality are opposites. Such an analysis assumes that different types of spirituality exist within Marxism, existentialism or Christianity but that, in each instance, it is a stress on the non-material element within human life that defines an activity or experience as spiritual (Kay, 1985). Yet others focus on the moral dimension of spirituality (SCAA, 1995), a focus often realized through responses to literature in a tradition that stretches back at least as far as Matthew Arnold (Pike, 2000). Here the moral dimension is concerned with the question of how we should live and, since spiritual responses inform answers to this question, spirituality is bound up with morality. Such moral concerns may coalesce with sexual morality or even sexual mysticism, of a kind manifested, according to Bertrand Russell, by D. H. Lawrence. As Lawrence put it, 'when I take a woman, then the blood-percept is supreme. My blood-knowing is overwhelming. We should realise that we have a blood-being, a blood-consciousness, a blood-soul complete and apart from a mental and nerve consciousness' (Russell, 1956).

Method

A large-scale questionnaire survey is the only way of drawing out representative information about religious experience from young people of secondary school age. Such information has the advantage of subsequently allowing precise analysis.

Sample: the sample comprised 33,135 young people, of whom 51.3% were male and 48.7% female. Just over half of the young people were in year nine (52.7%), or aged 13 to 14, and the remainder were in year ten (47.3%), or aged 14 to 15. The young people attended 180 secondary schools in England and Wales. The demographic characteristics of the schools indicate that their young people are representative of the secondary age population in England and Wales.

Questionnaire: the questionnaire was presented to the young people during their normal lessons in the form of a substantial booklet. The booklet was completed anonymously. Among many other things, the young people were asked 'Do you belong to a church or other religious group?' and given a wide range of choices that included *no* and a list of Christian denominations and world religions, as well as the category *other (specify)*. The young people were also asked 'Have you ever had something you would describe as a "religious experience"?' and given the options *no; perhaps, but I am not really sure; probably, but I am not certain;* and *yes, definitely.*

The young people were also asked about their expected academic qualifications on leaving school and given a series of options, from *none* to *3 or more A levels*. These options were scored on a seven-point scale, where *none* was 1 and *3 or more A levels* was 7. The young people were also asked about their father's job and these answers were then carefully classified according to the registrar general's descriptors, scoring 1 for the highest socio-economic group. Young people of unemployed fathers and fathers in the armed forces were excluded from this subsection of the analysis. In addition 128 statements were presented to the young people for response on a five-point Likert-type scale (Likert, 1932) ranging from *agree strongly* to *agree* through *not certain* to *disagree* and then *disagree strongly*. From these statements two scales were constructed, based on the groupings of items in Francis and Kay (1995). The first of these scales concerned sexual morality (six items, alpha .6108) and the second social morality (seven items, alpha .7779). As far as analysis is concerned, it is important to note that a high score on the sexual morality scale indicates agreement with a strongly puritanical position, whereas a high score on the social morality scale indicates agreement with a strongly amoral position.

Table 6.1 Sexual morality scale: item rest of test correlations

Item	r
Abortion is wrong	0.3092
It is wrong to have sexual intercourse outside marriage	0.4593
Divorce is wrong	0.3981
Contraception is wrong	0.3687
Homosexuality is wrong	0.2286
It is wrong to have sexual intercourse under the legal age	0.3404

Table 6.2 Social morality scale: item rest of test correlations

Item	r
There is nothing wrong in playing truant from school	0.5510
There is nothing wrong in shoplifting	0.5176
There is nothing wrong in buying cigarettes under the legal age	0.5471
There is nothing wrong in travelling without a ticket	0.5058
There is nothing wrong in cycling after dark without lights	0.4043
There is nothing wrong in buying alcohol under the legal age	0.5207
There is nothing wrong in writing graffiti (tagging)	0.4764

The young people were asked if they found it helpful to talk about their problems with their mother and with their father. They were also presented with the statements, 'Religious education should be taught in school' and 'Schools should hold a religious assembly every day', and again asked to respond to the statements, using the Likert-type format (Likert, 1932).

Results

For the purposes of analysis the sample was divided into four groups. The groups were constructed using polar opposites so that nobody could be assigned to more than one group. First, a distinction was made between pupils who reported membership of a religious group and those who reported no such membership. Second, a distinction was made between those who were either definitely or probably sure that they had had a religious experience and those who either denied that they had had a religious experience or were unsure about it. The result of this fourfold classification is as follows. Of the whole sample 43.7% had no membership of a religious group and had had no religious experience (of these 56% were boys); 42.7% had membership of a religious group but had had no religious experience (47% were boys); 3.2% had no membership of a religious group but had had a religious experience (55% were boys) and 10.4% had membership of a religious group and had had a religious experience (50% were boys).

When males and females were compared, 13.7% of girls and 13.4% of boys were found to claim a religious experience. However, of these young people 78.4% of girls and 74.5% of boys claimed religious membership. Thus, more girls reported religious experience and, of these girls, proportionately more claimed religious membership.

The four groups were then compared with each other. Responses to the items on religious education and collective worship or religious assembly were contrasted, using one-way analysis of variance and Bonferroni post-hoc comparisons. These results are given in Table 6.3. In each case the three other groups are compared with the small group that has religious experience but no religious membership. This is because it is this group that may in the long run be of most relevance in the extension of experiential methods on religious education.

Table 6.3 Group mean differences compared with the group which has religious experience and no religious membership

Issues group	Difference in means	P<
RE should be taught in school		
No religious experience and no religious membership	+0.41	.001
No religious experience with religious membership	−0.11	.05
Religious experience with religious membership	−0.65	.001
Schools should hold a religious assembly every day		
No religious experience and no religious membership	+0.39	.001
No religious experience with religious membership	+0.00	NS
Religious experience with religious membership	−0.45	.001
Social morality		
No religious experience and no religious membership	+0.00	NS
No religious experience with religious membership	+1.23	.001
Religious experience with religious membership	+2.39	.001
Sexual morality		
No religious experience and no religious membership	+0.63	.001
No religious experience with religious membership	+0.00	NS
Religious experience with religious membership	−2.01	.001
Expected academic qualifications		
No religious experience and no religious membership	+0.11	NS
No religious experience with religious membership	−0.31	.001
Religious experience with religious membership	−0.51	.001
Paternal social class		
No religious experience and no religious membership	+0.00	NS
No religious experience with religious membership	+0.26	.001
Religious experience with religious membership	+0.36	.001
Helpful to talk about problems with my mother		
No religious experience and no religious membership	+0.15	.01
No religious experience with religious membership	+0.00	NS
Religious experience with religious membership	+0.00	NS
Helpful to talk about problems with my father		
No religious experience and no religious membership	+0.11	.05
No religious experience with religious membership	+0.00	NS
Religious experience with religious membership	+0.00	NS

Note: In each case the score of the groups listed in the table have been subtracted from the scores recorded by the comparison group, namely the young people who have no religious experience and no religious membership.

Discussion

The first part of this discussion is focused on Table 6.3. The table shows that religious experience appears to have a positive effect on the evaluation by young people of religious education. When the two groups of young people with no religious membership are compared, it is those young people who have religious experience who are significantly more likely to be in favour of religious education in school. Yet, religious experience on its own is not able to lift favourability to religious education more than religious membership does. So religious membership emerges as the most powerful factor working in favour of young people's evaluation of religious education in school.

What these figures cannot predict is whether young people would become more favourable to religious education if, within the classroom, they entertained religious experience. Experiential methods of religious education, like those discussed in the opening sections of this chapter, may induce young people to receive religious experience within the confines of the classroom.

The effect of religious experience on evaluation of religious assembly is also noticeably positive. Young people who have had a religious experience, but no religious membership, are indistinguishable from young people with religious experience who also have religious membership. Certainly young people who have religious experience and a religious membership are more favourable to religious assembly than are young people who have neither membership nor experience. The group most positive toward religious assembly is that which has both experience and membership.

Religious assemblies have a huge range of possibilities inherent within them. They vary enormously in their content, style, ethos, size and enjoyability. Yet the possibility of religious experience within the religious assembly is in theory much greater than it would be within the classroom. Here within the assembly young people may be asked to pray, to reflect silently, listen intently to music or hear a scriptural reading that might stimulate fresh insights into the experiential side of religion.

Social morality within the analysis presented here is concerned primarily with theft, vandalism and lawbreaking. What is surprising in this analysis is the similarity between the groups who have no religious membership, whether or not they have had a religious experience. So we may say that religious experience *does* have an impact on the young people's view of religious education and assembly but does *not* have an impact on their social morality. It is evident that it is religious membership that has the greatest impact on social morality. Those who are members of religious groups (bearing in mind that there is no distinction here between different religions) are much more likely to consider that vandalism, theft and lawbreaking are wrong than are those who do not belong to a religious group.

It is clear from this that there are young people who are open to religious experience and yet who do not think this religious experience has a moral dimension. Their religious experience is something that is free-floating and detached from their general moral conduct. Yet, as Table 6.3 demonstrates, religious experience does impinge on sexual morality.

When comparisons are made over the issue of sexual morality it is clear that the young people with religious experience and no religious membership are nevertheless stricter in their sexual morality than the group who lack both religious experience and religious membership. It would therefore appear that religious experience does *sensitize* young people toward sexual relationships, even if it does not sensitize them toward public attitudes expressed in social morality.

Such sensitization is suggestive of the relational nature of spirituality. Speculation could posit a common sense of intimacy within sexual experience and religious experience. This would explain why religious experience has no impact on social morality, since this type of morality is protective only of the anonymous crowd and the impersonal institution. Moreover, this interpretation receives support from the finding that young people who reported religious experience (in the group that did not hold religious membership) were also more likely to report that they found it 'helpful' to talk to their parents about their problems. In this respect young people with a religious experience were similar to young people with religious membership in their feeling of closeness to their parents.

When expected academic qualifications are considered it is apparent that the two groups which have religious membership have the highest expectations of academic achievement and that the two groups without religious membership are not different from each other. So the group who have received religious experience but who lack religious membership are not different from their other generally irreligious contemporaries.

This picture is confirmed by inspection of paternal social class. It is the two groups with religious membership that have a higher social-class means. Thus, the group with religious experience but without religious membership is not drawn from disaffected middle-class young people. Rather, it is drawn from the great majority of young people within the maintained sector of education.

Having examined Table 6.3, it is now possible to comment on these findings briefly, using the three headings of psychology, pedagogy and spirituality mentioned earlier.

Psychological issues

The figures show that young women are more likely than are young men to report religious experience and that young women are more likely to choose religious membership than are young men. Altogether about 12% of the population report having received religious experiences. These experiences may or may not occur within the religious settings provided by religious membership. The figure of 12% reflects roughly what would be expected on the basis of belief-in-God figures, in the sense that religious experience is a little under half as frequent as is belief in God. The distribution of religious experience in the secondary school population appears to echo that found in the adult population.

This ratio deserves international testing. There is evidence in Gallup and Lindsay (1999: 24, 69) that this finding holds among adults in the United States of America. What is not clear is whether it would hold in a heavily secularized society.

Pedagogical issues

Experience is fostered as a matter of course within a large number of academic disciplines. Young people make and listen to music, make and look at paintings, visit historical buildings and enjoy virtual visits through digital media. Against this background it makes sense to offer experience within the classroom in religious education.

The presence of young people who claim religious experience

without religious membership indicates that such experiences are not dependent upon membership of religious communities. Although it is possible that young people who claim religious experience without religious membership may once have been members of religious communities, it is equally possible that many of them never shared in such community life and have simply experienced religion intensely within the ordinary process of living. Pedagogically this suggests that religious experience is accessible to young people within secular settings. If so, then religious experience is accessible to young people even within a classroom following an agreed and common curriculum of religion.

On the positive side of this balance is the possibility that young people may find religious education interesting and exciting because it is associated with experiences outside their normal range. On the negative side, the attempt to induce religious experience in young people by meditation, 'stilling', offering numinous objects, role-play or other forms of involvement might be alarming to parents of secular convictions. The impressionability of young people makes them vulnerable to manipulation. More than this, the inducement of religious experience demands the suspension of rational faculties so that the experience might be embraced fully. Pedagogically, when young people are asked to open themselves to religious experience in the classroom, they must not just 'bracket out' prejudices, in the way demanded by the phenomenological method, but also suspend critical reason and critical disbelief.

Spirituality
The model advanced here presumes that religious experience exists within the larger field of spiritual experience. Just as 'religious' is seen as a more specific adjective than 'spiritual', so religious experience should be seen as more specific than spiritual experience. The figures given here concerning religious experience should almost certainly be raised in the context of spirituality. What deductions may be made from the large sample reported on here about the openness of young people to religious experience and the prevalence of religious experience is almost certainly applicable *a fortiori* to spiritual experience.

The figures given here cannot settle the issue of whether spirituality ought to be seen as primarily religious or secular, although some kind of mixture between the two appears to be indicated by the notion that a religious experience is claimed by non-religious young people. To pursue this question more adequately and with greater empirical evidence it would be necessary to mount a project that asked religious people about their spiritual experiences (including humanistic 'peak' experiences) and non-religious people about the same range of experiences. We could then find out if religious people *also* reported non-religious spiritual experiences.

What is evident from the data here is that religious experience (whatever precisely that means to non-religious young people) is connected with sexual morality. This interpretation might be strengthened by the failure of religious experience to have any impact upon social morality. What seems evident here is that social morality is a function of membership of a religious group. By contrast religious experience does not change the expression of social morality. Consequently it is arguable that relational consciousness and spirituality (as evidenced by religious experience) have an affinity. Whether spirituality is also linked with non-materiality in relation to art or to holistic concerns cannot be answered from the data and ought also to be addressed by future research.

Conclusion

First, a significant proportion of English and Welsh secondary school young people claim religious experience. This experience is correlated with sexual morality. Young people with religious membership claim religious experience more frequently than others, but they are by no means the only young people to make this claim. Young people without religious membership have also had religious experience. These findings raise questions about the nature of religious experience and the social grouping needed to sustain it. Future research using empirical methods to explore the nature of spirituality ought to be able to tease out the network of concepts by which it is upheld and interpreted. Whereas previous quantitative research (Hay, 1987) has concentrated on the frequency of spiritual and religious experiences within various populations, and whereas qualitative research has been concerned with reports of spiritual experience so as to classify them in various ways (Robinson, 1977), there have been few, if any, attempts to investigate the *nature* of spiritual or religious experience among young people quantitatively and to connect the results of these findings to curriculum development.

Second, if one accepts that the teaching methods using experience belong to the progressive educational tradition and this tradition is suitable for mass education systems in the twenty-first century, then there is a logical case for extending the means by which experience of various kinds is elicited within the classroom. Agreed and rational safeguards would need to be put into place to avoid charges of indoctrination or exploitation, but such safeguards could be formulated either from philosophical or, better, from empirical research.

Third, this chapter provides evidence that, if religious experience were more widely achieved, there would be beneficial effects on young people's evaluation of religious education and collective worship.

References

Bainbridge, R. M. (2000), 'The spiritual and the intending teacher', *International Journal of Children's Spirituality*, 5, 163–75.

Chater, M. F. T. (2000), 'Spirituality as struggle: poetics, experience and the place of the spiritual in educational encounter', *International Journal of Children's Spirituality*, 5, 193–201.

Cooling, T. (1994), *Concept Cracking: Exploring Christian Beliefs in School* (Stapleford, Stapleford Project Books/Association of Christian Teachers).

Department of Education (1994), *Religious Education and Collective Worship* (London, HMSO).

Department of Education and Science (1977), *Curriculum 11–16* (London).

Dewey, J. (1926), *Science and the Modern World* (Cambridge, Cambridge University Press).

Erricker, C. and Erricker, J. (2000), *Reconstructing Religious, Spiritual and Moral Education* (London, RoutledgeFalmer).

Francis, L. J. and Kay, W. K. (1995), *Teenage Religion and Values* (Leominster, Gracewing).

Gallup, G. and Lindsay, D. M. (1999), *Surveying the Religious Landscape* (Harrisburg, Pa., Morehouse Publishing).

Grosch, P. (2000), 'Paideia: philosophy educating humanity

through spirituality', *International Journal of Children's Spirituality*, 5, 229–38.

Gruber, H. E. and Vonèche, J. J. (eds) (1995), *The Essential Piaget* (London, Jason Aronson).

Hammond, J., Hay, D., Moxon, J., Netto, B., Raban, K., Straugheir, G. and Williams, C. (1990), *New Methods in RE Teaching: An Experiential Approach* (Harlow, Oliver and Boyd).

Hay, D. (1987), *Exploring Inner Space* (London, Mowbray).

Hay, D. and Nye, R. (1998), *The Spirit of the Child* (London, Fount).

Hick, J. (1973), *God and the Universe of Faiths* (London, Macmillan).

Hood, R. W., Spilka, B., Hunsberger, B. and Gorsuch, R. (1996), *The Psychology of Religion* (London, The Guildford Press).

Hughes, T. (1856/1967), *Tom Brown's Schooldays* (London, Macmillan).

Hull, J. M. (2000), 'Religion in the service of the child project: the gift approach to religious education', in M. Grimmitt (ed.), *Pedagogies of Religious Education: Case Studies in Research and Development of Good Pedagogic Practice in RE* (Great Wakering, McCrimmons), pp. 112–29.

Inge, W. R. (1926), *Lay Thoughts of a Dean* (London, G. P. Putnam's Sons).

James, W. (1902), *The Varieties of Religious Experience* (New York, Longmans Green).

Kay, W. K. (1985), 'Variations on a spiritual theme: man in a multi-faith world', *British Journal of Religious Education*, 7, 128–33.

Kay, W. K. (1997), 'Belief in God in Great Britain 1945–1996: moving the scenery behind classroom RE', *British Journal of Religious Education*, 20, 28–41.

Likert, R. (1932), 'A technique for the measurement of attitudes', *Archives of Psychology*, 140, 1–55.

Marwick, A. (1998), *The Sixties* (Oxford, Oxford University Press).

Maslow, A. H. (1976), *Religions, Values and Peak-Experiences* (Harmondsworth, Penguin; first pub. 1964).

Montessori, M. (1964), *The Montessori Method* (New York, Schocken Books; first pub. in English 1912).

Newby, M. (1994), 'The spiritual development of children in a secular context: reflections on some aspects of theory and practice', *Spes*, 1, 17–19.

Newby, M. (1997), 'Literary development as spiritual development in the common school', *Journal of Philosophy of Education*, 31, 283–94.

Petersen, A. D. C. (1952), *A Hundred Years of Education* (London, Gerald Duckworth and Co.).

Pike, M. A. (2000), 'Spirituality, morality and poetry', *International Journal of Children's Spirituality*, 5, 177–91.

Priestley, J. G. (1985), 'Towards finding the hidden curriculum: a consideration of the spiritual dimension of experience in curriculum planning', *British Journal of Religious Education*, 7, 112–19.

Robinson, E. (1977), *The Original Vision* (Oxford, Religious Experience Research Centre).

Rusk, R. R. (1969), *Doctrines of the Great Educators* (4th edn) (London, Macmillan).

Russell, B. (1956), *Portraits from Memory and Other Essays* (London, George Allen and Unwin).

SCAA (1995), *Spiritual and Moral Development*, Discussion Paper 3 (London, School Curriculum and Assessment Authority).

Slee, N. M. (1993), 'Spirituality in education: an annotated bibliography', *Journal of Beliefs and Values*, 13 (3), 10–17.

Smart, N. (1968), *Secular Education and the Logic of Religion* (London, Faber and Faber).

Spencer, H. (1929), *Education* (London, Watts and Co.; first pub. 1861).

Wilson, B. R. (1996), *Religious Experience: A Sociological Perspective*, Occasional Paper 2 (Oxford Religious Experience Research Centre).

Wright, A. (1998), *Spiritual Pedagogy: A Survey, Critique and Reconstruction of Contemporary Spiritual Education in England and Wales* (Abingdon, Culham College Institute).

II

Quantitative and Qualitative Perspectives

7

Research on lifestyle, spirituality and religious orientation of adolescents in Germany

HEINZ STREIB

Summary

This chapter presents results from recent quantitative and qualitative empirical research designed to identify developments in the religious orientation of adolescents in Germany, which in turn can be compared with research in the United States of America. Interpretation of these results draws on German lifestyle research, especially the work of Schulze (1992), *Die Erlebnisgesellschaft* (*The Experience Society*). This perspective can help to explain the rise of hedonistic attitudes in German society which may have changed the pattern of the adolescent quest for spirituality and religious identity. This indicates the importance of reflection on the relationship between lifestyle and religion. These developments are relevant not only to the conceptualization of religion and the design of research, but also to religious education. The question is: how can religious education fulfil its task and meet the challenges which are presented by developments in youth culture and in the young person's spiritual quest?

Introduction

Here are two short portraits of adolescents which are derived, not from our own research, but from the qualitative section of the twelfth Shell survey (Shell, 1997: 105–21, 149–61).

Jana is 19 years old and lives in Munich. Jana has helped to introduce techno worship in her church and is happy that one of her dreams has become a reality. With permission from the bishop, techno-beat was heard in St John's Church in Munich on 27 October 1996.

Jana has a long Christian biography. Since her childhood, she has spent a great deal of time in the local Young Men's Christian Association, but as an adolescent she has become more critical of its organizational structures and has started to look for a form of religious involvement with which she would feel more comfortable. In the techno worship movement, she has found what she was looking for. 'We say hey, we are young Christians', says Jana, 'but we are not that much different from you. We also want to have fun, and our God does not forbid us to have fun.' Jana maintains that one ought to have fun in one's life, but that fun without meaning leads neither to fun, nor to meaning. Jana has made the decision to take the Bible as the foundation for her life.

Daniel is 18 years old and was born in Thüringen, which had been part of East Germany. Daniel is the oldest of four siblings of a rather strict and narrow Protestant family. Daniel lives with his parents; his father is an engine-driver and his mother is a cleaning lady in a home for the handicapped. Daniel has completed basic school education and goes to a vocational school to train to be a metalworker. His hobbies are going to the theatre, playing music and drinking beer.

Until he was 14 or 15 years old, Daniel went to church every Sunday. Then, recognizing the hypocrisy of the Church, he stopped going to church and joined the punk scene. For the past two years Daniel has played in several punk bands. In a song he wrote himself, he asks, 'Religion, what is your reality? Behind your mask, you are bewitched . . . Your Bible is a book full of lies; greed for money, if I look in your eyes . . . You lead yourselves into disaster! Nail your God on to the cross!'

I have chosen Jana and Daniel from the numerous biographical portraits in the Shell study because these two case-studies reflect the kind of adolescent everyday aesthetic orientation and sensation-seeking in relationship to religion. The relation to religion, however, is totally different in the two biographies. In Jana's life there is a simultaneous intensification of both religiosity and sensational experience, while in Daniel's life there is movement away from his family's religion in order to find excitement and some sense of identity.

Imagine that Jana and Daniel are students in the religious education class. What do their different life-stories mean for communication in the classroom? Will the teacher's words address the everyday aesthetic preference of the students and their self-determined search for either a religious or a non-religious identity? Or will the classroom communication be marked by conflicting lifestyles which impede or actually prevent learning? It is my suspicion that at least some of the communication problems in the classroom can be explained by a model of 'conflicting lifestyles' which takes into account the attitudes of religious educators, as well as those of their students.

Classroom communication in religious education is only one practical application for the topic to which I wish to draw attention, namely the relationship between lifestyle, spirituality and religious orientation among adolescents. To unfold this theme, I will proceed in four steps. First, I shall start by presenting selected results from empirical research on the religious orientation and socialization of adolescents in Germany, presenting results on 'spirituality' as far as we have relevant data. Second, based on the observation of the increasing privatization and invisibility of adolescent religion, together with a significant number of self-assessments of 'being spiritual', research on the 'spiritual quest' is examined. Third, building on results from the German lifestyle research, which takes 'experience', 'event' or 'everyday aesthetical orientation' as key factors in sociological analysis, the following question is addressed: 'Has this become a significant pattern in the adolescent quest for religious identity or spirituality?' Fourth, I conclude this presentation of empirical research on religious, spiritual and lifestyle orientation of German adolescents with a discussion of questions, implications and hypotheses for further research.

Empirical research on adolescent religion and spirituality

Quantitative evidence for the rise of invisible religion

Since we have neither a comprehensive study of the religious landscape of Germany as a whole, nor a representative portrait of the religious socialization of German adolescents, I need to refer to results from more selective studies and from broader youth surveys. I begin with the Shell studies because they provide an outstanding youth survey in Germany that not only has a comprehensive design and large samples of thousands of adolescents, but also presents us with longitudinal data that embrace almost half a century, as a result of regularly asking the same questions. Table 7.1 presents some data from the Shell survey (Shell, 1985, 1992, 2000) on church membership (mainly Protestant and Catholic), Sunday worship participation, youth group membership, belief in life after death and personal prayer. These results document the continuous decline of church membership in West Germany. Despite the alarming long-term effects of this decline, church membership still appears relatively high (81% in 1999), at least when compared with the data from East Germany after reunion, where the figure is about 20% church membership among adolescents.

These data agree with results from other research. In a more detailed analysis, which casts light on the socialization dynamics, Schmidtchen (1997: 149–50) talks about 48% of 15- to 30-year-old East German citizens who have never had any church affiliation in their families, plus another 25% who were never church members themselves, although their parents belong or have belonged to a church. Pollack (1996: 605–6) points to an even more problematic difference between East and West, in regard to the readiness to change one's world-view and to engage in religious mobility. While 91% of Catholics and 85% of Protestants in West Germany have kept the religious affiliation of their family of origin, only 63% of Catholics and 53% of Protestants in East Germany have remained loyal to their family tradition. The others have left the churches. The German churches, therefore, have reason to be concerned about membership stability of the younger generation, especially in the East.

Church membership is only one factor and, especially for the West German adolescents, a rather formal one. The Sunday worship participation figures indicate this very clearly. The percentage of adolescents who go to church at least once a month has dropped from 59% in the 1953 study to 16% at the end of the century. In East Germany Sunday worship participation is higher relative to church membership (which still reflects the tradition of a minority church situation), but only 7% of adolescents attend church at least once a month. Compared with formal church membership and Sunday worship participation, membership in church youth groups has been relatively stable over the decades; this perhaps indicates that, for adolescents, youth groups are a more attractive way of participating in church life.

Table 7.1 Results for the Shell studies from 1953, 1984, 1991 and 1999

Item	West 1953 %	West 1984 %	West 1991 %	East 1991 %	West 1999 %	East 1999 %
Are you a member of a Christian church?	97	94	90	21	81	20
Have you worshipped in the last four weeks?	59	27	21	10	16	7
Are you a member of a church youth group?	10	6	7	3	7	4
Do you believe in life after death?	43	49	56	22	32	18
Do you pray sometimes or regularly?	50	36	39	17	28	11

A different dynamic is seen in the data about belief in life after death and personal prayer. In contrast to the enormous decline in worship participation, personal prayer has declined more slowly; the number of adolescents who confess that they 'pray sometimes or regularly' has even increased slightly between 1984 and 1991. Adolescents who pray occasionally or regularly amount to almost twice the number of adolescent worshippers. Indeed, as Fuchs-Heinritz (2000: 163) reports, in 1999 8% of the male and 26% of the female adolescents who never go to church reported that they prayed sometimes or regularly. Thus, despite some decline, personal prayer among adolescents outside any official religious context has emerged as a factor that needs to be taken seriously. There has also been an increase in belief in life after death from the 1953 survey to the 1991 survey, but there is some reason to assume that beliefs about reincarnation, inspired by eastern religions, may have influenced these results.

These results regarding personal prayer can be examined alongside other facets of religion which appear to be part of the present-day adolescents' orientation toward religion. The Shell study in 2000 asked additional questions, 'Do you intend to raise your children religiously?' and 'Do you believe in a higher justice?' I have compiled the results in Table 7.2. This not only indicates the close relationship to scores on personal prayer, but also the significant difference between male and female adolescents with regard to religion. Since this Shell survey has, for the first time, included samples of immigrant youth (including those without a German passport), we have some data which allow for a comparison. The data demonstrate that Italian and Turkish immigrant adolescents have higher scores in all items, the female Turkish adolescents being the most religious.

These results on the religious membership, participation, private practice, intentions and beliefs of adolescents in Germany can be checked against a single question in the Shell survey, 'Do you consider yourself as religious?' Just over half the total sample (52%) responded that they did not consider themselves religious. Despite some differences between males (57%) and females (47%), which are not particularly surprising, and also between East Germany (78%) and West Germany (47%), the real surprise is the total number of adolescents who say that they are 'not religious'. Looked at from the other perspective, however, these data mean that 48% of German adolescents still, more or less, declare themselves as being religious.

Table 7.2 Religiosity of German, Italian and Turkish adolescents from the Shell study 2000

Item	German male %	German female %	Italian male %	Italian female %	Turkish male %	Turkish female %
Do you pray sometimes or regularly?	18	31	30	50	41	52
Do you intend to raise children religiously?	29	37	49	56	64	74
Do you believe in *higher* justice?	36	44	58	68	72	78

As we can see from these results, a decline of participation in worship and in religious groups does not necessarily mean a decline in private religious practice and in religious orientation. Even terminating membership of the Church does not mean giving up private religion or the search for religious meaning. On the contrary, as the 1993 survey of Protestant church members (Engelhardt, von Loewenich and Steinacker, 1997: 327) documents, 52% of West Germans and 31% of East Germans who have left the Protestant Church maintain that they 'can be Christian without the Church', and about 20% (East and West) deny that they have left the Church because they 'did not need religion in their lives'.

These results can be taken as evidence that religiosity among German adolescents has more stability and continuity than may be inferred from the decline of church membership and church participation. These results certainly contradict any general secularization hypothesis that assumes the decline and eventual disappearance of religion in Western societies. Rather, these results indicate that the religiosity of German adolescents may have changed significantly. Religion has become a matter of individual practice and preference. The religion of adolescents, because of its retreat from the public sphere, has become more invisible: that is, invisible to the public sphere and to the type of surveys that ask questions about membership and participation on the institutional and macro-sociological level. Religious orientation, belief and practice continue to be a dimension of some importance in adolescents' lives and self-understanding, although in a different way.

Biographical research and new types of religious socialization

Quantitative survey data document supposedly reliable surface indicators for a solid and supposedly representative number of subjects, but they are not designed to tell us much about motivational conditions and biographical developments. Therefore, we need the complementary help of qualitative analysis. Qualitative approaches have become increasingly utilized in German research on religious socialization and development, since, despite their very small samples, they yield valuable insights into the depth dimension of a person's life. This method can help us to understand better the motivational and developmental dynamics of religious identity formation and transformation (see, for example, Schöll, 1992; Comenius-Institut, 1993; Fischer and Schöll, 1994; Klein, 1994; Sandt, 1996; Sommer, 1997; Schöll, 1998; Streib, 1998; Fuchs-Heinritz, Heinritz and Kolvenbach, 1998; Augst, 2000; Tietze, 2001). Drawing on these studies, how can we characterize the new way of searching for religion or of being religious, and what is the better label: religion or spirituality?

The gradual development of Albrecht Schöll's typology can be taken as an example of how qualitative research is engaged in the struggle to come to terms with religious identity formation in an ever-changing environment.

In 1992 Schöll identified a new emerging type of religious socialization in which the pluralization of religious meaning was influential, but at the same time he identified ways in which religion was being used for crisis prevention. Interviewees who were members of new religious movements inspired the construction of this new type (see Schöll, 1998). But already in 1994, in a new and larger research project on adolescents' religion, Schöll felt the need to expand the typology and include what he then called the 'occasional' type of religious socialization. The reason for this was a number of case studies of people for whom religion had in fact the function of structuring life, not as a permanent commitment to one religion, but as occasional appropriations of religious meaning selected from a plural supply.

This can be taken as an example of how qualitative biographical-reconstructive research is learning and progressing as a result of its attempt to embrace the biographies under investigation. In this way a new type of religious socialization has emerged and come into the foreground. We are very likely to encounter this new type of religious socialization, as consumer attitudes increasingly influence religious meaning-making. Such emergence and development of a new type may help to interpret the quantitative data from the surveys outlined above. While, from the quantitative results, we derive some indication about a tendency of adolescent religiosity toward individualization and privatization, qualitative analysis helps us to differentiate various types of individualized religious search and to understand more clearly some of the dynamics of such religious searching. The new type of 'occasional' appropriation could be characterized as *bricolage* type, since the *bricoleur*, in contrast to the professional or experienced expert, looks around 'occasionally' to find material for the project under construction. This search may be focused on one's own religious tradition, but it is not necessarily limited to one's own religion. In my own research on 'So-called sects and psycho-groups' for the Enquête Commission of the thirteenth German Parliament I have identified a similar type of religious biographical trajectory which I have called the 'accumulative heretic' (Streib, 1999a, 1999b, 2000, 2001b). The obvious characteristic of the accumulative heretic is a tour through various religious orientations. Conversion here is not a once-in-a-lifetime occurrence that leads to commitment; conversions and deconversions may occur more than once. The motivations and biographical dynamics for this accumulative search are not so obvious and need to be discovered by careful interpretation. On closer scrutiny, we may discover that the religious search is structured by biographical forces and desires, rather than by concern with religious truth claims, belief systems or cognitive dissonance. Biography is determining religion. We may also identify, as major factors, the availability of a variety of religious orientations and respective groups, the access to the religious marketplace, and the customer competence necessary for shopping for religion. Eventually our accumulative-heretical subjects may identify themselves as searchers, not for religion, but for *spirituality*: as people on a *spiritual quest*. There is thus some evidence for the emergence and rise of a new type of religious socialization for German adolescents.

In closing my sketch of qualitative research on religious orientation in Germany, I should mention briefly another project, the study on the *Religion of Religious Educators* (*'Religion' bei ReligionslehrerInnen*) reported by Feige, Dressler, Lukatis and Schöll (2000). This study is interesting not only because it gives us biographical studies of seventeen religious educators, but also because it provides a portrait of their teaching which gives us some insight into, and allows for some prognosis about, the future influence of religious education on adolescents' biographies. The 'lived religion' (*die 'gelebte religion'*) of these seventeen religious educators differs greatly and includes cases of close association with traditional religion and the Church. In my reading, however, I would label at least four of these cases as a 'search for spirituality', since they characterize their 'lived religion' as a search for 'aesthetic enjoyment of religious feelings', for 'a holding wholeness' or for 'future possibilities of a divine power', or describe themselves as 'vagabonds in search of intact life' (see portraits in Feige, Dressler, Lukatis and Schöll, 2000: 179–86).

The typology which has emerged from these seventeen case-studies contains three types of religious biographies and related teaching habits in religious education: type A takes 'institution' and 'tradition' as regulative principle; type B features 'self-guidance' with the occasional inclusion of religious resources; whereas type C features 'experience-rational' preference in their incorporation of religious resources. These biographical developments of religious educators, I conclude, reflect the dynamics of change in religious socialization which can be characterized as a tendency to include a search for spirituality rather than religion, a feature of the *bricoleur* who 'occasionally' includes the religious resources at hand. In the absence of any longitudinal study on the effect of religious educators on the religious socialization of their students, I can only speculate that this new type of religious educator will also have a long-term effect, increasing the number of adolescents who understand religion as spiritual quest and *bricolage*.

'Being spiritual' and 'being religious' among adolescents in Germany

Results from our own research supports the occurrence of a type of religious socialization among German adolescents that can be characterized as 'spiritual quest' and provides some first indications about the incidence of its occurrence. Since these data have been collected simultaneously in Germany and the United States of America, the results allow for a comparison. The questionnaire with 158 questions included some demographic questions, the 'Big Five' personality factors, the Religious Fundamentalism Scale (Altemeyer and Hunsberger, 1992), and the Right-Wing Authoritarianism Scale (Altemeyer, 1996). It was administered to 202 German university students who were just beginning their course of study and to 295 freshmen in the United States of America. In the demographic section subjects were asked to mark one of the following statements: *I am more religious than spiritual, I am more spiritual than religious, I am equally religious and spiritual* and *I am neither religious nor spiritual.* Leaving aside many aspects of our results, I focus here on the religious/spiritual assessment. The results are shown in Table 7.3.[1]

Table 7.3 Self-assessment of adolescents in the United States of America and the Federal Republic of Germany of being spiritual/religious

Item	United States of America	Germany
	%	%
I am neither religious nor spiritual	5.8	32.8
I am more spiritual than religious	31.3	20.7
I am equally religious and spiritual	48.2	16.7
I am more religious than spiritual	14.8	29.8

Table 7.3 shows that 21% of the German adolescents identify themselves as being more spiritual than religious. In comparison with the American adolescents, it stands out that almost one-third of the German adolescents describe themselves as neither spiritual nor religious, and the number of subjects who describe themselves as *more religious than spiritual* is twice as many in the German sample. Therefore the percentage of self-identified 'more spiritual' adolescents in the American sample is significantly higher (31%) than in the German sample (21%).

However, when we compare our results with the Shell survey results, which document a 52% agreement with the self-assessment of being 'not religious', an interesting issue emerges. Either our sample contains fewer self-declared non-religious (33%) and more self-declared religious (67%) adolescents, or we have to draw the line between self-declared religious and self-declared non-religious adolescents in the middle of the column, which means that the subjects who describe themselves as *more spiritual than religious* would answer *no* when they were asked in the Shell survey if they were religious. Surprisingly, the 'neither/nor' and the 'more spiritual' group, when taken together, amount to the same percentage as we have for self-declared non-religious adolescents in the Shell survey: 52% and 54% are very close. From these results, the question emerges whether self-declared 'spiritual' adolescents have been invisible to research so far which has asked for a self-assessment of 'being religious' only. Tentatively, we advance the hypothesis that there is a new type of German adolescent religiosity which has been neglected in research and which we were able to identify and preliminarily quantify: the type of 'spiritual seeker' who self-describes as 'more spiritual than religious'.

Our sub-sample from the United States of America can be compared with many findings of surveys on the spirituality/religion question. Table 7.4 brings together these research results (Zinnbauer, Pargament, Cole, Rye, Butter, Belavich, Hipp, Scott and Kadar, 1997; Roof, 1999; Scott, 2001; Marler and Hadaway, 2002). It shows that there is an overall correspondence with our results, when we take into account that, in these studies, the statements read: *I am neither spiritual nor religious, I am spiritual but not religious, I am spiritual and religious* and *I am religious but not spiritual.*

Table 7.4 Being religious and being spiritual (five studies in the United States of America)

Item	Boomers (Roof) 1995–1996	Institutional (Zinnbauer) 1995	National (Scott) 2001	Protestants (Scott) 2001	Protestants (Marler/Hadaway) 1991
	%	%	%	%	%
Religious and spiritual	59	74	61	67	64
Spiritual only	14	19	20	18	18
Religious only	15	4	8	9	9
Neither	12	3	11	6	8
N	*409*	*346*	*487*	*270*	*1,884*

Adapted from Marler and Hadaway (2002: 292).

These quantitative results allow for an initial résumé on the question of the religious and spiritual orientation of German adolescents. Though, as the data suggest, German adolescents differ from their American peers in that they have more of a traditional attitude toward 'religion', at the same time they distance themselves in greater numbers from both spirituality and religion. We can conclude, nevertheless, that the developments in the religiosity of adolescents in Germany follow the same path as we see in the United States of America, although with some delay: there *is* a certain portion of German adolescents who identify them-selves as 'more spiritual than religious'. Further research may confirm or correct the exact percentage, but it is justified to assume that between a fifth and a third of German adolescents redefine or explicate their religious search as a *spiritual quest*.

Spiritual quest

Most of what has been discussed so far of the results from empirical research on adolescent religiosity in Germany can be understood as 'invisible religion', as defined by Luckmann (1963, 1967, 1991). Or, referring to a more recent proposal, much of our German adolescents' religious orientation can be understood along the lines of the 'neosecularization paradigm' (Yamane, 1997), since it displays the declining influence of religious authority structures. This may be an adequate characterization of German adolescent religiosity, but it states primarily what it is not and uses negative propositions. We should, however, be able to indicate the direction of such religious transformation and what characterizes the new type of adolescent religious search. What are present-day adolescents searching for when they search for religion? And what are the reasons for their new type of religious search? Is it appropriate to adopt a new label and call this a 'spiritual quest'?

To talk about 'spiritual quest' is not my invention. Recent book titles such as *Virtual Faith: The Irreverent Spiritual Quest of Generation X* (Beaudoin, 1998), *A Generation of Seekers: The Spiritual Journeys of the Baby Boom Generation* (Roof, 1993), or *Spiritual Marketplace: Baby Boomers and the Remaking of American Religion* (Roof, 1999) suggest such a label for certain developments in the religious landscape of the United States of America. In these titles the time of this turning point is also specified: it is the 'baby boomer' generation or the cohort called Generation X who supposedly inaugurate a new era of religious socialization. Roughly speaking, persons in the United States of America who are now in their late twenties and thirties belong to cohorts for which pop music (for example, the Woodstock festival), television and increasing virtual reality have been at least as influential in their socialization as has traditional religion.

Wade Clark Roof presents us with results from a large number of interviews, partially in longitudinal research. Roof proposes to redraw the map of the religious landscape: 'the boundaries of popular religious communities are now being redrawn, encouraged by the quest of the large, post-World War II generations, and facilitated by the rise of an expanded spiritual marketplace' (1999: 10). His characterization of the new situation reads as follows:

> A great variety of terms now in vogue signal such a shift in the centre of religious energy: inwardness, subjectivity, the experiential, the expressive, the spiritual. Inherited forms of religion persist and still influence people but, as Marty says, 'the individual seeker and chooser has come increasingly to be in control'. Nowhere is this greater emphasis upon the seeker more apparent than in the large chain bookstore: the old 'religion' section is gone and in its place is a growing set of more specific rubrics catering to popular topics such as angels, Sufism, journey, recovery, meditation, magic, inspiration, Judaica, astrology, gurus, Bible, prophecy, Evangelicalism, Mary, Buddhism, Catholicism, esoterica, and the like. Words like *soul, sacred,* and *spiritual* resonate to a curious public. The discourse on spiritual 'journeys' and 'growth' is now a province not just of theologians and journalists, but of ordinary people in cafés, coffee bars, and bookstores across the country. (Roof, 1999: 7)

Spirituality, Roof wrote (1993: 64) by way of definition, 'gives expression to the being that is in us; it has to do with feelings, with the power that comes from within, with knowing our deepest selves and what is sacred to us'.

Roof's new map of the religious landscape includes five major subcultures: as well as dogmatists, mainstream believers, and born-again Christians, he identifies metaphysical believers/spiritual seekers and secularists. And Roof explicitly divides the different types of religious orientations along the axes of 'religious identity' and 'spiritual identity'.

Tom Beaudoin's book makes a valuable contribution to a 'thick description' of the type of spiritual seeker. Beaudoin does not present a single statistic, but provides a well-done characterization of this spiritual quest of Generation X (GenX). Beaudoin (1998: 36) claims the 'emerging GenX theology, a lived theology', cannot be understood apart from its context in a culture heavily prone to simulating reality. Generation X uses the wider culture's fascination with 'virtual' reality as we practise religiousness. It is appropriate, then, to turn to a discussion of the 'virtually' religious. Additionally, ambiguity is central to the faith of Generation X. According to Beaudoin (1998: 121) 'Xers make great heretics.' Then he continues:

> When Madonna – and Xers – practice their religiosity with sacramentals, from prayer cards and holy water to ripped jeans, piercings, crucifixes, and dark makeup, they challenge the authority of the official sacraments and the institution that 'dispenses' them. They threaten to displace the centre with the margins. This is just the beginning of a larger blurring of what is considered orthodox with what was considered heterodox, or heretical. (Beaudoin 1998: 122)

However, in the midst of such heretical adventure, Beaudoin identifies a search for a unique spirituality, a 'spiritual quest', which nevertheless is characterized by irreverence:

> A central dynamic and challenge emerging for Generation X is that of 'bricolating' their own spirituality and carrying forward religious traditions. *Bricolage* means making do with the materials at hand to solve particular (in this case religious) problems and questions. This term describes the way GenX pop culture brings together diverse religious symbols and images, forever recombining and forming new spiritualities. GenX pop culture does not respect the boundaries of tradition or religious dogma. At the same time that such bricolating and reassembling become even more widespread in GenX pop culture, Xers are challenged to renew their own spiritualities and those of their religious traditions by giving the concept of tradition itself a fresh look. (Beaudoin, 1998: 178)

Roof and Beaudoin have advanced an interesting thesis which may be helpful for a better understanding of our German subjects: it is in the younger generations of baby boomers and Generation X that greater numbers of adolescents have departed from the religious ways of their parents and transformed their religious orientation and practice. Their results suggest that this emerging type of 'spiritual seeker' has some affinity to the lifestyle of the cohort which finds such new avenues. Religion and lifestyle have at least some kind of 'family resemblance'. We may even ask if religion, at least this type of religious or spiritual quest, has become a question of preference, a question of lifestyle. It can be hypothesized that the typical irreverence and *bricolage* model has influenced the handling of religion and spirituality in a marketplace type of situation.

This hypothesis calls for detailed empirical investigation in the European and German context, which, to my knowledge, has not been completed so far. Research on religious *bricolage* in adolescence is one of the important tasks of empirical theology in the coming years; but we need to attend closely to the motivations of adolescents who turn away from the religion or the world-view of their families of origin and to the trajectories which they develop in their own search for their own religion and in their own spiritual quest. Thereby, a more decisive focus on *motivation* and *biographical trajectories*, which could lead beyond the interpretation proposals of Roof and Beaudoin, should be implemented in the research design. From German lifestyle research we derive a suggestive proposal for understanding this motivational aspect. To assess the question of whether this search for religion or spirituality has become a question of style, and is motivated like lifestyle preference, lifestyle research could be valuable. Lifestyle research will be my next point of discussion here, because we find there some evidence about the motivations and attitudes which characterize this cultural change.

Lifestyle research

There are some indications that religious socialization has changed significantly in recent years. The question now is how to explain this and how to shed some light on the motivational forces of such change. I believe that lifestyle research has a contribution to make. Of course, lifestyle research does not focus exclusively on contemporary adolescents, nor on religion. What makes these results interesting, however, is that they describe cultural changes for which we are tempted to use a new vocabulary. 'Spiritual quest' is one such term in the new vocabulary; another interpretative phrase is 'religion as everyday aesthetical preference', or perhaps 'experience-religion' (in German, *'Erlebnisreligion'*).

Contemporary lifestyle research is a prominent branch of research in sociology (see, for example, Garhammer, 2000;

Hartmann, 1999). Usually we do not expect results about leisure activities or consumer behaviour to elicit much attention beyond the community of researchers and the interest groups who fund such research. However, this changed in 1992 with Gerhard Schulze's *Die Erlebnisgesellschaft* (Schulze, 1992). Now, not only sociological and psychological literature databases, but also databases in the field of religious studies, produce a considerable number of references when you search for *'Erlebnisgesellschaft'* (experience society).[2] What is associated with this new catchphrase?

Schulze's portrait of *Erlebnisgesellschaft* (experience society) is based upon a comprehensive survey and its interpretation in a book of more than 750 pages. More than 1,000 persons aged from 18 to 70 in the city of Nuremberg were interviewed in the spring of 1985, using an extensive questionnaire which had been designed to investigate leisure activities, music preferences, favourite books, favourite television shows, political affiliations, inclinations and so on. The focus of this research rests upon 'everyday aesthetical preferences', as Schulze calls them. 'Everyday aesthetics' embraces everything a person enjoys, what elevates him or her from the grey everyday, what makes life worthwhile.

More interesting and more important than the mere statistical registration and presentation of everyday aesthetical preferences is their interpretation. Schulze is determined to provide a thorough-going interpretation of his data when he seeks to identify a depth structure or, as he calls it, a 'fundamental semantic of cultural codes'.

At the surface, we can identify the 'styles'. Schulze defines 'style' as the 'commonalities of repetitions in the everyday aesthetical episodes of a person'. Beneath the surface, he constructs the everyday aesthetical schemata in which the interpreter condenses or reduces the plurality of styles into a number of 'types of styles': 'high culture schema', 'trivial schema', and 'tension schema' (see Schulze, 1992: 124ff.). 'Tension schema' is the youngest and most interesting development.

In this depth structure the fundamental semantics of our times comes to light: 'experience orientation' or 'experience rationality'. This is an 'inward orientation', which means that the person no longer relates him or herself *to the world* to find status, conformity or security, but relates the world *to the self* and attempts to utilize the world for self-realization and stimulation (see Schulze, 1992:

261).Though this happens in an immense variety of ways, Schulze is able to design a clearly arranged map of milieus.

Using educational status and age as basic parameters, Schulze constructs five milieus of present-day society: (1) entertainment milieu; (2) self-realization milieu; (3) high culture milieu (*'niveau'* milieu); (4) integration milieu; and (5) harmony milieu. These milieus are characterized by the above-average occurrence of one (or two) everyday aesthetical schemata. For example, the tension schema is over-represented in the entertainment milieu; both the tension schema and the high culture schema are over-represented in the self-realization milieu; the trivial schema is over-represented in the harmony milieu; the high culture schema and the trivial schema are over-represented in the integration milieu; and the high culture schema is over-represented in the high culture or *niveau* milieu.

Despite this rather comprehensive map of milieus in German society, Schulze's book title, *The Experience Society* (*Die Erlebnisgesellschaft*), appears to highlight particularly *one* of these milieus, the entertainment milieu, in relation to the tension schema for which the search for excitement, entertainment and action is most characteristic. In his book title, and in a great portion of his writings, Schulze has explicated what had been the latent awareness of many in our society: that we have become a society governed by hedonistic attitudes of sensation-seeking, event excitement and everyday aesthetical preferences. Schulze's message may be sound, despite the suspicion that this is an over-interpretation of his data.[3] Before addressing Schulze's provoking message, especially in respect to religion, I will address the question of milieu formation and mention some critical objections which have been voiced against Schulze's analysis.

Milieus in society and religion

To what extent has Schulze inspired religious research? Schulze's research design and typology has certainly influenced further research. Within lifestyle research, a kind of experience-society research tradition is taking shape (see Hartmann, 1999; Hölscher, 1998; Walter, 2001). Things are different in research on religion, however. This is perhaps due to the fact, which is heavily under criticism, that as in most lifestyle research we find little attention to questions of social justice or life conduct in Schulze's research.[4] This may be one reason why Schulze's approach has not been used so far in research on religion. Before we could use it for elaborating a map of religious milieus, Schulze's perspective would need some qualification by an implementation of socio-economic factors and dimensions. However, after such qualification, lifestyle research, and not least Schulze's approach, could help us to open the focus of research for these types of 'invisible religion', 'spiritual quest' and '*bricolage* religiosity', which do not pay much attention to church affiliation, but assemble in new milieus or religious scenes.

Lifestyle-related milieu studies are important not only in respect of society, but also in respect of religion, because we should then be able to identify milieu limitations and blind-spots in church work and religious education. To my knowledge, the only milieu study on religion in Germany is Michael Vester's research project on 'Milieus in der Kirche' (Vögele, Bremer and Vester, 2002) which decidedly has *not* been based upon Schulze's approach, but on Vester's own milieu map of German society (see Vester, 1997) which in turn is based upon the SINUS lifestyle results. Vester has investigated the attitudes, expectations and participation behaviour of members of the Protestant Church of Hanover. This is a step in the right direction and could encourage further church surveys (for example, the church membership surveys in the Protestant Church/*EKD-Mitgliedschaftsuntersuchungen* which have been quoted above) to attend more closely to the milieus in society. As one of the important results of this study, a 'modernization problem' has been identified, which consists not only in the decline of the church-supporting core milieu of petty bourgeois, but also in the fact that the humanistic education milieu and the hedonistic milieus of adolescents are mainly outside the focus of church work. Here we have one of the very few results of empirical research which addresses the question whether adolescents' declining participation in established religious institutions is possibly related to their affinity to specific milieus and lifestyles. However, it also needs to be mentioned that Vester's study has severe limitations: the mapping of religion has focused on church affiliation and church-based religiosity and largely ignored the new type of religiosity or spirituality, as outlined in the first part of this chapter. Here, Schulze's milieu map could help us greatly.

Is the religious quest experience-oriented?

Schulze's work contains a straightforward culture-analytic hypothesis, which is expressed in condensed form in the title of his book. *Erlebnisgesellschaft* (experience society) is defined as 'a society which (in historical and intercultural comparison) is determined by inward orientation' (1992: 54). We find a powerful statement about this new 'inward orientation' in the Introduction (Schulze, 1992: 17) where Schulze rhetorically asks if, in the 'experience society', we have entered a final state of individualization. His portrait of experience society is rather negative when he describes metaphorically a crushing machine, in which we have destroyed even the last remnants of group experience and solidarity remaining after the decline of the economic class structures and the diversification of neighbourhoods, leaving the individual as a social atom.[5]

It cannot be overlooked that, behind this prognosis of our culture, a developmental model comes to light which we have come to call the 'individualization theorem', and which has attained some prominence through the work of the sociologist Ulrich Beck (1986, 1992). In defending this work against those who criticize the neglect of socio-economic conditions in Beck's perspective, an 'elevator effect' has been discussed, which means that the less privileged participate increasingly in the economic resources and the freedom that comes with them. Schulze (1992: 531–53) gives a portrait of the German post-war culture and economy which has produced the egalitarian multi-dimensionality of autonomous milieus in the 1980s. According to Schulze (1992: 541), in experience society 'groups of taste exist side by side without relating to each other in their thinking'.

What does this mean for religion? While Schulze does not have much data about religion, his findings on lifestyle and milieu formation raise questions about religion. Is it not true that we have undergone a process of 'inward orientation' in the last decades? Is it not true that 'experience rationality' has spread and affected attitudes toward religion? Is it not true that the religious milieus exist side by side, with little relation to each other in their thought systems? The thesis of 'experience society' gives rise to the question of whether religion has become a matter of individual everyday aesthetical preference, and thus that Peter Berger's (1979) *Heretical Imperative* has come to its full realization with only one innovation:

the main stalls in the crowded spiritual marketplace (cf. Roof, 1999) have changed and consumers appear motivated by an inward-oriented quest for experience, event and action. This series of questions conveys a strong and clear thesis, which could help us to answer the problem raised by the quantitative results and left open in most of the qualitative research. The invisible religion of adolescents (as made visible in personal prayer and tacitly held beliefs), the (sometimes irreverent) spiritual quest of younger generations and the *bricolage* character of many adolescents' religious search trigger the question of what kind of motivations and intentions, what kind of developmental dynamics and drives, determine this specific type of religious socialization (which is supposedly quite new in our culture). Schulze's bold thesis could be the answer: it is the increasingly attractive lifestyle of inward-oriented everyday aesthetical preferences in experience society which has come to dominate the religious search of adolescents. Since we have little empirical evidence for this thesis, at least from research in Germany, I restrict myself to stating this in the form of questions. Only further research can help to confirm or qualify this assumption.

Hedonistic orientation as religion?
Going one step further, we could ask if experience orientation itself has a religious quality. Everyday aesthetical preference could be understood *as* religion. Schulze (1999) appears to be open to such an interpretation. In his book *Kulissen des Glücks* (*Sceneries of Luck*), the theses appear more pointed when Schulze identifies a 'universal imperative' – the rule 'Experience your life!' Here Schulze characterizes 'experience orientation' explicitly *as* religion.

> In the post-metaphysical age, the highest thing for which we may call recognition in discourse, is human life. One regards one's own life as a kind of God, we should serve Him, we should take from Him our fundamental guidelines. His highest command is this: 'Do something with me!' Instead of the old concept of sin, the God 'Life' has stated the imperative: 'Don't mess me up!' . . . The discourse on luck has captured our social world like a worship. (Schulze, 1999: 9)

Schulze here explicitly describes 'experience orientation' as a kind of new religion, a cult of the individualistic-hedonistic life. If Schulze had not offered this interpretation himself, it would have been my task to suggest such an interpretation. Although the sociologist leaves it at that, it is the task of the religious educator to take this further. The sociologist could have taken this further, however, as it is from sociology that we derive approaches to a concept of religion which understand the aestheticization of the everyday *as* religion or, more cautiously, as *equivalent* to religion. According to Thomas Luckmann (1967, 1991), religion originates in 'everyday transcendations'. Therefore, religion has the form of experiences which are invisible both before they are communicated and again after their age of visibility in religious institutions. From this concept of religion, Luckmann was able to suggest, back in 1963, that religion has not disappeared, but in part has become invisible; and also that forms of religion outside the religious institutions could be addressed *as* religion. Based on this concept of religion, Hubert Knoblauch (1996) has analysed adolescent experiences and worlds of meaning, especially the experiences in Schulze's tension or action schema, such as the adolescent escape into music, drugs, risk sports and other types of sensation-seeking activities, as equivalents of religion.[6] From this point of view, Schulze's cult of individualistic-hedonistic life could be understood *as* everyday religion.

Summary

Even though Schulze's generalization, his limited focus on leisure and consumer activity, and his marginalization of religion, might provide reasons to question the validity of his thesis, and although there could be reason to doubt that his data fully support his message, his texts pose questions and challenges for theology, religious education and church work. They also suggest some answers to the question of what motivates the religious and spiritual quest of adolescents. Four main conclusions emerge.

First, we have to pay attention to the potential danger that theology, religious education and church work have a rather limited milieu focus and exclude the milieus and scenes which have emerged in the adolescent generations.

Second, lifestyle research suggests an interpretation model for religious plurality which has not been used and tested so far, namely that the pluralization of religious orientations which we encounter in German society, especially in the younger generations, may be the effect of, and function in the same way as, the pluralization of lifestyles.

Third, from Schulze's work we derive the question regarding whether the adolescents' approach toward and their appropriation of religion are influenced and motivated by their general attitude and manner of adopting a lifestyle, namely by everyday aesthetical preference.

Fourth, Schulze characterizes the aestheticization of the everyday as having itself some kind of a religious quality; the aestheticization of the everyday could have become equivalent to religion.

Schulze's most provocative message is his interpretation of German culture and society in terms of 'experience orientation' and 'everyday aesthetical preferences'. Thereby, he appears to have articulated what many in our society feel and assume. His work, however, also appears to indicate what many in church, theology and religious education are concerned about: that the religious domain may not make an exemption here, and that 'everyday aesthetical preference' has become the motivational pattern of how a growing portion of Germans approach religion.

There are still many open questions, not only in regard to lifestyle research but also with respect to the larger field of social scientific research on religion. One of these questions is whether 'religion' has been conceptualized adequately in the present research. A second question is whether 'religion' should be considered only as a dependent variable, or whether 'religion' itself is a style-forming and transforming factor, producing or proposing a 'Protestant Style' (see Korsch, 1997). Finally, my own proposal for a modification of James Fowler's (1981) structural-developmental differentiation of 'faith', in which I propose to distinguish 'religious styles' (Streib, 1997, 2001a, forthcoming a, forthcoming b), would need to be brought into discussion.

Conclusion

In closing this examination of research on the religious, spiritual and lifestyle orientation of German adolescents, I shall try to summarize open questions, implications and hypotheses which may be important for further research, and also for reflection in theology and religious education.

The quantitative results, as they are presented in the first part of this chapter, provide empirical evidence that the religiosity of German adolescents has more stability and continuity than can be deduced from the decline of church membership and worship participation. Around 30% of adolescents reported praying privately, more than 30% intended to raise their children religiously, and almost 50% described themselves as 'being religious'. Such data indicate that affinity to religion is still widespread among German adolescents. At the same time, these results also indicate that the religiosity of German adolescents may have changed significantly, because this religiosity, to a large extent, does not take place in organized religion and has become a matter of individual practice and preference. It has become privatized religion. The religion of German adolescents, because of its retreat from the public sphere, has thus become more invisible, invisible for the public and for the type of survey which attends mainly to questions of membership and institutional participation. While these results are convincing because of their representative nature, they cannot lead us further than documenting that privatized religious orientation, belief and practice are still dimensions of some importance in adolescents' life and self-understanding; we can only speculate about what exactly these adolescents mean by 'being religious' or by 'praying'. This is one of the open questions of these quantitative results.

Our own research results about the 'being spiritual/being religious' question identify and add another 20% to the group of adolescents who indicate that they are open toward and deal with religion or spirituality; but these results also may indicate the complexity and ambiguity of the more recent transformation of adolescent religiosity. It is very likely that this indicates that an even larger number of German adolescents have moved away from the religious tradition of their own culture and are sailing in their 'spiritual quest' toward new shores, in order to anchor their religious or spiritual identity and to find a different language for their ultimate concerns.

Qualitative research, as we have seen, sheds some light on the biographical developments and search strategies that adolescents employ. It is especially interesting to find qualitative evidence of the existence of an 'occasional' type of religious orientation and praxis in German adolescents. This type of 'occasional' appropriation implements the pluralization of religious meaning and thus can be characterized as a *bricolage* type. The accumulative heretic type of religious identity formation emerges. Without being able, at this state of research, to give any quantitative account of this type of religious identity among German adolescents, this is another one of the open questions. I maintain that we need to pay attention to this rather new development in youth culture and to formulate and test the relevant hypotheses. It is my conviction that biographical-reconstructive research is the best way to bring to light the motivational and biographical dynamics involved in the development of religious socialization.

This characterization of adolescent religiosity, which has focused on the concepts religion, spirituality and *bricolage*, has so far traced the paths of the increasing ambiguity of religious quest, with an increasingly loose relation to one specific religious tradition. So far, however, less research attention has been given to the question of *motivation*. What motivates adolescents to engage in pluralistic and heretical quest for religion or spirituality? This is the point to bring lifestyle research into discussion, and it is particularly Schulze's lifestyle research that suggests some answers: 'everyday aesthetical preference' may have become the motivational pattern for how a growing portion of Germans approach religion.

In the project on the religiosity of religious educators (Feige, Dressler, Lukatis and Schöll, 2000), a type has been characterized as 'experience-rational preference and incorporation of religious resources'. Although this is research with adults, it also provides evidence about the motivational dynamics leading to the *bricolage* type of spiritual and religious quest. Explicitly, in this type characterization, Schulze's lifestyle perspective has been taken up. This recent detail from qualitative research also indicates that Schulze's perspective and proposal is gaining plausibility among German researchers, who recognize this pattern in their interpretation of religious biographies. To maintain that 'experience rationality' or 'everyday aesthetical preference' is an adequate characterization of adolescent religious or spiritual quest is an hypothesis which we may dare to advance. But the task of providing more solid empirical evidence, proof or falsification, is still ahead of us.

Notes

[1] I thank Ralph Hood and Christopher Silver for collecting the data in Tennessee and for their work on the quantitative analysis of the data.

[2] Since the author himself has decided to translate 'Erlebnis' by 'experience', I follow this path, but would like to add the connotation of 'event'. For the reception and discussion of Schulze's *Die Erlebnisgesellschaft*, see journal issues of *Wege zum Menschen* (WzM, 1996) and *Concilium* (Concilium, 1999), and also some contributions in practical theology and religious education (Wegenast, 1994; Koch, 1995; Sobiech, 1995; Schliep, 1996; Blasberg-Kuhnke and Kuhnke, 1997; Engemann, 1997; Kochanek, 1998; Kurz, 2000).

[3] For Schulze it appears justified to talk about 'experience society', even if he appears to overstretch his data: as Vester and Vögele (1999: 22) note, only 25% of Schulze's subjects fall into 'experience-oriented' milieus.

[4] This raises questions about Schulze's map of milieus and some have proposed to stand Schulze's design on its head. In 1994, Mörth and Fröhlich (1994) criticized the lack of attention in Schulze's research to socio-economic factors. They posed a great sociological tradition of lifestyle research against Schulze's approach, namely the work of Bourdieu (1984). We could also, with Lüdtke (1996), propose a model in which lifestyle is only the fourth and final layer, which rests on social situation, social milieu and mentality. Alheit (1995: 94), to refer to a third critical voice, reveals 'amazing congruence' between Schulze's and Bourdieu's milieu maps and proposes to continue to work with Schulze's map, but under one condition: that we locate his milieus in Bourdieu's social space. Schulze's self-limitation on leisure activities and consumer behaviour and his ignoring questions of social justice are also the critique of Michael Vester (see Vester and Vögele, 1999: 22).

[5] 'Tritt nicht durch die volle Entfaltung des Erlebnismarktes Individualisierung in ein finales Stadium ein? Geraten nicht die letzten Reste von Gruppenerfahrung und Solidarität, die übriggeblieben sind nach dem Verschwimmen ökonomischer Klassen, nach der Entstandardisierung der Lebensläufe, nach der Durchmischung der Wohngebiete, auf dem Erlebnismarkt in eine Zertrümmerungsmaschine, die nur noch den einzelnen als soziales Atom zurückläßt?' (Schulze, 1992: 17ff.).

[6] In similar ways, Baacke (1990) has talked about the 'tacit ecstasies of adolescents'. The thesis that the religious educator has to attend to the religious and religion-equivalent everyday experiences of adolescents has been put forth, for example by Sauer (1990, 1995), Biehl (1998) or Heimbrock (1998). And Biehl (1998: 36) suggests that religious education should attend to 'the new and manifold forms of lived religion as not-everyday experiences in everyday'.

References

Alheit, P. (1995), 'Aufbruch in die "Erlebniskultur"? Kritische Überlegungen zur zeitgenössischen Kultursoziologie', *Das Argument*, 208, 91–104.

Altemeyer, B. (1996), *The Authoritarian Specter* (Cambridge, Mass., Harvard University Press).

Altemeyer, B. and Hunsberger, B. (1992), 'Authoritarianism, religious fundamentalism, quest and prejudice', *International Journal for the Psychology of Religion*, 2, 113–33.

Augst, K. (2000), *Religion in der Lebenswelt junger Frauen aus Sozialen Unterschichten* (Stuttgart, Kohlhammer).

Baacke, D. (1990), 'Die stillen Ekstasen der Jugend: Zu Wandlungen des religiösen Bezugs', *Jahrbuch der Religionspädagogik*, 5 (Neukirchen-Vluyn, Neukirchener Verlag), 3–25.

Beaudoin, T. (1998), *Virtual Faith: The Irreverent Spiritual Quest of Generation X* (San Francisco, Calif., Jossey-Bass).

Beck, U. (1986), *Risikogesellschaft: Auf dem Weg in eine andere Moderne* (Frankfurt/M, Suhrkamp).

Beck, U. (1992), *Risk Society: Towards a New Modernity* (London, Sage Publications).

Berger, P. L. (1979), *The Heretical Imperative: Contemporary Possibilities of Religious Affirmation* (New York, Doubleday).

Biehl, P. (1998), 'Der phänomenologische ansatz in der religionspädagogik', in H.-G. Heimbrock (ed.), *Religionspädagogik und Phänomenologie: Von der Empirischen Wendung zur Lebenswelt* (Weinheim, Deutscher Studienverlag), pp. 15–46.

Blasberg-Kuhnke, M. and Kuhnke, U. (1997), 'Szene oder Netzwerk? Bedingungen und aufgaben der pfarrei in der erlebnisgesellschaft', in A. Schifferle (ed.), *Pfarrei in der Postmoderne?* (Freiburg, Herder), pp. 83–92.

Bourdieu, P. (1984), *Distinction: A Social Critique of the Judgement of Taste* (Cambridge, Mass., Harvard University Press).

Comenius-Institut (ed.) (1993), *Religion in der Lebensgeschichte: Interpretative Zugänge am Beispiel der Margret E* (Gütersloh, Gütersloher Verlag).

Concilium (1999), 'Die Erlebnisgesellschaft', *Concilium* (thematic issue), 35, 401–508.

Engelhardt, K., Loewenich, H. von and Steinacker, P. (1997), *Fremde Heimat Kirche: Die Dritte EKD-Erhebung über Kirchenmigliedschaft* (Gütersloh, Gütersloher Verlag).

Engemann, W. (1997), 'Die Erlebnisgesellschaft vor der Offenbarung – ein ästhetisches Problem? Überlegungen zum Ort und zur Aufgabe der praktischen Theologie heute', in A. Grözinger (ed.), *Gelebte Religion* (Rheinbach, CMZ-Verlag), pp. 329–51.

Feige, A., Dressler, B., Lukatis, W. and Schöll, A. (2000), *'Religion' bei ReligionslehrerInnen: Religionpädagogische Zielvorstellungen und religiöses Selbstverständnis in empirisch-soziologischen Zugängen* (Münster, Lit-Verlag).

Fischer, D. and Schöll, A. (1994), *Lebenspraxis und Religion: Fallanalysen zur subjektiven Religiosität von Jugendlichen* (Göttingen, Vandenhoeckand and Rupprecht).

Fowler, J. W. (1981), *Stages of Faith: The Psychology of Human Development and the Quest for Meaning* (San Francisco, Calif., Harper and Row).

Fuchs-Heinritz, W. (2000), 'Religion', in Deutsche Shell (ed.), *Jugend*, 1 (Opladen, Leske and Budrich), pp. 157–80.

Fuchs-Heinritz, W., Heinritz, C. and Kolvenbach, R. (1998), 'Psychokulte/Esoterik', in Deutscher Bundestag: Enquête-Kommission, Sogenannte Sekten und Psychogruppen (ed.), *Neue religiöse und ideologische Gemeinschaften und Psychogruppen* (Hamm, Hoheneck-Verlag), pp. 231–95.

Garhammer, M. (2000), 'Das Leben: eine Stilfrage. Lebensstilforschung hundert Jahre nach Simmels "Stil des Lebens" ', *Soziologische Revue*, 23, 296–312.

Hartmann, P. H. (1999), *Lebensstilforschung: Darstellung, Kritik und Weiterentwicklung* (Opladen, Leske and Budrich).

Heimbrock, H.-G. (1998), 'Gelebte Religion im Klassenzimmer?', in W.-E. Failing and H.-G. Heimbrock (eds), *Gelebte Religion wahrnehmen, Lebenswelt, Alltagskultur, Religionspraxis* (Stuttgart, Kohlhammer), pp. 233–55.

Hölscher, B. (1998), *Lebensstile durch Werbung? Zur Soziologie der Life-Style-Werbung* (Opladen, Westdeutscher Verlag).

Klein, S. (1994), *Theologie und empirische Biographieforschung: methodische Zugänge zur Lebens- und Glaubensgeschichte und ihre Bedeutung für eine erfahrungsbezogene Theologie* (Stuttgart, Berlin, Köln, Kohlhammer).

Knoblauch, H. (1996), 'Die unsichtbare Religion im Jugendalter: Geschlossene Sinngebiete, symbolische Universa und funktionale Äquivalente der Religion bei Jugendlichen', in W. Tzscheetzsch and H.-G. Ziebertz (eds), *Religionsstile*

Jugendlicher und Moderne Lebenswelt (München, Don Bosco), pp. 46–65.

Koch, H. (1995), 'Kirche in der Erlebnisgesellschaft: Anpassung oder Widerstand?', *Kirche und Gesellschaft*, 217, 1–16.

Kochanek, H. (1998), 'Die Erlebnisgesellschaft als Herausforderung an die Katechese', in P. A. Franz (ed.), *Katechese im Umbruch* (Freiburg im Breisgau, Herder), pp. 439–57.

Korsch, D. (1997), *Religion mit Stil: Protestantismus in der Kulturwende* (Tübingen, Mohr).

Kurz, W. (2000), 'Erlebnisorientierung und Bildung: Zur Sinnfrage im Kontext der Erlebnisgesellschaft', in L. Duncker and H. Hanisch (eds), *Sinnverlust und Sinnorientierung in der Erziehung: Rekonstruktionen aus pädagogischer und theologischer Sicht* (Bad Heilbrunn, Klinkhardt), pp. 107–36.

Luckmann, T. (1963), *Das Problem der Religion in der Modernen Gesellschaft: Institution, Person und Weltanschauung* (Freiburg, Rombach).

Luckmann, T. (1967), *The Invisible Religion: The Problem of Religion in Modern Society* (New York, Macmillan).

Luckmann, T. (1991), *Die unsichtbare Religion* (Frankfurt/M, Suhrkamp).

Lüdtke, H. (1996), 'Methodenprobleme der Lebensstilforschung: Probleme des Vergleichs empirischer Lebenssitiltypologien und der Identifikation von Stilpionieren', in O. G. Schwenk (ed.), *Lebensstil zwischen Sozialstrukturanalyse und Kulturwissenschaft* (Opladen, Leske and Budrich), pp. 139–63.

Marler, P. L. and Hadaway, C. K. (2002) ' "Being Religious" or "Being Spiritual" in America: a zero-sum proposition?', *Journal for the Scientific Study of Religion*, 41, 289–300.

Mörth, I. and Fröhlich, G. (1994), 'Lebensstile als symbolisches Kapital? Zum aktuellen Stand kultureller Distinktionen', in I. Mörth and G. Fröhlich (eds), *Das Symbolische Kapital der Lebensstile: zur Kultursoziologie der Moderne nach Pierre Bourdieu* (Frankfurt/M, New York, Campus), pp. 7–30.

Pollack, D. (1996), 'Zur religiös-kirchlichen Lage in Deutschland nach der Wiedervereinigung: Eine religionssoziologische Analyse', *Zeitschrift für Theologie und Kirche*, 93, 586–615.

Roof, W. C. (1993), *A Generation of Seekers: The Spiritual Journeys of the Baby Boom Generation* (San Francisco, Calif., Harper and Row).

Roof, W. C. (1999), *Spiritual Marketplace: Baby Boomers and the Remaking of American Religion* (Princeton, NJ, Princeton University Press).

Sandt, F. O. (1996), *Religiosität von Jugendlichen in der multikulturellen Gesellschaft: Eine qualitative Untersuchung zu Atheistischen, Christlichen, Spiritualistischen und Muslimischen Orientierungen* (Münster, Waxmann).

Sauer, R. (1990), *Mystik des Alltags: Jugendliche Lebenswelt und Glaube. Eine Spurensuche* (Freiburg, Herde).

Sauer, R. (1995), 'Religiöse Phänomene in Jugendkulturen', in P. Biehl, R. Degen, N. Mette, F. Rickers and F. Schweitzer (eds), *Jahrbuch der Religionspädagogik*, 10 (Neukirchen-Vluyn, Neukirchener Verlag), pp. 17–30.

Schliep, H. J. (1996), 'Kirche in der Erlebnisgesellschaft: Soziologische Beobachtungen und theologische Bemerkungen', *Pastoraltheologie*, 85, 211–24.

Schmidtchen, G. (1997), *Wie weit ist der Weg nach Deutschland? Sozialpsychologie der Jugend in der postsozialistischen Welt* (Opladen, Leske and Budrich).

Schöll, A. (1992), *Zwischen Religiöser Revolte und Frommer Anpassung: Die Rolle der Religion in der Adoleszenzkrise* (Gütersloh, Gütersloher Verlag).

Schöll, A. (1998), 'Fernöstliche Gruppen, Bewegungen und Organisationen', in Deutscher Bundestag: Enquête-Kommission, Sogenannte Sekten und Psychogruppen (ed.), *Neue religiöse und ideologische Gemeinschaften und Psychogruppen* (Hamm, Hoheneck-Verlag), pp. 159–230.

Schulze, G. (1992), *Die Erlebnisgesellschaft: Kultursoziologie der Gegenwart* (Frankfurt, New York, Campus).

Schulze, G. (1999), *Kulissen des Glücks: Streifzüge durch die Eventkultur* (Frankfurt, New York, Campus).

Scott, R. O. (2001), 'Are you religious or are you spiritual? a look in the mirror', *Spirituality and Health* (Spring), 26–8.

Shell (1985), Jugendwerk der Deutschen Shell (ed.), *Jugendliche und Erwachsene '85. Generationen im Vergleich*, vols 1–5 (Opladen, Leske and Budrich).

Shell (1992), Jugendwerk der Deutschen Shell (ed.), *Jugend '92. Lebenslagen, Orientierungen und Entwicklungen im vereinigten Deutschland*, vols 1–4 (Opladen, Leske and Budrich).

Shell (1997), Jugendwerk der Deutschen Shell (ed.), *Jugend '97.*

Zukunftsperspektiven, gesellschaftliches Engagement, politische Orientierungen, 12. Shell Jugendstudie (Opladen, Leske and Budrich).

Shell (2000), Deutsche Shell (ed.), *Jugend 2000, 13. Shell Jugendstudie* (Opladen, Leske and Budrich).

Sobiech, F. (1995), 'Konfirmanden und Konfirmandinnen in der Erlebnisgesellschaft und die Themen des Konfirmandenunterrichts: Ein Erfahrungsbericht', in T. Böhhme-Lischewski (ed.), *Engagement und Ratlosigkeit* (Bielefeld, Luther-Verlag), pp. 207–16.

Sommer, R. (1997), *Lebensgeschichte und gelebte Religion von Frauen: Eine qualitativ-empirische Studie über den Zusammenhang von Biographischer Struktur und Religiöser Orientierung* (Stuttgart, Kohlhammer).

Streib, H. (1997), 'Religion als Stilfrage: Zur Revision struktureller Differenzierung von Religion im Blick auf die Analyse der pluralistisch-religiösen Lage der Gegenwart', *Archiv für Religionspsychologie*, 22, 48–69.

Streib, H. (1998), 'Milieus und Organisationen christlich-fundamentalistischer Prägung', in Deutscher Bundestag: Enquête-Kommission, Sogenannte Sekten und Psychogruppen (ed.), *Neue religiöse und ideologische Gemeinschaften und Psychogruppen* (Hamm, Hoheneck-Verlag), pp. 107–57.

Streib, H. (1999a), 'Off-road religion? A narrative approach to fundamentalist and occult orientations of adolescents', *Journal of Adolescence*, 22, 255–67.

Streib, H. (1999b), 'Biographies in Christian fundamentalist milieus and organizations', in Deutscher Bundestag: Referat Öffentlichkeitsarbeit (ed.), *Final Report of the Enquête Commission on 'So-called Sects and Psycho-groups'* (Bonn, Deutscher Bundestag), pp. 402–14.

Streib, H. (2000), *Biographies in Christian Fundamentalist Milieus and Organizations (Report to the Enquête Commission of the 13th German Parliament on 'So-called Sects and Psycho-groups')* (Bielefeld, University of Bielefeld).

Streib, H. (2001a), 'Faith development theory revisited: the religious styles perspective', *International Journal for the Psychology of Religion*, 11, 143–58.

Streib, H. (2001b), 'Is there a way beyond fundamentalism? Challenges for faith development and religious education', in

L. J. Francis, J. Astley and M. Robbins (eds), *The Fourth R for the Third Millennium: Education in Religion and Values for the Global Future* (Dublin, Lindisfarne Books), pp. 177–99.

Streib, H. (forthcoming a), 'Religion as a question of style: revising the structural differentiation of religion from the perspective of the analysis of the contemporary pluralistic-religious situation', *International Journal for Practical Theology*.

Streib, H. (forthcoming b), 'Faith development research revisited: accounting for diversity in structure, content, and narrativity of faith', *International Journal for the Psychology of Religion*.

Tietze, N. (2001), *Islamische Identitäten: Formen muslimischer Religiosität junger Männer in Deutschland und Frankreich* (Hamburg, Hamburger Ed).

Vester, M. (1997), 'Soziale Milieus und Individualisierung: Mentalitäten und Konfliktlinien im historischen Wandel', in U. Beck and P. Sopp (eds), *Individualisierung und Integration: Neue Konfliktlinien und neuer Integrationsmodus?* (Opladen, Leske und Budrich), pp. 100–23.

Vester, M. and Vögele, W. (1999), 'Das Projekt "Kirche und Milieu" ', in W. Vögele and M. Vester (eds), *Kirche und die Milieus der Gesellschaft*, vol. 1 (Loccum, Evangelische Akademie), pp. 9–35.

Vögele, W., Bremer, H. and Vester, M. (2002), *Soziale Milieus und Kirche* (Würzburg, ERGON Verlag).

Walter, V. (2001), *Virtualität und Lebensstil: Über die Virtualisierung der Gesellschaft* (Mering, R. Hampp Verlag).

Wegenast, K. (1994), 'Erlebnisgesellschaft', *Der Evangelische Erzieher*, 46, 3–8.

WzM (1996), 'Herausforderung Erlebnisgesellschaft', *Wege zum Menschen*, 48, 445–512.

Yamane, D. (1997), 'Secularization on trial: in defense of a neosecularization paradigm', *Journal for the Scientific Study of Religion*, 36, 109–22.

Zinnbauer, B. J., Pargament, K. I., Cole, B., Rye, M. S., Butter, E. M., Belavich, T. G., Hipp, K. M., Scott, A. B. and Kadar, J. L. (1997), 'Religion and spirituality: unfuzzying the fuzzy', *Journal for the Scientific Study of Religion*, 36, 549–64.

8

Exploring the religious life-world and attitude toward Islam among British Muslim adolescents

ABDULLAH SAHIN

Summary

This chapter reports the findings of a three-year research project investigating the construction of religious identity and attitudes toward Islam among a group of Muslim adolescents in three sixth-form colleges in Birmingham. A phenomenology-based post-structural research framework is utilized to explore participants' religious life-world. The concept of religious life-world is defined in its two interrelated aspects: attitudes toward Islam and religious subjectivity. The degree of intergenerational difference concerning the perception of Islam constituted a central aspect of this investigation. The project aimed at grounding the Islamic education of British Muslim adolescents in their life experiences. By drawing upon the religious experiences of Muslim adolescents the research offers an empirical critique to the overwhelmingly teacher/text-centred discourse of traditional Islamic pedagogy.

Introduction

There are approximately two million Muslims in Britain, mainly living in the metropolitan cities of London, Birmingham, Manchester and Glasgow (Peach, 1997; Ballard and Kalra, 1994). Families of the majority of British-born Muslims originated in Pakistan, India and Bangladesh. Post-war Britain's need for manual workers to help to rebuild the country was the main motive behind the mass immigration of Muslims to the country during the 1950s and 1960s.

The inclusion of a specific question on religious affiliation in the 2001 census provided for the first time a much more accurate picture of the demographic profile of British Muslims. It appears that few other European countries collect data on the ethnic and religious affiliations of their citizens (Brown, 2000). Although it is difficult to be exact, various studies estimate that there are between 15 and 20 million Muslims in western Europe (Nonneman, Niblock and Szajkowski, 1996). According to some estimates, the vast majority of European Muslims are young. For example, according to the 2001 census for England and Wales (*http://www.statis-tics.gov.uk*) the statistics are as follows. The Muslim population in England and Wales has a very high proportion of young people, compared with the national average: 33.8% of Muslims are under 15 years of age, while the national average is 20.2%, and 18.2% of Muslims are aged between 16 and 24 years of age, while the national average is 10.9%.

In Britain during the last three decades, research on minority communities has been overwhelmingly carried out within the 'race–ethnicity' paradigm. It was only after the public unrest caused by Muslims' strong reaction to the Rushdie affair and the Gulf War during the late 1980s and early 1990s that the import-ance of the religious dynamic in the collective psyche of the Muslim community, and its potential threat to secular polity, have been recognized. It appears that these events were also among the key forces behind a new Islamic awareness within the British Muslim community itself. If the Gulf War signified the internal turmoil within the worldwide Muslim society, *umma*, the Rushdie affair symbolized the uncomfortable position of Islam in the midst of secular and multicultural life in the west.

Within the social scientific research on immigration focused on race and ethnicity, settlement of diaspora Muslim communities and their interaction with the wider society have been the subject of numerous studies (Visram, 1995; Werbner, 1990; Rex and Moore, 1971). Acculturation, integration and assimilation consti-tuted the central themes in these studies, which were mainly inter-ested in the question of how the British Muslim community will be absorbed into the secular democratic cultural life of the wider society. It was assumed that gradual socio-economic upward movement within the British Muslim community would guarantee their 'integration'. The assumption was that once second and third generations of British Muslims developed their English skills and obtained better levels of education, they would identify with the values of late modern capitalist western society, and consequently grow out of their so-called primitive, religiously-based culture.

Despite the more recent recognition that communities that make the totality of society have been leading 'segregated parallel lives' British Muslims are still addressed within a naive assimilationist frame of reference. Thus, the official discourse of policy-makers does not pay sufficient attention to the religious dynamic of the linguistically and ethnically diverse Muslim communities in Britain (Foner, Rumbaut and Gold, 2001; Bacal, 1991). Only after the horrific events of 11 September 2001 has the religious question begun to be seen as an important structural factor, like those of economic deprivation and racism, that hinders the emergence of a meaningful interaction between Islam and secular multicultural life in the west. It must be stressed that this recognition has not yet been coupled with constructive educational intervention strategies, but it seems to be creating a reactionary racist and anti-Islamic backlash in the western world.

A recent ethnographic study by Jacobson (1998) has focused more sharply on the religious/Islamic dimension of the Muslim community in Britain. Jacobson uses the well-known social boundary approach to ethnicity (Barth, 1994; Tajfel, 1981), while studying the formation of 'ethnic identity' among Muslim young people. Without exploring the personally construed nature of Islamic identity, that is, how participants express and interpret their religious belonging, Jacobson claims that because orthodox Islamic faith possesses a fixed nature, her subjects showed a very limited awareness of change in their Islamic identity. Jacobson suggests that this rigidity is very evident in Islam's resistance to secularization. However, despite this overall unsubstantiated conclusion about the so-called 'immutable character' of Islamic self-understanding, she entitled her study *Islam in Transition*.

Lewis (1994), in his general observations about the future of Islam in Britain, much more accurately grasps the difficulties facing Muslim young people. He sees the widening gap between the experiences of Muslim youth and the experience of their parents, and sharply identifies the key question facing the contemporary Muslim community: 'How much traditional South Asian religiosity is accessible, relevant and transferable to today's Muslim youth?'

As the above brief literature review demonstrates, neither the religiosity of the young British Muslims nor their attitudes toward

Islam have been properly researched. Islamic education and other classical Islamic sciences have also neglected the exploration of the religious life-world of young British Muslims. The British Muslim community, like the rest of the Islamic world, is still not ready to acknowledge the religious question in its life-world. In some ways a rigid religious subjectivity hinders development of a meaningful Islamic response to sociocultural change.

Research in Islamic education tends to be historic and normative in character; in other words, it has no empirical research dimension. Thus, Muslim educators do not seem to be interested in understanding how Muslims receive Islamic teachings in the contemporary conditions of their lives. This research project aimed at problematizing religious commitment and modes of Islamic subjectivity. It argues that exploration of the religious life-world of young Muslims should be given priority if we want to see the development of a mature Islamic identity among young generations of Muslims in the west. Most importantly, Muslim educators must face the difficult question of *what it means to be Islamicly educated* in a multicultural society. The present research project was initiated to address these urgent, but so far neglected, issues in Islamic education.

Phenomenology-based post-structural research framework

A phenomenology-grounded interdisciplinary research framework is utilized to investigate the religious life-world of British Muslim youth. As such, the study aims to provide a critique of the central modernist assumptions underpinning the structural-developmental theories that have dominated research on religiosity. Structural-developmental theories in psychology have been widely used to understand the course of human faith development (Fowler, 1981), religious thinking (Goldman, 1964) and religious judgement (Oser and Gmunder, 1991). What is common to structuralist theories of religious development is the assumption that the process of development is underlined by certain invariant stages, which express qualitative differentiation in the ways people relate themselves to what they regard as the centre of their meaning in life (faith) or the ultimate Being. Religious subjectivity is reduced to psychosocial faith construct/structure. Such a structuralist research framework rarely takes into account the culturally embodied nature of a religiously ordered life-world, and the power-laden character of religious discourse.

The recognition of language not merely as a mediating device but as a sign system that actually *constitutes* the reality in our consciousness is central to postmodern thinking. As such, the movement is generally conceptualized as the *linguistic-turn* (Lafont, 1999). Language has come to be seen, not as an apparatus that mirrors external reality in human consciousness as certain universal, ahistorical structures, but as a complex self-referential sign system that renders reality arbitrarily. The ambiguous nature of the sign is expressed by Derrida, probably the most influential contemporary postmodern thinker, as *différance*; meaning both to defer and to differ (see, for example, Derrida, 1967, 1982). These functions of the sign compel meaning to be already and always incomplete, both present and absent. Reality, construed through language, reveals itself as a set of discourses that are relative to our social and cultural conditions. While the former approach is associated in general terms with 'structuralism' the latter is often conceptualized as 'post-structuralism'.

Phenomenology refers literally to the study of what appears to us in our diverse life-experiences. Thus, any systematic attempt to make sense of psychosocial reality as it becomes concrete, 'thematized' in different life domains and realms, can be thought of as phenomenological. Since Brentano's seminal work, *Psychology from an Empirical Standpoint*, was first published in 1874 (reprinted 1995), the idea of describing the life-world (*lebenswelt*) of individuals has been at the centre of phenomenology. In the work of his pupil, Husserl, the phenomenological project became, for a long period, focused on achieving the ultimate aim of foundationalist Cartesian philosophy: namely, to capture the 'pure essences' which were presumed to be constituting the content of human consciousness. Phenomenology as a scientific framework to study reified essences in human cognition has received considerable criticism (Adorno, 1982). However, it did not take Husserl long to go beyond such strict epistemological concerns and to recognize the temporal and historical character of human self-understanding.

If we trace the trajectory of Husserl's phenomenology we will see that his focus moved from essences to a concern with meanings, and from there to the concept of transcendental subjectivity

(Mohanty, 1997). Finally, he was engaged with the phenomenology of the life-world (for the notion of life-world see Habermas, 1981; Carr, 1977; Lotz, 2001). The early Husserlian phenomenology that is focused on describing essences and the way they are constituted in consciousness is called 'static' or 'constitutive' phenomenology, while life-world-centred phenomenological enquiry is called 'generative' or 'generic'. The subject matters of generative phenomenology were inter-subjectivity, historical becoming of 'home-world' (self-understanding) and 'alien-world' (understanding the other), together with the interaction between them (Carr, 1999; Makkreel, 1982). In his last major work, *The Crises of European Sciences*, Husserl (1970) explores what he called the intricate paradox of inter-subjectivity. Husserl's phenomenological method is an ambitious attempt to combine empiricism, intellectualism, idealism and realism within a broad phenomenological framework.

It is true that the 'static' or 'constitutional' analysis that was used by Husserl early in his career led him to a kind of structuralist position which aimed at investigating the invariant configurations and formal essences in consciousness. However, Husserl, by suggesting that the idea of *generativity* be taken to refer both to the process of becoming (generation process) and to the process that occurs over the generations (historical social becoming), goes beyond the strictures of structuralist thinking. The idea of generativity has ecological, hence social contextual, recognition. As such, Steinbock (1995) observes that Husserlian phenomenology offers a non-foundational research framework for investigating the sociocultural phenomena.

Modes/statuses approach to religious subjectivity

Within such a non-foundational phenomenological approach, subjectivity refers to a person's overall being in the world and signifies the processes of synthesizing diverse life experiences into a personally constructed 'singularity'. Subjectively ordered singularity takes shape within the concrete conditions of diverse life experiences that constitute the totality of a life-world. Any life-world is composed of phenomenologically discernible dimensions/domains. Domains are culturally embodied and linguistically embedded realms of experience and expressions of different forms and practices, in which humans engage within life. In this sense we can talk of sexual, religious or occupational realms of life. Naturally, subjectivity in these domains takes on a sexual, religious or occupational character. However, domains possess a semi-autonomous existence; they should not be thought of as separate realms hermetically sealed off from each other. On the contrary, they arise as a result of the *emergent* nature of human subjectivity; human experience of reality remains constantly open to new and fresh interpretations.

Structural-developmental theories assume a stage-based linear progression in self-development. According to the phenomenology-grounded statuses/modes approach, self is subject to a multi-directional change process in which not only is progress or growth a strong possibility (as an outcome), but equally so is regression. The conception of subjectivity as modes and statuses suggests a taxonomy rather than a scheme of hierarchically organized stages and structures. In such a taxonomy, statuses/modes signify observable clusters of interrelations, meanings construed within a certain domain of a life-world as certain discourses and storylines. The self gains certain statuses and modes in the contingency of each discourse and narrative.

Two interrelated levels of phenomenological analysis
As indicated earlier, phenomenology-informed theoretical design of the present research has two major interrelated levels. The *constitutive/static* level of phenomenological analysis enables us to understand the large-scale characteristic of a given research concern, a life-world in which mainly conventional quantitative instruments and analysis procedures can be utilized, such as large-scale surveys and questionnaires. On the other hand, the *generic/generative* level of phenomenological analysis explores subjectively ordered historical cultural dynamics in a given life-world.

In this research the constitutive aspects of the religious life-world of participants are investigated through the implementation of the Sahin Scale of Attitude toward Islam (see Table 8.1). The theoretical construct of 'religious attitude' is operationalized within both the empirical research tradition of attitude measurement in the psychology of religion and the main components of Islamic religiosity.

The Scale of Attitude toward Islam is modelled upon Francis's cross-culturally validated Scale of Attitude toward Christianity (Francis and Stubbs, 1987; Francis, 1989). The Sahin Scale of Attitude toward Islam includes both negative and positive statements, concerned with an affective response among Muslim young people to four central components of Islamic faith, recognized by the participants and traditionally known as *Itiqad* (belief), *Ibadaat* (worship), *Mu'amalat* (interpersonal relationships) and *Akhlaq* (ethics). Each of the twenty-three items is assessed on a five-point scale (Likert, 1932) with responses (*agree strongly, agree, not certain, disagree, disagree strongly*) producing a range of scores from 23 to 115. Age, gender and frequency of performing prayer were the independent predictors of scores recorded on the scale.

The second main theoretical construct of research, modes of religious subjectivity, is operationalized by critically appropriating the psychosocial model of adolescent identity development suggested by Erikson (1965) and by Marcia, Waterman, Matteson, Archer and Orlofsky (1993). In the latter book, *Ego Identity: A Handbook for Psychological Research*, the process of identity construction is investigated through conducting a semi-structured interview schedule. Thus, based upon Marcia's model, a semi-structured *Modes of Muslim Subjectivity Interview Schedule* is constructed to explore the modes of religious (Islamic) subjectivity among young British Muslims.

Method

Research instruments
Two different kinds of research instruments were employed in this study. The first method was questionnaire-based in order to obtain quantitative data, using the *You and Your Faith Questionnaire*. The second method was interview-based in order to generate qualitative data, employing the semi-structured *Modes of Muslim Subjectivity Interview Schedule*.

Sample
The *You and Your Faith Questionnaire* was administered to a randomly selected sample of 400 Muslim students in three sixth-form colleges in inner-city Birmingham. A total of 383 questionnaires were

completed. Participants had diverse ethnic, linguistic and cultural family backgrounds, but all of them identified themselves as Muslims and were born and brought up in Britain. The majority of the students' parents originated in south Asia, primarily in Pakistan, Afghanistan, India, Bangladesh and Kashmir. The questionnaire sample consisted of 219 male and 163 female participants, and the age range was from 16 to 20.

A total of fifteen randomly selected students (nine male and six female) aged from 19 to 21 completed the semi-structured *Modes of Muslim Subjectivity Interview Schedule*. Each interview took approximately 45 to 60 minutes and was tape-recorded. Comparison between the performance of interviewed and non-interviewed participants on the *You and Your Faith Questionnaire* did not reveal any statistically significant differences between the two groups. This indicates that the interviewed group was fairly representative of the rest of the study sample.

Results

Participants' attitudes toward Islam
The questionnaire study consisted of 383 students, with a slightly higher percentage of male (57%) participants compared with female participants (43%). Although there are, as yet, no reliable statistics, there appear to be more Muslim young men than Muslim young women in the mainstream sixth-form colleges in Britain. One of the reasons behind this is that within Muslim communities in Britain young men, rather than young women, are likely to be encouraged to enter post-16 education. Muslim parents often feel uncomfortable sending their daughters to predominantly secular mainstream colleges. The age distribution demonstrates that 13% of participants were 16 years of age, 23% were 17, 33% were 18, 26% were 19 and 5% were 20 years of age.

The majority of participants did not pray regularly (prayer frequency here refers to the obligatory five-times prayer in Islam, *salaat*): 23% prayed at least five times a week, 18% prayed several times a week, 11% prayed on Fridays but not on other days, and 41% prayed less than weekly. This left 7% who never prayed. These findings about the frequency of prayer can be interpreted as indicating emergence of *an implicit secularization* process in the life-world of young Muslims. The data clearly demonstrate that on the whole young women were engaged in prayer less frequently than were young men. This difference between young men and young girls' performance of prayer is found to be statistically significant (t = 4.3, P<.001).

Apart from gender, age also appeared to be making statistically significant difference as it interacts with prayer frequency. The older members of the sample prayed more frequently than did the younger members (r = .15, P<.001).

The initial non-rotated factor analysis revealed a single general factor, indicating that almost all items in the questionnaire are highly significant and homogeneous. These items are presented in Table 8.1. The data presented in Table 8.1 demonstrate that the majority of study participants have quite a high positive attitude toward Islam.

Intergenerational differences
Two additional items were included in the questionnaire, to assess the extent to which the adolescents participating in the survey considered their own attitude toward Islam to coincide with that of their parents. These items read as follows: 'My understanding of Islam is the same as that of my parents' and 'My understanding of Islam is not the same as that of my parents'. The data demonstrate that 54% of the Muslim adolescents agreed that their understanding of Islam was the same as that of their parents, 24% agreed that their understanding of Islam was not the same as their parents, and that the remaining adolescents were not sure one way or the other.

The majority of students' parents came mainly from rural areas in their countries of origin. Thus, although they have a strong emotional attachment to Islam, the level of their knowledge and understanding of Islam has remained quite restricted. This contextual background concerning the lack of adequate Islamic religious literacy among parents is thought to be a fairly common phenomenon. It is assumed that the extent to which the young people in the study identified themselves with this traditional Islamic religiosity would reveal the degree of their personal construction of Islamic faith. Similarity with the parents' faith construction is thought to indicate identification with a traditional form of Islam, while dissimilarity is assumed to indicate the presence of a personal construction of faith. It is possible that dissimilarity may indicate alienation (secularization) from parental culture and faith perception. However, knowing that children position themselves differently vis-à-vis parents' religious understanding clearly shows the presence of a *personal investment* in their faith perception.

Table 8.1 Item rest of test correlations and factor loadings

Scale item	% item endorse-ment	r	Factor loading
I find it inspiring to listen to the Qur'an	95	0.4567	0.5029
I know that Allah/God helps me	98	0.6081	0.6709
Saying my prayers/*du'a* helps me a lot	93	0.5435	0.6075
Attending the Mosque is very important to me	76	0.3884	0.4235
I think going to the Mosque is a waste of my time★	2	0.4641	0.4880
I want to obey Allah/God's law/*shari'a* in my life	95	0.4068	0.4533
I think Mosque sermons/*khuba* are boring★	6	0.4224	0.4511
Allah/God helps me to lead a better life	96	0.6099	0.6691
I like to learn about Allah/God very much	98	0.5697	0.6304
Allah/God means a lot to me	98	0.6455	0.7113
I believe that Allah/God helps people	98	0.6621	0.7306
Prayer/*salaat* helps me a lot	92	0.6564	0.7060
I feel that I am very close to Allah/God	66	0.3881	0.4454
I think praying/*salaat* is a good thing	98	0.6319	0.6845
I think the Qur'an is out of date★	2	0.5084	0.5632
I believe that Allah/God listens to prayers/*du'a*	95	0.6445	0.6969
Allah/God doesn't mean anything to me★	2	0.5328	0.5907
Allah/God is very real to me	92	0.4966	0.5569
I think praying/*du'a* does no good★	2	0.4313	0.4977
Belief in Allah/God means much to me	96	0.5855	0.6630
I find it hard to believe in Allah/God★	3	0.5063	0.5600
I am happy to be a Muslim	98	0.5287	0.5902
I love to follow the life/*sunnah* of the Prophet	93	0.6578	0.7014
alpha/per cent variance		0.9012	35.9%

Note: ★These items are reverse coded.

Having a personal interpretation of Islam which is different from the parental (traditional) conception of Islam does not seem to indicate a lack of performing regular prayers. A substantial percentage of those who pray regularly also appear to disagree with the traditional interpretation of Islam. It should be noted that an important percentage of those who pray regularly indicate uncertainty with parental faith construction.

Modes of Islamic subjectivity

The *constitutive* level of phenomenological analysis concerning the general characteristics of participants' religious life-world has already revealed important aspects of their religious subjectivity. The *generative* phenomenological analysis, carried out through the *Modes of Muslim Subjectivity Interview Schedule*, explored participants' modes of religious subjectivity.

The analysis identified a fourfold typology of religious subjectivity, in which the four modes are characterised as 'foreclosed commitment', 'achieved commitment', 'diffused commitment' and 'moratorium non-commitment'. The four modes of religious subjectivity are centred around the phenomenologically observable signs and characteristics of 'commitment' and 'exploration' processes as experienced in participants' religious life-world. According to this, having a religious commitment that is not informed by an exploration process reveals the 'foreclosed' mode of religious subjectivity, while arriving at a commitment that is preceded by an exploration process results in an 'achieved' mode of religious subjectivity. On the other hand, displaying no observable signs of interest in religion, which rules out the presence of both exploration and commitment in one's religious life-world, is identified as being in a 'diffused' mode of religious subjectivity. Being in a constant exploration process regarding one's position vis-à-vis religion, and active engagement with a given religious content, are taken to be indicators of the 'moratorium' mode of religious subjectivity.

It is possible that some features of the four modes can be observed with varying degrees of significance in one's overall religious life-world. While the fourfold model acknowledges this possibility, it also asserts that one of these modes will define the overall character and style of being religious. Although each mode produces a distinct theology and a faith construct, the emphasis in this model is on understanding the *subjectively ordered relational process* resulting from a person's continual interpretation of his/her religious life-world. The model is post-structural, as the person's religious subjectivity is not reduced to faith structures or constructs as such.

The limitations of this chapter do not allow a full discussion of the theoretical properties of the *Modes of Muslim Subjectivity Interview Schedule* and of the criteria for assessing each subject's position on the exploration/commitment continuum in detail. It is also not possible to present adequately participants' religious subjectivity. We can only illustrate briefly the most common modes of Islamic subjectivity observed among participants.

The *Modes of Muslim Subjectivity Interview Schedule* revealed that three interviewed participants (Arif, Betul and Tulay) experience Islam in a diffused mode and expressed that they were 'culturally Muslims'. They did not involve themselves with any significant religious practice. A 19-year-old female participant, Betul (in order to protect participants' privacy they were given pseudonyms), clearly articulated this increasing alienation from Islamic practice: 'I, and many of my Muslim friends, think that it is not cool to read *namaz* (obligatory prayers) and to go to mosque.'

However, Arif (aged 18), while acknowledging that compared with his parents he was less involved with religious practice, criticized his parents' understanding of Islam:

> My parents are fully Muslims but I am not. They pray regularly and I do not. My mother always reads the Qur'an. But she does not understand it, because . . . she does not know Arabic. That is the way she only taught us – how to read the Qur'an but not to have an understanding of what we were reading.

Analysis of both Arif's and Tulay's religious subjectivity showed that they were not completely uninterested in Islam, as Islam constituted their cultural background. There was a strong emotional tie between them and Islam. Both of them believed in the basic teachings of Islam but clearly did not participate in Islamic practice. In other words, they seemed to lack *personal commitment* to Islam; they both wanted to preserve Islam as a cultural element in their lives, as an identity marker that enabled them to resist assimilation into what they called 'white culture'.

Three male participants showed general features of a foreclosed type of religious subjectivity. Their religious discourse showed strong *predestinarian* and *ahistoric* features, in which the idea of having an 'understanding/interpretation' of Islam as such seemed unacceptable. As far as they were concerned, the divine nature of

Islamic revelation prevented any contamination with human ideas and interpretations. This pure form of Islam has been handed down across generations without any addition or alteration. They felt that they were passive agents of this divine message. In their view the rules and regulations of Islam, *shari'a*, were applicable for all times and places. Islam should not be forced to be suited to the changing social conditions, but un-Islamic life conditions should be Islamized.

The religious discourse of Hasan (aged 19) indicated the above basic features:

> My parents tell me that Allah planned everything in our lives, took care of everything for us . . . This makes me feel comfortable, and accept whatever happens to me in life . . . I do not feel confused . . . I know my *iman* (faith) will always protect me . . . Islam is not a human-made religion; it is from God and most importantly I believe in *qadar* (preor-dination of life events by God).

The religiously foreclosed participants were clear that there was an unbridgeable gap between the Islamic community and the rest of the society. They expressed the view that they were living in the land of the infidel, *dar al Kufr*, and that interaction with the outside culture, which they deemed to be morally decadent, should be avoided. Thus, they felt that they were *in* and not *of* the multicultural society that surrounded them.

However, the majority of participants showed general features of an exploratory mode of Islamic belonging. They felt it necessary to interpret Islam in a *multi-layered relatedness matrix of belonging*. Unlike their parents they found it difficult to separate their lives at home from their lives outside their homes. There was a strong emphasis on being *British Muslims*.

Aqil (aged 19) expressed this newly emerging phenomenon of multi-layered mode of relatedness as having an *outside home world*:

> My parents, I think, do not appreciate that I have (an) outside home world . . . my friends that I play with particularly when I am at the college. I see different religious people. I came to see that there are dif-ferent religions and I am every day actually meeting them . . . that makes a lot of difference.

It is important to note that many of these young people were aware that a cultural multiplicity informed their life-world and they had to interpret Islam within such a reality. It is significant to observe that none of the participants had an 'achieved' mode of Islamic subjectivity, which primarily indicated lack of knowledge and understanding of Islam among the younger generation of Muslims. Most of the female participants were experiencing Islam in an exploratory, questioning mode of Islamic subjectivity. This finding complements young Muslim women's increasing detachment from Islamic religious practice, as mentioned earlier. The fact that female Muslims are subject to much more control in the Muslim community can be seen as an important element behind the exploratory features in their Islamic subjectivity.

Conclusion

Exploration of the religious life-world of a selected group of British Muslim young people revealed that Islam on the whole remains an important factor structuring their lives. The result of the attitude survey showed that the great majority of British Muslim youngsters hold very high positive attitudes toward Islam. However, despite this strong emotional attachment to Islam the actual degree of religious practice is found to be low, which is interpreted as an emergence of *an implicit secularization* process among young British Muslims.

A statistically significant positive relationship is recorded between religious behaviour and attitudes toward Islam. The positive influence of religious behaviour on attitudes toward religion has already been well established (Francis, 1989; Tamminen, 1991). The findings of the present study, however, did not support the other well-established observation in the research literature on attitudes toward religion, namely that females and younger age-groups have a more positive attitude toward religion. According to the findings of the present study no statistically significant difference was recorded between attitudes to Islam and age or gender.

The overall findings indicate that young British Muslims interpret Islam differently from their parents. The majority of the interviewed participants had an exploratory mode of Islamic subjectivity. They were aware that they had to make sense of Islam in their changing life conditions, and also stressed that they were British Muslims.

The study found that high positive attitudes toward Islam did not predict an achieved mode of Islamic subjectivity.

Many of the young British Muslims who participated in the research expressed views that could not be captured and adequately explained by assuming either that they were victims trapped between two cultures or that they easily 'switched' between cultures. They felt the need to initiate a meaningful dialogue among the different cultural practices that they had internalized. Many of them were conscious that they were the first real generation of British Muslims.

Because participants are in a volatile/fluid cultural context and are in their late adolescent years, the observed modes of Islamic subjectivity remained *emergent*. It is primarily the task of Islamic education to help young Muslims to come out of this exploratory mode with a mature understanding of Islamic faith. It is quite possible that a resolution of the exploratory process could lead them toward a more foreclosed or a diffused religious subjectivity.

The real question is this: can traditional Islamic education, with its teacher-text centred approach and memorizing-based methods, help young British Muslims to develop a mature Islamic subjectivity? The situation in Britain of supplementary mosque schools suggests that the answer to this question is, unfortunately, no. Islamic education, and in fact nurture, is overwhelmingly based on the outward teaching of Islam: memorizing a body of religious knowledge, rather than creating a dialogue. A case in point is the way in which young Muslims are introduced to the Qur'an. Despite the fact that many British young Muslims speak and think in English, there is not a well worked-out Qur'anic pedagogy in English. Thus, many of these young people are left either ignorant of this fundamental source of Islam or at the mercy of radical transnational Islamic groups, which try to indoctrinate them into a rigid ahistorical understanding of Islam.

At this stage we can ask a further question: is Islamic education inherently a conservative enterprise, in which concepts like criticality, rationality and dialogue are unthinkable? As a Muslim theologian I am very much convinced that the answer to this question must be no. A brief look at the conception of education in the Qur'an and at its understanding of human development will reveal that the educational process is identified with facilitating a person's overall capacities, primarily his or her religious subjectivity. Let me explain why I believe that Islamic education should be critical and dialogic.

The Qur'an uses several concepts to describe the educational process. The concept of *tarbiyya*, which in its etymological origin means increase, growth, being in an existential transitional mode, came to shape the Islamic approach to education. In Arabic anything that facilitates a growth process has an educative, *tarbawi*, function. For example, in Arabic the word *As-sahab*, meaning cloud, is imaged to be having an educative mission for it enables grass to grow, thus it is also called *ar rabab*, that which has *tarbiyya* quality.

God in the Qur'an, particularly in early revelations, is expressed with the word *Rabb*, the educator par excellence. As the famous opening chapter of the Qur'an declares, 'He is the educator of all worlds.' He nurtures, looks after and is in constant dialogue with all realms of existence, with all different life-worlds. Thus, according to the Qur'an, the educational process cannot be reduced to a mechanical process of training or indoctrinating, one-way transmission. On the contrary, it must be a dialogic process that produces a qualitative change in the subjectivity of the learner.

Let us look at the theological anthropology of the Qur'an, how it views being human. There are many passages in the Qur'an that describe the developmental character of human nature in cognitive terms (*ilm*, *marif*) and similarly in terms of religious subjectivity (*iman*) (Sahin, 1996). According to the Qur'an, humans are created incomplete and the task of defining oneself during the course of one's life is an open-ended process; one either purifies (*tazkiyya*) or corrupts (*fucur*) one's existence. If we take this essentially person-oriented developmental Qur'anic model of education, together with the strong Qur'anic emphasis upon thinking, it becomes clear that a critical dialogic process is in fact at the very heart of Islamic educational self-understanding.

Let us now turn to the question of whether Islamic education can cope with cultural religious plurality. The Qur'anic educational principle of *at-Taaruf* (knowing each other) should be taken into consideration here. According to the Qur'an, humanity is created as different genders, nations and tribes, and with different languages. God did not plan this multiplicity to *confuse* humanity but in order to enable humans to enter into the process of 'knowing each other' or *taaruf* (the Qur'an, chapter 49, verse 13).

Religious plurality is clearly endorsed by the Qur'an, for it declares that many nations have received God's guidance and many nations were 'enabled to have access to divine knowledge and wisdom'. The Qur'an uses the symbolic expressions, *ahl al Kitab, Kitab, utu nasiban min al Kitab*, to express this educational idea of different nations being introduced to God's divine curriculum (for these two symbolic terms see Madigan, 2001).

In addition, it is well known that the Qur'anic revelation took twenty-three years to be completed, during which God replaced many verses with new ones, as the conditions of Muslims changed. This dynamic notion of revelation is expressed with the concept of *naskh*, the phenomenon of abrogation, which clearly reflects that the Qur'anic discourse is aware of its own historicity.

Unfortunately, if we look at the literature produced in contemporary Islamic education, particularly in western languages, we can see very little evidence that a Qur'anic philosophy of education is mentioned in them. For example, if we look at the biggest idea of the last two decades among Muslim educators, the *Islamization of knowledge project*, we can easily see that not only the conception of Islamic education but also the understanding of Islam in this attempt is monolithic. In fact, the literature on Islamic education would be hardly recognized as 'educational' by western educationalists. Thus, when many open-minded western European educationalists who want to initiate a meaningful dialogue between Islam and western civilization read this literature, they naturally become pessimistic about the possibility of such a dialogue.

For example, Meijer's writings (2002a, 2002b) symbolize such an educational effort of creating a mutual understanding between Islamic and western educational world-views. As a Muslim educator, I have tried in this chapter to show that critical openness is a strong feature of the Islamic faith and Islamic educational self-understanding. Such an openness is not only the prerequisite for a meaningful dialogue between Muslim and non-Muslim educators, but also the necessary condition for the possibility of responding adequately to the Islamic educational needs of the new generation of European Muslims.

References

Adorno, T. W. (1982), *Against Epistemology: A Meta-Critique: Studies in Husserl and the Phenomenological Antinomies* (Blackwell, Oxford).

Bacal, A. (1991), *Ethnicity in the Social Sciences: A View and Review of the Literature on Ethnicity* (University of Warwick, Coventry, Centre for Research in Ethnic Relations).

Ballard, R. and Kalra, B. (1994), *The Ethnicity Dimension of the 1991 Census: A Preliminary Report* (Manchester, Census Dissemination Unit, University of Manchester).

Barth, F. (1994), 'Enduring and emerging issues in the analysis of ethnicity', in H. Vermeulen and C. Govers (eds), *The Anthropology of Ethnicity Beyond Ethnic Groups and Boundaries* (Amsterdam, Het Spinhus).

Brentano, F. C. (1874/1995), *Psychology From an Empirical Standpoint*, trans. A. Rancurello, D. B. Terrell and L. L. McAlister (London, Routledge).

Brown, M. (2000), 'Quantifying the Muslim population in Europe: conceptual and data issues', *The International Journal of Social Research Methodology: Theory and Practice*, 3, 87–102.

Carr, D. (1977), 'Husserl's problematic concept of life-world', in F. Elliston and P. McOrmic (eds), *Husserl: Expositions and Appraisals* (Notre Dame University, Notre Dame Press), pp. 202–12.

Carr, D. (1999), *The Paradox of Subjectivity: The Self in the Transcendental Tradition* (Oxford, Oxford University Press).

Derrida, J. (1967), *Speech and Phenomena* (Evanston, Ill., Northwestern University Press).

Derrida, J. (1982), *Margins of Philosophy* (Brighton, Harvester Press).

Erikson, E. (1965), *Childhood and Society* (Harmondsworth, Penguin).

Foner, N., Rumbaut, R. G. and Gold, S. J. (eds) (2001), *Immigration Research for a New Century* (New York, Russell Sage Foundation).

Fowler, J. W. (1981), *Stages of Faith: The Psychology of Human Development and the Quest for Meaning* (London, Harper and Row).

Francis, L. J. (1989), 'Monitoring changing attitudes towards Christianity among secondary school pupils between 1974 and 1986', *British Journal of Educational Psychology*, 59, 89–91.

Francis, L. J. and Stubbs, M. T. (1987), 'Measuring attitudes towards Christianity from childhood into adulthood', *Personality and Individual Differences*, 8, 741–3.

Goldman, R. (1964), *Religious Thinking from Childhood to Adolescence* (London, Routledge and Kegan Paul).

Habermas, J. (1981), *Life-World and Systems: A Critique of Functionalist Reason* (London, Polity).

Husserl, E. (1970), *The Crises of European Sciences* (Evanston, Ill., Northwestern University Press).

Jacobson, J. (1998), *Islam in Transition: Religion and Identity among British Pakistani Youth* (London, Routledge).

Lafont, C. (1999), *The Linguistic Turn in Hermeneutic Philosophy* (London, MIT Press).

Lewis, P. (1994), 'Being Muslim and being British: the dynamics of Islamic reconstruction in Bradford', in R. Ballard (ed.), *Desh Pardesh: The South Asian presence in Britain* (London, Hurst) pp. 58–87.

Likert, R. (1932), 'A technique for the measurement of attitudes', *Archives for Psychology*, 140, 1–55.

Lotz, T. A. (2001), 'Life-world: a philosophical concept and its relevance for RE', in H. Heimbrock, C. Scheilke and P. Schreiner (eds), *Towards Religious Competence: Diversity as a Challenge for Education in Europe* (London, Lit Verlag), pp. 74–85.

Madigan, D. A. (2001), *The Qur'an's Self-image: Writing and Authority in Islam's Scripture* (Princeton, NJ, Princeton University Press).

Makkreel, R. A. (1982), 'Husserl, Dilthey, and the relation of the life-world to history', in J. Sallis (ed.), *Research in Phenomenology* (Atlantic Highlands, Humanities Press), pp. 39–59.

Marcia, J. E., Waterman, A. S., Matteson, D. R., Archer, S. L. and Orlofsky, J. L. (eds) (1993), *Ego Identity: A Handbook for Psychological Research* (London, Springer-Verlag).

Meijer, W. A. J. (2002a), 'East and West in education: shifting dichotomies', unpublished paper at the International Seminar on Religious Education and Values, Kristiansand, Norway.

Meijer, W. A. J. (2002b), 'Education and literacy in Islam: the case of 20th century Morocco', in T. Kvernbekk and B. Nordtug (eds), *The Many Faces of Philosophy of Education: Traditions, Problems and Challenges*, Conference Proceedings of the 8th International Network of Philosophers of Education (Oslo, Norway), pp. 196–205.

Mohanty, J. N. (1997), *Phenomenology between Essentialism and*

Transcendental Philosophy (Evanston, Ill., Northwestern University Press).

Nonneman, G., Niblock, T. and Szajkowski, B. (eds) (1996), *Muslim Communities in the New Europe* (Reading, Ithaca).

Oser, F. and Gmunder, P. (1991), *Religious Judgement: A Developmental Approach* (Birmingham, Ala., Religious Education Press).

Peach, C. (1997), *Estimates of the 1991 Muslim Population of Great Britain*, working papers (Oxford, School of Geography, Oxford University).

Rex, J. and Moore, R. (1971), *Race, Community and Conflict: A Study of Sparkbrook* (Oxford, Oxford University Press).

Sahin, A. (1996), 'Faith development and its educational implications: an Islamic perspective', unpublished MEd thesis, University of Birmingham.

Steinbock, A. J. (1995), *Home Development and Beyond: Generative Phenomenology after Husserl* (Evanston, Ill., Northwestern University Press).

Tajfel, H. (1981), *Social Psychology and Intergroups Relations* (Cambridge, Cambridge University Press).

Tamminen, K. (1991), *Religious Development in Childhood and Youth: An Empirical Study* (Helsinki, Suomalainen Tiedekatemia).

Visram, R. (1995), *The History of the Asian Community in Britain* (Hove, Wayland).

Werbner, P. (1990), *The Immigration Process: Capital, Gifts and Offerings among British Pakistan* (London, Berg).

9

Change in religious behaviour and beliefs among Israeli religious high-school seniors, 1990–1999

YISRAEL RICH AND AVRAHAM LESLAU

Summary

The purpose of this chapter is to report on an important component of a comprehensive study of the religious and educational 'worlds' of students completing their last year of study in public religious Israeli high schools (Leslau and Rich, 2001). This chapter will focus on the changes occurring among these young people in some key aspects of their religious behaviour and beliefs over the last decade of the twentieth century. This was an especially tumultuous period in Israel's political and religious cultural life and had the potential to spawn significant change in the religious behaviour and beliefs of young people. We investigated two relatively large cohorts of students, one of which graduated from high school in 1990 (Leslau and Bar-Lev, 1993) and the other of which graduated from high school in 1999 (Leslau and Rich, 2001). Similarity of sampling procedures and in the contents of the questionnaires to which students responded facilitated comparison of the two cohorts. Results of these comparisons enabled us to draw conclusions about differences in the two groups, and to offer some conjectures regarding the sources of the changes in the religious behaviour and beliefs of these young people.

Introduction

Results of several earlier studies concerned with examining changes in the religious beliefs and behaviour of secondary school students over a significant period of time have appeared in the scientific literature. For example, in Ireland, Turner, Turner, and Reid (1980) investigated attitudes toward religion among boys in one Catholic and one Protestant secondary school in 1969, and again in 1979. They found some erosion of positive attitudes toward religion among the Catholic students but not among the Protestant students. Greer (1990) also reported on the religious beliefs, practices and moral judgements of Protestant pupils from several religious denominations in Northern Ireland. Questionnaires were administered in 1963, 1968 and 1978 to a relatively large number of male and female secondary students from tens of schools. Religious beliefs tended to remain stable, with some indices showing a strengthening trend. Reports on religious practice were also quite stable, but with decline in a few notable areas, such as church attendance. These studies were conducted in a period of significant social unrest. Francis (1992) monitored attitudes toward Christianity among students in two comprehensive secondary schools in East Anglia. The same brief scale was administered to students in 1974, 1978, 1982, 1986 and 1990. Francis noted a progressive deterioration of positive attitudes from survey to survey until 1990. In that year, some enhanced attitudes toward God and toward the Bible were found, whereas commitment to religious practice continued in its weakened state. The present study adds important new dimensions to this literature by examining recent changes in the religious beliefs and behaviour of Jewish students in Israel who attended secondary schools that are mandated to educate in accordance with the traditions of modern Orthodox Judaism.

The remainder of this introduction is divided into two sections. First, we familiarize the reader with Israeli public education, with special emphasis on public religious education. Second, we explain why the decade examined was especially ripe for the emergence of changes in the religious behaviour and beliefs of young people attending religious schools.

Public religious education in Israel

Public education in Israel provides separate educational programmes for four different sectors of the population (Iram and Schmida, 1998). Most Jewish students choose the 'general public' programme, which serves children from secular homes or those that are mildly observant of religious tradition. Mixed-gender classes are the norm. Very little study of religious topics is provided. Those few subjects related to religion that are part of the curriculum (for example, the Bible, Jewish history) are presented through cultural or historical lenses, rather than from a religious perspective.

Almost 20% of the Jewish young people opt for 'public religious' schools, where they study general academic subjects, as well as special religious topics, such as Jewish law and the Talmud. A large majority of school staff members and the families of most students in this group seek to blend a modern lifestyle with moderate to strict religious observance. The social and religious climate in these schools generally reflects the strivings of their constituencies. A variety of organizational structures can be found among these secondary educational institutions. Some of the schools are single-gender only. Others schools are mixed-gender, but the genders are usually separated for religious subjects. Lifelong religious observation is an important schooling outcome for graduates of this group, alongside academic achievements, and vocational and personal contributions to society.

A third group of Jewish families opt for the 'independent' system, where religious studies are dominant and general studies are undertaken less extensively than in the other two school systems. Stringent religious practice is the norm and modernity is often viewed with suspicion. Schools are almost always separated by gender.

Finally, most Arab families, Muslim and Christian, send their children to 'Arab' public schools that have a distinct curriculum, consisting of general academic subjects and some special topics that reflect their unique culture, including the study of Islam and the Qur'an. Religious and cultural perspectives are presented in the instruction of topics related to religion. Most schools are mixed-gender, although separate-gender schools have recently become more common. A significant minority of Arab families, Muslim and Christian, send their children to private high schools sponsored by various Christian denominations.

We will now turn to a closer inspection of the public religious school system, the setting in which this study takes place. Three types of public religious high schools have evolved over the years, each serving a somewhat different student constituency and each having distinct characteristics (see Bar-Lev, 1991). First, there are *comprehensive* high schools with a mixed-gender student body. Most religious subjects in these schools are taught in classes separated by gender, with male and female students exposed to only partially overlapping curricula. Boys and girls attend mixed-gender classes for general subjects. Comprehensive high schools offer a variety of academic curricula, ranging from those that are scholastically demanding to vocational programmes not leading to matriculation. These schools are frequently located in lower-middle and low socio-economic status communities. Compared with the two other types of schools, comprehensive school students, in general, have historically been less successful academically and less observant of religious practices.

A second type is the *academic* high school, which is similar to the comprehensive high school regarding the participation of boys and girls, but differs in other ways. Usually there are fewer curricular programmes offered and all are geared to advanced-level matriculation exams. Students in these schools are usually quite successful in their academic studies; the large majority obtain post-secondary education after army service. Many academic high schools serve a largely middle- and upper-middle-class population. Religious observation varies widely from modern Orthodox to relatively non-observant.

The third school type is the *yeshiva* high school, for boys only, and the parallel *ulpana*, for girls only. Many of these are boarding schools, and all students attend classes throughout the especially long school day. Additionally, as compared with comprehensive and academic high schools, these schools have more strict religious standards and more curricular hours are devoted to religious studies. As might be expected, student religious observance is relatively stringent. Academic standards in most of these schools are quite high and the percentage of children from low socio-economic backgrounds is rather small. However, a not insignificant percentage of these schools cater to academically weaker students while striving to maintain high religious standards.

A period of change

As noted above, the main purpose of this study was to investigate changes occurring over a ten-year period in the religious practice and beliefs of two cohorts of Israeli Jewish students who were about to complete their religious high school education. We compared high school seniors who graduated in 1990 with their counterparts who graduated in 1999. Senior personnel in the

Education Ministry and many educational researchers and practitioners expressed the opinion that this was an especially appropriate period to examine this topic, because of the occurrence of dynamic events and the spread of intellectual trends that could have brought about significant decay in the degree to which young people attending public religious schools conformed to traditional religious behaviour and beliefs.

During this period, at least four factors could have contributed to this change in the behaviour and thinking of young people. First, an important shift occurred in the public climate of Israel toward greater openness to political solutions to the conflict with Palestinians. As a result of the end of the first *intifada*, peace negotiations began with the Palestinians and several agreements with the Palestinian Authority were made. The assassination of Prime Minister Rabin and its socio-political aftermath also occurred during this time. These events led to a weakening of the Greater Israel ideology, and perhaps also to the religious fervour it generated among modern Orthodox teenagers (Sheleg, 2000).

Second, cracks in the doctrine of blending traditional Orthodox Judaism with a modern world-view were increasingly being felt. *Charedi* (ultra-Orthodox) political and social institutions appeared to gain strength, while political and social institutions associated with moderate modern Orthodoxy seemed to weaken. As a result, it would not be surprising if increasing numbers of young people would either turn toward more fervent forms of Orthodoxy, or turn away from religious observation.

Third, public discussions, often acrimonious debates accompanied by little or no evidence, cropped up frequently in well-publicized and respected forums. Public religious schools were often accused of being ineffective and derelict in their duty of preparing students to enter adult society with a firm religious foundation, in light of the observation that so many graduates seemed to encounter great difficulties in maintaining religious beliefs and practices after leaving school. This argument seemed to portray young people's alienation from religious practice as a natural outcome of inferior public religious schooling, thereby further legitimizing disaffection from religion.

Finally, postmodernist thinking made inroads into educational and religious circles, with concomitant justification for the primacy of realizing individual goals and for avoiding long-term commitment. This orientation could have provided an intellectual base for some young people to weaken their religious commitment.

All four of these factors had the potential to contribute to an erosion of allegiance to modern Orthodox religious beliefs and practice, the desired religious outcome of public religious schooling. Accordingly, we anticipated that the 1999 graduates would demonstrate lower levels of religious observance in both beliefs and practice, as compared with their counterparts who graduated almost a decade earlier.

The present research was based on the 1990 study by Leslau and Bar-Lev (1993) that examined the 'religious world' of twelfth-grade students in the public religious sector. The 1990 research was an exhaustive study that investigated a large number of participants and used a range of instruments. Researchers administered a lengthy questionnaire to 5,345 graduating seniors (2,939 females and 2,406 males) in 130 schools. This constituted over 60% of the entire population of relevant students. Results of that study indicated significant variation in religious behaviour and beliefs among twelfth-grade public religious students, ranging from anti-religious to ultra-Orthodox positions. As anticipated, the type of school was related to the level of religious observance. Students in the *yeshiva* and *ulpana* were most observant, while their counterparts in comprehensive schools were least observant. Of particular importance was the finding that in all types of schools there were significant percentages of young people who were strictly observant, as well as significant numbers of students who were completely non-observant. This latter result gave rise to much public discussion and soul-searching, because it suggested that no type of modern religious school can immunize all of the students against adopting a secular lifestyle.

Method

As noted above, the present study arose out of the frequently expressed concern that a significant trend toward lowered levels of religious beliefs and practice was widespread among students in public religious high schools. Accordingly, we sought to investigate this assumption by comparing students graduating from these schools in 1999 with their counterparts in 1990. In order to maximize the validity of the comparison, our strategy was to use the same general sampling procedures as well as the same questionnaires employed in the 1990 study, if the psychometric properties proved adequate.

In the present study, schools were randomly sampled from virtually the entire population of relevant public religious high schools, stratified for type of school, socio-economic level of student body and student gender. For each of these three parameters the distribution of actual participants in the study was compared with that of the intended sample and with the population. These comparisons indicated relatively minor discrepancy. Sampling procedures in this study thus enabled a smaller sample than that in the earlier study, approximately 22% of the entire relevant population. A total of 2,306 students participated, 1,283 females and 1,023 males.

The questionnaire used in the Leslau and Bar-Lev study (1993) adopted items from previously existing scales and, when necessary, new items were generated. We administered the same questionnaire in the present study except for several modifications: some background questions on the student and his/her parents were eliminated, as well as some questions regarding religious beliefs. The questions and sub-scales that were eliminated suffered from weak psychometric characteristics or were no longer relevant, due to the passage of time. A few short scales were also added that examined students' future plans after high school. Each of the new indices constructed underwent factor analysis and demonstrated adequate internal reliability. The questionnaire was administered by trained personnel, usually in the classroom, after receiving permission from the relevant educational authority. All responses were anonymous.

Results

In the following analysis comparisons of the two cohorts will be reported that reflect changes in student religious practice and beliefs from 1990 to 1999. Because even small differences between such large samples can yield statistical significance, and in order to ease comparison among groups, we report percentages of religious practice and beliefs rather than statistical tests.

Table 9.1 Religious self-definition of male students by type of school – 1999

School	Very religious %	Religious %	Somewhat religious %	Not so religious %	Not religious %	Very much not religious %	N
Yeshiva	23	43	17	12	5	1	536
Academic	5	38	26	18	12	2	215
Comprehensive	5	29	23	29	11	3	265
Total	14	38	20	18	8	2	1,016

Table 9.2 Religious self-definition of male students by type of school – 1990

School	Very religious %	Religious %	Somewhat religious %	Not so religious %	Not religious %	Very much not religious %	N
Yeshiva	14	55	19	9	3	1	1,090
Academic	3	40	24	17	11	4	373
Comprehensive	3	24	23	30	15	4	851
Total	8	41	21	18	9	3	2,314

Religious practice was determined by global self-definition of religiosity, self-reports of observance of positive religious practices, and prohibitions that are considered appropriate in public religious schools. Tables 9.1 to 9.4 relate to religious self-definition. Table 9.1 provides data for males in the 1999 cohort according to the three types of schools investigated, while Table 9.2 provides the same information for the 1990 cohort. Perusal of these tables reveals, as anticipated, that both in 1990 and 1999 *yeshiva* students defined themselves as more religious than did their counterparts in the other two types of schools. Furthermore, young men in the academic high schools reported greater religiosity than those in comprehensive high schools. This result was more pronounced in 1990 than in 1999. Another interesting finding is that, as compared with the 1990 group, more *yeshiva* students in the 1999 cohort defined themselves as 'very religious' while fewer students characterized themselves as 'religious'. Finally, males in comprehensive schools reported greater observance in 1999 than they did in 1990. In brief, as compared with the 1990 cohort, the 1999 cohort of young men in *yeshivas* demonstrated greater divergence, while comprehensive school students defined themselves as more religious. Little change occurred among academic high school males.

Tables 9.3 and 9.4 provide comparable information for young women. Similar to the results among males for both cohorts, young women in the *ulpana* were more religious than were those in the other two types of schools, and they were more religious in academic as compared with comprehensive schools. Overall, more young women than young men defined themselves as likely to be religious . Comparing the two cohorts of young women, we see that a higher proportion described themselves as 'very religious' in 1999 than did in 1990. Also, among 1999 *ulpana* young women there is a greater tendency to characterize themselves as non-religious, although this remains a relatively uncommon occurrence. Finally, a moderate trend toward increased religiosity in 1999 from 1990 appears among young women in the academic and comprehensive high schools. In brief, a modest but inclusive trend toward greater religiosity in 1999 is apparent among virtually all the groups of young women.

Table 9.3 Religious self-definition of female students by type of school – 1999

School	Very religious %	Religious %	Somewhat religious %	Not so religious %	Not religious %	Very much not religious %	N
Ulpana	25	55	11	6	2	1	545
Academic	10	60	13	13	3	1	320
Comprehensive	5	42	17	24	11	2	401
Total	15	52	13	14	5	1	1,266

Table 9.4 Religious self-definition of female students by type of school – 1990

School	Very religious %	Religious %	Somewhat religious %	Not so religious %	Not religious %	Very much not religious %	N
Ulpana	19	65	11	3	1	0	698
Academic	6	56	20	12	5	1	871
Comprehensive	3	37	22	26	11	2	1,269
Total	8	50	19	16	7	1	2,838

We now turn to an examination of specific religious practices and of how rates of observance differ between respondents in the 1990 and the 1999 cohorts. It is important to note that earlier research demonstrated high correlations (r = .70+) between self-definition of religiosity and self-reports of specific religious practices among Jewish Israeli young people (Kedem, 1991; Leslau and Bar-Lev, 1999; Rich and Iluz, 1999). Thus, we anticipated similar patterns of results, despite the different ways of measuring religiosity. Tables 9.5 to 9.8 present data for young people in three types of public religious schools, who report on their affirmation of observance of six religious practices or prohibitions during an extended vacation from school. School vacation was the focus of the questions in order to extract information that reflected religious observance based more on personal volition than on social or school pressure. Three practices were the same for young men and young women, and three were gender-specific. The particular practices and prohibitions were chosen because of their religious and/or social meaning and because they formed a Guttman scale.

Analysis of the data in Tables 9.5 and 9.6 indicates that most male students in all three types of schools were careful to avoid eating non-kosher food and not to desecrate the Sabbath by lighting electricity. However, there are meaningful differences among the three types of schools regarding the other religious practices. As reported above, young men in the *yeshiva* reported the highest levels of observance. Also, academic as compared with comprehensive high school males were more observant of most practices in 1990, but not in 1999. Of particular importance are the changes appearing among both *yeshiva* and comprehensive school boys. Regarding the former group we note a small but consistent drop in observance of all practices. By contrast, religious observance strengthened among comprehensive school young men from 1990 to 1999 for five of the six practices, and for two of them, refraining from lighting electricity on the Sabbath and donning phylacteries, the change was quite large. Little change was apparent among academic high school young men. Thus, from 1990 to 1999 we see some enhanced religious observance among young men attending comprehensive school, a slight regression among young men attending *yeshiva* schools and stability characterizing young men in academic high schools.

Table 9.5 Male students observing ritual practices by type of school – 1999

Ritual practice	Yeshiva %	Academic %	Compre-hensive %	Total %
Not eat non-kosher food	94	91	93	93
Not 'use' electricity on Sabbath	92	86	73	86
Put on phylacteries every day	79	61	66	72
Pray evening prayer	71	36	33	46
Daily morning services with a quorum	58	30	32	45
Not bathe in mixed pool	49	14	19	34

Table 9.6 Male students observing ritual practices by type of school – 1990

Ritual practice	Yeshiva %	Academic %	Compre-hensive %	Total %
Not eat non-kosher food	95	92	89	93
Not 'use' electricity on Sabbath	95	82	62	82
Put on phylacteries every day	86	64	42	70
Pray evening prayer	78	40	32	56
Daily morning services with a quorum	62	31	30	47
Not bathe in mixed pool	51	15	24	37

Tables 9.7 and 9.8 provide comparable information for young women. There is a high level of observance of major kosher and Sabbath prohibitions among all groups of females, while for the remaining practices observance remains relatively high for *ulpana* girls, but less so among academic and comprehensive school female students. From 1990 to 1999 little change is observed in five of the six practices among *ulpana* students, while among the other two groups of young women there is greater observance in 1999, especially among those attending academic high schools. In brief, there is evidence of increased religious observance over the decade for many of the young women.

Table 9.7 Female students observing ritual practices by type of school – 1999

Ritual practice	Ulpana	Academic	Compre-hensive	Total
	%	%	%	%
Not eat non-kosher food	98	95	97	97
Not 'use' electricity on Sabbath	96	92	72	87
Makes blessing after meal	81	67	55	69
Does not wear trousers	80	58	30	58
Not bathe in mixed pool	69	43	32	51
Attends Sabbath morning prayer	43	36	17	33

Table 9.8 Female students observing ritual practices by type of school – 1990

Ritual practice	Ulpana	Academic	Compre-hensive	Total
	%	%	%	%
Not eat non-kosher food	97	98	97	98
Not 'use' electricity on Sabbath	96	86	69	81
Makes blessing after meal	71	44	30	46
Does not wear trousers	84	56	30	53
Not bathe in mixed pool	69	36	32	44
Attends Sabbath morning prayer	44	24	13	25

The last four tables report on religious beliefs. Even more than religious practices, there is much disagreement within Jewish tradition regarding those beliefs that are at the core of Orthodox Judaism. Nevertheless, there was general agreement among many religious educators polled that the beliefs appearing in these tables are appropriate belief outcomes for students in the public religious system. It is immediately apparent from these tables that there was relatively little variation in beliefs among young men and young women in both 1990 and 1999. Four points are worthy of note. First, overall levels of religious belief were higher than levels of religious practice. There are many possible reasons for this phenomenon, but they are not directly relevant to the issue at hand. Second, level of religious belief drifted only slightly lower from 1990 to 1999 for all student groups on virtually all measures. Third, students in comprehensive schools expressed levels of religious belief that are almost as high as those of the *yeshiva* and *ulpana* students. Academic high school students had lower belief levels, but even in this group a majority of young people affirmed their belief in every item. Finally, affirmation of core religious beliefs among young women was consistently higher, albeit only slightly, as compared with that of the young men.

Table 9.9 Male students affirming belief by type of school – 1999

Affirm belief	*Yeshiva*	Academic	Compre-hensive	Total
	%	%	%	%
God exists	95	81	97	92
God gave the Torah to Moses on Sinai	92	76	93	89
Jews are 'chosen' people	89	69	88	85
Soul exists after death	88	67	87	83
God guides Jewish history	88	66	85	83
Divine providence	86	64	86	81
Coming of Messiah	85	62	83	80
Resurrection of the dead	80	55	77	74

Table 9.10 Male students affirming belief by type of school – 1990

Affirm belief	*Yeshiva*	Academic	Compre-hensive	Total
	%	%	%	%
God exists	98	94	98	97
God gave the Torah to Moses on Sinai	97	94	97	96
Jews are 'chosen' people	94	88	92	91
Soul exists after death	92	81	82	84
God guides Jewish history	97	87	88	90
Divine providence	95	86	89	90
Coming of Messiah	94	85	88	89
Resurrection of the dead	89	74	77	79

Table 9.11 Female students affirming belief by type of school – 1999

Affirm belief	*Ulpana*	Academic	Compre-hensive	Total
	%	%	%	%
God exists	98	93	96	96
God gave the Torah to Moses on Sinai	96	88	92	93
Jews are 'chosen' people	92	79	88	87
Soul exists after death	90	79	82	85
God guides Jewish history	93	79	86	87
Divine providence	90	75	86	85
Coming of Messiah	89	73	80	82
Resurrection of the dead	80	65	68	72

Table 9.12 Female students affirming belief by type of school – 1990

Affirm belief	*Ulpana*	Academic	Compre-hensive	Total
	%	%	%	%
God exists	98	94	98	97
God gave the Torah to Moses on Sinai	97	94	97	96
Jews are 'chosen' people	94	88	92	91
Soul exists after death	92	81	82	84
God guides Jewish history	97	87	88	90
Divine providence	95	86	89	90
Coming of Messiah	94	85	88	89
Resurrection of the dead	89	74	77	79

Conclusion

In conclusion, we detected relatively little overall change in the state of religious practice and belief of students in public religious Israeli high schools from 1990 to 1999. However, closer examination of the various sub-groups reveals variation in behaviour that may prove increasingly meaningful if the existing trend continues. There was some attrition in the religious practice of *yeshiva* students, who generally come from religiously and socially solid families. Also evident was a concomitant increment in the religious behaviour of students from comprehensive high schools, who are usually the children of *Sepharadi*, lower middle-class families with less commitment to religious practice. In contrast to the *yeshiva* young men, *ulpana* young women remained steadfast in their religious observance, while there was a strengthening of observance among comprehensive and academic high school young women, especially among the latter. It is noteworthy that the increase in observance among academic high school young women is not apparent among their male counterparts. The young men in these schools often displayed a relatively low level of observance.

Implications for public religious education

We will now briefly consider some of the possible reasons for the change and the stability revealed by the data. One area of change regarding religious practice relates to increased, or at least stable, levels of observance for most student groups, with some deterioration among *yeshiva* students. We anticipated lowered levels of observance, due to various social and political events mentioned in the introduction. However, we apparently did not consider sufficiently other socio-political dynamics that create forces toward greater observance. Chief among these is an ongoing movement of return to religious roots that has had a major influence on the Israeli public in all walks of life (see Sheleg, 2000). This influence has been especially prominent among *Sepharadi* persons living away from urban centres, and has been spearheaded by the Shas political movement. Although much of the 'return to roots' movement is toward a more fundamentalist stance than that favoured by public religious schools, it has provided an aura of legitimacy and a sense of community to its adherents that spills over to young men and young women served by public religious schools. It could well be that the effects of this social and religious phenomenon, combined with other factors, counterbalance the forces toward reduced practice. This does seem to be likely, in light of the fact that the largest change toward increased practice occurred in comprehensive schools, which are often located outside the large urban centres and where the student body is comprised of relatively large percentages of *Sepharadi* children. These are the populations who were most likely affected by this movement.

This line of reasoning may also help to explain why *yeshiva* students' religious observance was not enhanced. First, they come from more observant homes and thus they are less likely to be targets for the 'return to roots' movement. Also, they are less likely to be affected by the Shas party, because a large percentage are of western origin and middle class. Indeed, not only are *yeshiva* students less exposed to the 'return to roots' movement, but being largely from western, middle-class, well-educated families, they are possibly more inspired by the social and political phenomena described above (for example, intellectual debates, post-modernism) that steer young people to reduced religious observance.

It is of special interest that in many cases the public debate rested on the assumption that there is increasing abrogation of religious commitment among young people, an assumption proved false by data in this study. Yet it appears that these discussions, conducted by the well educated and relatively affluent, paid special attention to the disappointments rendered by their own children, who were probably not registered in comprehensive schools, where a revitalization of religious commitment is ongoing. The *yeshivas*, and to a lesser extent the *ulpanas*, the schools of choice for many of these families, have experienced some rise in the number of students who define themselves as non-religious. The public debates have paid less attention to the improved lot of comprehensive school students. Although such bias in public discussions may be inevitable, the introduction of objective up-to-date data may prove valuable in enabling less egocentric discussions that can affect educational policy decisions.

Another phenomenon appearing in this study is increased polarization of religious observance within religious school settings. This is apparent in the relatively greater percentage of *yeshiva* students declaring themselves as 'very religious', alongside a relatively larger number who see themselves as non-religious. It is apparent in the academic high school, where young men are becoming less observant, as compared with their counterparts in other types of schools, while their female classmates amplify their religious commitment. It is also obvious in the comprehensive school, where religious observance is on the rise and coexists alongside the fairly large numbers of students who see themselves as relatively non-observant. This suggests that school personnel will need to design formal and informal curricula for a more varied student body and will need to be increasingly sensitive to the unique religious needs of students. Indeed, educators' concern about the heterogeneity of the student body (for example, Ben Ari and Rich, 1997) should also relate to the diversity of religious beliefs and practice, as well as to the more traditional interest in academic and cultural variation. One certainly should not make assumptions about the religious tendencies and inclinations of young persons based solely on demographic information, such as their socio-economic characteristics or the type of schools they attend.

References

Bar-Lev, M. (1991), 'Tradition and innovation in Jewish religious education in Israel', in Z. Sobel and B. Beit-Hallahmi (eds), *Tradition, Innovation, Conflict* (Albany, NY, State University of New York Press), pp. 101–31.

Ben Ari, R. and Rich, Y. (eds) (1997), *Enhancing Education in Heterogeneous Schools: Theory and Application* (Ramat Gan, Israel, Bar Ilan University Press).

Francis, L. (1992), 'Monitoring attitudes toward Christianity: the 1990 study', *British Journal of Religious Education*, 14, 178–82.

Greer, J. (1990), 'The persistence of religion: a study of sixth-form pupils in Northern Ireland, 1968–1988', *Journal of Social Psychology*, 130, 573–81.

Iram, Y. and Schmida, M. (1998), *Educational System of Israel* (Westport, Conn., Greenwood Press).

Kedem, P. (1991), 'Dimensions of Jewish religiosity in Israel', in Z. Sobel and B. Beit-Hallahmi (eds), *Tradition, Innovation, Conflict* (Albany, NY, State University of New York Press), pp. 251–77.

Leslau, A. and Bar-Lev, M. (1993), *The Religious World of Graduates of Public Religious Education* (Ramat Gan, Bar Ilan University, Israel Sociological Institute for the Study of Communities) (in Hebrew).

Leslau, A. and Bar-Lev, M. (1999), 'Religious schooling, family, and pupils' religious commitment', in Y. Rich and M. Rosenak (eds), *Abiding Challenges: Research Perspectives on Jewish Education* (Tel Aviv, Israel, Freund), pp. 341–56.

Leslau, A. and Rich, Y. (2001), *Survey of 12th Grade Students in*

Public Religious Education-5759 (Ramat Gan, Bar Ilan University, Israel, Stern Institute for the Study and Advancement of Religious Education) (in Hebrew).

Rich, Y. and Iluz, S. (1999), *Attitudes of Students in Religious Teacher Education Institutes* (Ramat Gan, Bar Ilan University, Israel, Stern Institute for the Study and Advancement of Religious Education) (in Hebrew).

Sheleg, Y. (2000), *The Newly Religious* (Jerusalem, Israel, Keter) (in Hebrew).

Turner, E., Turner, I. and Reid, A. (1980), 'Religious attitudes in two types of urban secondary schools: a decade of change', *Irish Journal of Education*, 14, 43–52.

10

Models of inter-religious learning: an empirical study in Germany

HANS-GEORG ZIEBERTZ

Summary

To a large extent, denominational religious education is standard practice in Germany today. However, there are also processes of secularization, religious change and religious plurality taking place, as in other western countries. How religious education should keep up with the times is a matter of public discussion. Thus, for example, the question arises, whether in the future religious education should be Christian-ecumenical, or even completely non-denominational. What sort of education would we have if the pupils concerned had to decide? So as not merely to speculate about the answer to this question, we have carried out an empirical study at various schools in Germany. We wanted to establish how pupils assessed the traditional mono-religious denominational principle of religious education, and how they judged the alternatives, which we have called 'multi-religious' and 'inter-religious'. We shall first introduce the models and then proceed to the results of the empirical study.

Introduction

Religious education as mono-religious education

What does the mono-religious model imply? So as to avoid misunderstanding we want to make it clear from the start that people who prefer this model do not think that there is only one true religion (*'religio vera'*) and that the other religions are completely without justification, wrong or even inferior, imperfect, incomplete or temporary. Perhaps fundamentalist thinking tends this way; fundamentalists cling to an exclusive view: there is only one absolute and universal religion, which is their own, and that is how they interpret their religion. From a fundamentalist perspective the term 'mono-religious' is a pleonasm, as it presupposes the existence of other religions and one's own as just one among many, whereas from a fundamentalist point of view this is not possible. If there is a point of contact between the true personal religion and the other mistaken and inferior 'religions' it is the 'denominational dialogue', as described by John Hick (1982).

Following on from this, it seems that the mono-religious model is based on the concept that one should take many different religions into account and that they actually communicate with one another, and rightly so. Nevertheless, the question then is, how *is* this exchange developed and realized, or, better still, how *should* it be developed and realized? A first basis of the mono-religious model is the so-called 'inclusive approach'. This allows us to adopt a concept that was introduced in Karl Rahner's work and which can be found explained in more detail in the relevant records of the Second Vatican Council (Rahner, 1975, 1978). Behind this view lies the recognition that one should adopt a positive attitude toward members of other religions and approach them with an open mind, because their personal faith may contain stimulating ideas and elements of the Christian faith, even if they are not aware of them. Within the bounds of this concept people of other religious faiths could be described as 'anonymous Christians'. This is the reason why they can be redeemed and live in God's mercy. This interpretation can be described as 'soft inclusion', as it takes into consideration the personal faith of the religious individual as a member of a non-Christian religion (Waldenfels, 1987).

A different emphasis is represented by the idea of 'hard inclusion'. This term, applied to non-Christian religions, does not concern itself so much with individual faith (*'fides qua'*) as with the systems of faith of these religions (*'fides quae'*). The motivation, however, is the same. One has to take a positive approach toward the non-Christian religions because their systems of faith contain certain valuable ideas, elements and components that belong to the core of Christianity, although the Christian aspects of these systems of faith are not recognized as such. Against this background the non-Christian religions can, at least partly, be described as forms of anonymous Christianity. The basic ideas of 'soft' and 'hard' inclusion recur in the principle of the incarnation, in which Christ is universally present in everything that is considered valuable in this world. From a critical fundamentalist point of view, the incarnation of Christ has a merely gnostic-cognitive character in this model, as its purpose is to make visible those Christian elements of redemption and grace that are already present in the other religions.

Religious education as multi-religious education

The multi-religious model differs in many aspects from the mono-religious one. This applies not only to the aims of religious inter-action but also to the separate steps necessary to achieve them. The objective is not, as it is in the mono-religious model, 'religious truth', for instance, the truth about God's real existence, about attributes such as omnipotence, justice and love, as well as God's actions in the history of humanity. The objective of the multi-religious model is comparison. It aims at neither diligence in the search for the truth nor the search for the real meaning. The actual motive is curiosity and the pursuit of knowledge. The aim is to receive cultural information about religious experiences, feelings and the behaviour of believers, so as to understand the motivation of religious people to whom one may or may not feel personally attracted. A comparison of these data is made so that an insight into differences between religions may be gained, on the one hand, and points of resemblance determined, on the other. Against this background it is not possible to classify the various religions in a particular hierarchical order, as the criterion for this classification is not the individual's involvement in a particular religion, but the so-called 'objective criteria' (for example, attitude toward women). One could therefore say that one religion is more progressive than another. Looking, for example, at the process of religious evolution we see that only the strongest religion will survive, for religions come and go (Mostert, 1989). One can also discuss the 'family grouping' of religions: some religions are considered to be closer to the core of the family than others (Edwards, 1972). Finally, perspectives of rationality and abstraction can also be used in the comparison and characterization of the images of God. The separate steps toward the realization of the multi-religious model are distinct from the mono-religious one, as they are based on the assumption that the world religions have, in principle, been conceived in a similar way.

One extreme of the equality principle is to say that all religions are 'branches of the same genealogical tree'. The roots of this tree reach down into the same 'primal ground', which is to say that all religions are founded on human objectives, which point to the absolute (philosophical balance) or to the fact that all religions are an emotional expression of the human search for complete happiness and joy (psychological balance) (see Ziebertz, 1993, 2002). Instead of the metaphor of the genealogical tree and its branches we can also use another – the 'lens' metaphor. One could say that religions represent different 'lenses', through which people see their relationship to the philosophically absolute or to psychologically perfect joy (see Knitter, 1985).

The other extreme of the equality principle is that of religious relativism, which means that individuals' religious involvement can be reduced to the cultural environment within which they live, for example, the cultural environment of Christians 'in the west', of Muslims in Arab and African countries, of Hindus within the Indian environment, and so on. Strictly speaking, one can take the equality principle one step further. Religious relativism can result in religious indifference, when people feel it is not important which religion they have, or if they have a religion at all. The equality principle thus leads to religious agnosticism, in which a religion appears to be a purely cultural phenomenon which can, nevertheless, arouse our curiosity to find the answers to urgent cognitive needs.

One frequently comes across this kind of distanced curiosity among young people in Northern Europe. We found it in empirical studies (see for example Ziebertz, Kalbheim and Riegel, 2003). Young people, including those who are often described as secularized and completely atheist in the Christian sense, were not 'against religion' on principle; on the contrary, many regarded religion as an interesting historical and cultural phenomenon. 'Interesting' and 'highly interesting' were recurring keywords. It is surprising that the number of students who participate in religious activities is dropping in the northern west European countries, while the academic interest of students in various aspects of religion, which, after all, does not require any religious involvement, appears to be remaining stable.

Religious education as inter-religious education

We can begin our description of the inter-religious model by putting forward the main arguments against the mono-religious and multi-religious models. This should account for the fact that, according to a number of theological authors, yet another model is needed.

The fundamental weakness of the mono-religious model is that it does not examine the other religions from the starting point of their fundamental principles, their presuppositions or their self-perceptions. In the mono-religious perspective, the encounter with other religions takes place within a framework that corresponds to the views of the Christian religion. The other religion is placed within the limits of Christian concepts and weighed and judged in terms of the incarnation of Jesus Christ in the world. One could argue that there is too much Christianity in the mono-religious model, or, in other words, that the criteria of this model correspond too much to the 'I-perspective' of Christian believers. There is no 'you-perspective' directed at other religions. There is no exchange of perspectives, no coordination between the 'I' and the 'you' (see Habermas, 1982). So the objective is not the exclusiveness of the I-perspective; nor is it the surrender or abandoning of this perspective. The objective is the *relationship*, because the assumption is that different perspectives can enrich one another. In other words, the strongly defined mono-religious model can, from various religious points of view, develop into an ethnocentric model, which, in the most extreme case, will favour one's own religious group and relegate other religious groups to a position of no relevance. These are not tentative considerations, as is proved only too clearly by fundamentalist movements in all religions (see van der Ven and Ziebertz, 1994, 1995).

The fundamental weakness of the multi-religious model lies in the fact that it reduces the variety of religious human experience to another dimension, which could be the philosophical dimension of humanity's pursuit of the absolute or the psychological dimension of its search for perfect happiness. Mircea Eliade has warned us against this reduction of the religious (Eliade, 1969). To make our position quite clear, we would like to point out that every religious phenomenon always implies historical, literary, psychological, sociological and cultural aspects. However, it should not be reduced to those aspects, because we are first and foremost concerned with a religious phenomenon. The phenomenon represents human interaction with 'a reality' that cannot be empirically established; it is the human answer to transcendence (see van Baal, 1971; van Beek, 1982). This transcendence can adopt many forms of expression, such as, for instance, those of theism, panentheism and pantheism or, as Krüger claims, in his interesting description of early Buddhism and early Christianity, metatheism (see Krüger, 1989).

If we consider the communicative view of the multi-religious model, another objection can be formulated in connection with the dangers of reductionism. As the mono-religious model confines itself to the I-perspective while ignoring the you-perspective, so the multi-religious model runs the risk of the restrictively neutral 'it-perspective'. It distances itself from the religious involvement of the individual, it abstracts and places itself above religions, in order to weigh and judge such questions as evolutionary processes, family adherence or rationality from a non-subjective viewpoint. The academic question which arises here is whether one does not lose the essence, the inner worth of every religion, by using such an approach. What matters is the human encounter with transcendence. What could be more fundamental?

To put it even more critically: is there a neutrally objective it-perspective at all which does not include the I-perspective and the you-perspective? Proponents of this so-called objectivity and abstraction think so. We believe, though, that the it-perspective is as much bound by situation and context as the I-perspective and you-perspective. To push the argument a little further: is the it-perspective something different, then, from the I-perspective of academically educated and 'enlightened' people in the western hemisphere? Is not every form of knowledge whatsoever a personal and cultural knowledge construct? Does not the fundamental idea behind constructivism in itself rule out the idea of the it-perspective (see Bruner, 1992)?

The question is, therefore, is there some model for an encounter with the various religions, other than on the basis of the criteria of the I-perspective of one's own religion? In other words, is there an alternative to the I-perspective being every time and repeatedly placed in a situation of reciprocity with the you-perspective of other religions? Is there an alternative to the exchange of perspectives? An apposite discussion following on at this point would have to conclude: no, there is no such thing. Thus, an exchange of perspectives is the foundation of the inter-religious model.

However, what is meant by 'exchange of perspectives'? On the one hand, this concept describes an activity and, on the other, it states an aim. Implicit in this aim is the notion that those who participate obtain the ability, through practical involvement, to understand their own religion, not just from its own perspective but also from the perspectives of the other religions thus encountered. This means that one is capable of interpreting one's own religion from one's own, as well as from other less familiar points of view. However, this is only one side of the coin. The exchange of perspectives also means that one is capable of seeing the other religion, not just through one's own eyes, but also through the eyes of others. The inter-religious model thus includes the doubly reciprocal interpretation of one's own and of another's religion by oneself and the other (Camps, 1984). Inter-religious study would, in this sense, be the practice of this model as a function of organized religious education (Selman, 1984). It not only implies the pursuit of mutual understanding, tolerance and respect, but also stands for reflection about oneself and for self-criticism. Religions do not meet in a static way; they have a history and an inner plurality. The requirement for reflection about, and criticism of, the self has to do with the view that one's own religion is also a contextual construct throughout history, which, in retrospect, can even demand partial self-destruction at certain moments. Knitter and Pannikar, who have described the process of 'passing over', show the benefit which this process can have for a more profound understanding of one's own religious tradition (Dunne, 1977).

No matter how one wishes to determine the value of the models described, in our postmodern age there will probably be no 'religion without inter-religious commitment' in future. This, then, reinforces the argument that this aspect will, in future, deserve a place of elemental significance in our considerations of the possibilities of religious education in schools.

Method

In the study under discussion, about 3,000 pupils, 16 or 17 years of age, from secondary schools all over Germany, were invited to complete a questionnaire in spring 2002. In the following analysis we include the responses of 1,912 pupils. The questionnaire contained, among others, sixteen items designed to operationalize the three models of religious education outlined above. We have assumed that there is little distinction between the basic assumptions of the two models defined as mono-religious (soft inclusion) and denominational (hard inclusion) (see Ziebertz, 1993). Furthermore, we assume that the distinction between a mono-religious, multi-religious and inter-religious model may be empirically tested. The multi-religious model should be distinguished from the mono-religious model, as it rejects the notion that one religion could be superior to another and that the criteria of *one* religion could be used for judging others. These models also differ regarding personal commitment. Whereas the multi-religious model not only makes 'inner distance' possible, but believes it to be a necessary method, in the mono-religious model commitment is, if not taken for granted, at least aimed at. From this we can clearly see that the inter-religious model is not further removed from the mono-religious than the multi-religious is; on the contrary, the inter-religious model is closer to the mono-religious model. Nor does the inter-religious model simply stand 'between' the other two, but in a number of respects it offers more than either. It implies (as does the multi-religious model) a distancing of the believer toward his or her own tradition, albeit temporarily and partially, so as to allow an exchange of perspectives to take place. At the same time, it implies commitment without rejecting the normative obligation of dialogue in the light of an exchange of interpretations of the truth. The inter-religious model could be summarized in the following formula: having recognized that no religious tradition can simply extend claims of hegemony over all other religious traditions, we know that each religion needs the others for the interpretation of its own tradition in the present and for the future.

Items conceptually linked to the models described above were rated on a five-point Likert scale (Likert, 1932) of *agree strongly, agree, not certain, disagree* and *disagree strongly*. We need to make explicit that this scale system not only records values obtained for the three working models, but also represents a potential for the empirical recognition of new models within the continuum between the mono-religious and multi-religious models and, indeed, between any other models. It is to be expected that the pupils questioned will not be unequivocally in favour of one particular model and reject all the others. Perhaps none of the models appeals to them, or perhaps all do. Perhaps they see the boundaries we have set between the three models quite differently.

Our main intention in the phrasing of these items was that they should be clearly distinguished from each other and that they should cover a certain spectrum of items. Should there be intermediate forms in the minds of those interviewed they are not excluded, and can become apparent should the total spectrum be large enough. We think that this will prove to be the case when the relevant literature is consulted.

Results

We now test our theoretical assumptions against the empirical data. Our first hypothesis proposed that there is a difference between the mono-religious and the denominational model, but that both can be regarded empirically as one element. Our second hypothesis proposed that, in an empirical sense, the three models (mono-religious, multi-religious and inter-religious) could be distinguished one from another. A study from 1994, in which we used the same scale, confirmed these hypotheses (see Ziebertz, 1996). We will test the hypotheses further with the help of factor analysis on the new data.

The results presented in Table 10.1 demonstrate that we are indeed dealing with three factors. The first major factor is created out of the items concerned with 'mono-religious education'. The two elements 'hard inclusive' (MOHA) and 'soft inclusive' (MOSO) combine to form a single construct which represents our notion of mono-religious education (MONO). In the respondents' perception there is no distinction between hard and soft inclusion. The second important factor is formed from the four items of the inter-religious model (INTER). All factor loadings are located in the area of 0.80. The third factor consists of the four items of the multi-religious model (MULTI). One item only reaches a loading of 0.48 and has, moreover, a loading in factor two (INTER), so it has been eliminated. In all three scales the reliability is between good and very good. Thus we can work empirically

Table 10.1 Dimensions of models of religious education (factor analysis – oblimin-rotation)

Item	MONO religious	INTER religious	MULTI religious
(MOHA) My religion contains the one, true light of redemption	0.921		
(MOSO) Compared to other religions, my religion contains the supreme salvation	0.917		
(MOHA) Only in my religion can people attain true salvation	0.914		
(MOHA) Only in my religion do people have access to true redemption	0.907		
(MOSO) Compared to other religions, the deepest truth lies locked in my religion	0.896		
(MOHA) The only way to true salvation is revealed to mankind in my religion	0.896		
(MOSO) My religion is the best way to salvation compared to other religions	0.837		
(MOSO) Compared to my religion, other religions contain only part of the truth	0.775		
(INTER) The real truth can only be discovered in the communication between religions		0.820	0.158
(INTER) Before finding authentic (real) redemption, religions must enter into dialogue with each other		0.830	0.160
(INTER) God may only be found in the meeting between religions		0.755	0.192
(INTER) The way to real salvation can only be found in a dialogue between the religions		0.769	0.191
(MULTI) Religions are equal to each other; they are all directed at the same truth			0.758
(MULTI) There is no difference between religions, they all stem from a longing for God	−0.155		0.736
(MULTI) All religions are equally valuable, they are different paths to the same salvation	−0.223	0.309	0.679
(MULTI) Within religion as a whole, my religion is only one possible way to redemption	−0.204	0.352	0.579
alpha	0.96	0.83	0.73

Note: Method of extraction: Main component analysis. Method of rotation: 'Varimax'. Eigenvalue: factor 1 = 6.7; factor 2 = 3.4; factor 3 = 1.2. Var. = 71%.

from mono-religious, multi-religious and inter-religious models. There is no real difference between these findings and the findings produced from the 1994 data.

First, we have further assumed that there is a difference between the mono-religious and multi-religious models, but also between the mono-religious and inter-religious models. Second, we have assumed that the inter-religious model lies 'closer' to the mono-religious model than the multi-religious one does, because 'inter' always requires a certain degree of commitment. These assumptions can be tested by means of examining the correlations between the three indices.

The correlation coefficient shows a strong association between the multi-religious and inter-religious models (r = +0.49). This correlation is considerably stronger than in the previous study eight years earlier (r = +0.30). This means that both models belong very closely together for today's respondents. There is a statistical probability that the respondents who endorse one model also endorse the other relevant model.

That there is a negative association between the multi-religious and mono-religious models (r = –0.28) could be presumed after theoretical considerations. The difference between the two models is slightly more strongly pronounced than it had been eight years earlier (r = –0.23). That means that in the eyes of the respondents both models seem to be more incompatible today than they were eight years earlier.

Finally, it has been assumed that there is a difference between the mono-religious and inter-religious models. The hypothetical assumption proposed that this difference would not be as pronounced as between the multi-religious and mono-religious models. Eight years earlier, the correlation was slightly positive (r = +0.14); now it is reversed and lies in the negative area (r = –0.06). Our theoretical assumption is reflected fully in the 1994 outcome, but only partially in that of 2002. Today, the mono-religious model seems to be isolated from the other two. However, the inter-religious model is on the whole less 'distant' from the mono-religious model than is the case for the multi-religious model. From that point of view, the theoretical consideration that 'multi-religious' is more strongly differentiated than is 'inter-religious' from 'mono-religious' holds true. The shifts within the eight-year comparison period are nevertheless striking. What does that mean for religious commitment, which is implicit in the inter-religious model and which should justify the proximity of this model to the mono-religious one? We may assume that fewer and fewer respondents consider it necessary to express commitment in terms of exclusivity or inclusivity. It appears that diversity, in and for itself, is the platform from which accord and unity are sought. This shows itself in that, for the respondents, 'inter-religious' corresponds strongly with 'multi-religious'. With this change, are we looking at a move in the direction of postmodern religiousness?

Before we draw any further conclusions, let us take a look at the mean values presented in Table 10.2, which compares the scores recorded in 2002 with the scores recorded on the same scales by the earlier study, conducted in 1994. The analysis of the mono-religious model demonstrates that the German students reject this model. In 2002 their response rated 1.89 on a five-point scale. The pupils are critically opposed to the fundamental assumptions of a line of thought that no longer seems plausible to them within the context of contemporary society. The analysis shows that the mono-religious model is now more negatively evaluated than was the case eight years earlier. The shift into the negative part of the scale corresponds to more than half a point (0.55).

In place of the mono-religious model the pupils prefer something rather different. For them the multi-religious model is clearly in the positive range of the scale. To the statement 'all religions are equally valuable, they point to different roads leading to the same salvation' they respond positively, with a mean value of 3.35. Here a comparison with the data from 1994 demonstrates a small shift of 0.07 in the positive direction.

And what do our pupils think of the inter-religious model? Have they discovered any difference at all between the inter-religious model and the other views proffered? The answer is, to some extent, 'yes'. With a value of 3.03 the inter-religious model is valued more positively than the mono-religious model, but not as positively as the multi-religious model. However, the value of 3.03 demonstrates that the inter-religious model is viewed neither positively nor negatively. Here a comparison with the data from 1994 demonstrates a small shift of 0.15 in the negative direction.

Table 10.2 Mean values for the mono-religious, multi-religious and inter-religious models: 1994 and 2002

	MONO		MULTI		INTER	
	mean	sd	mean	sd	mean	sd
German pupils 2002 (n = 1,912)	1.89	0.94	3.35	0.88	3.03	0.91
German pupils 1994 (n = 916)	2.44	0.90	3.28	0.87	3.18	0.88

The above analyses show that German pupils clearly have a preferred model: the multi-religious education model, which excludes considerations of the value and truth of religions. The pupils are less convinced by the inter-religious model, which is concerned with dialogue between the religions. They are even less convinced by the standpoint of commitment reflected in the mono-religious model. They themselves do not want to be too preoccupied with religion. In comparison with the data from 1994, this intention is clearer today. The best way of 'dealing' with religion in education seems to them to be offered by the multi-religious model, which admits to 'interest at a remove'. In 1994 the German pupils, by contrast, registered a 'double peak': for them the inter-religious (an objective approach to religion) and multi-religious model (participation in the inter-religious dialogue) seemed to be nearly of equal importance. The denominational ties are now weaker and the presence of ideological diversity has become the norm.

Let us now link these results to those of another analysis. We want to find out what influence religious self-determination has on the attitude toward the three different models. First, we used two items designed to assess the religiosity of the pupils' mother and father on a five-point scale. Statistically it was possible to put these two items together. We then asked the pupils to assess their own religiosity on a similar scale. A cross-tabulation of both parents' and pupils' religiosity allows five types to be identified, and of the total sample 1,349 pupils could be placed within these types.

- In type 1 both pupils and parents are non-religious (n = 428).
- In type 2 pupils are religious and parents are non-religious (n = 92).
- In type 3 pupils are non-religious and parents are religious (n = 185).
- In type 4 both pupils and parents are religious (n = 564).

- In type 5 both pupils and parents are indifferent to religion (n = 460).

The question is whether and how the evaluation of the three educational models is related to the five religious types. First, we will analyse the mono-religious model, which had a mean value of 1.89 for the whole group. Table 10.3 shows that four sub-groups rate the mono-religious model more negatively than the average. Only group 4 have a less negative attitude, and these are respondents who describe themselves and their parents as religious. There are significant differences between group 4 and all the other groups. Nevertheless, the value of group 4 is also in the negative half of the scale.

Table 10.3 Religious types and the mono-model

	N	mean 1	sd	mean 2	sd
Group 3 pupils are non-religious and parents are religious	185	1.61	0.80		
Group 2 pupils are religious and parents are non-religious	92	1.76	0.89		
Group 1 both parents and pupils are non-religious	428	1.78	0.91		
Group 5 both pupils and parents are indifferent	460	1.80	0.86		
Group 4 both pupils and parents are religious	564			2.17	1.04
significance (Scheffé procedure)		0.34		1.00	

Note: Sub-groups for alpha = .05.

The inter-religious model is evaluated negatively by two groups. First, it is evaluated negatively by pupils who are themselves non-religious and whose parents are religious. This is perhaps because too much commitment is expected in the inter-religious approach. Second, the attitude toward this model is a little less negative among the group of respondents whose parents were also non-religious. The other three groups view the inter-religious model slightly positively. In particular, group 4 (both parents and pupils are religious) are more in accordance with this model. They are at significant odds with the non-religious ones.

Table 10.4 Religious types and the inter-model

	N	mean 1	sd	mean 2	sd
Group 3 pupils are non-religious and parents are religious	185	2.85	0.93		
Group 1 both parents and pupils are non-religious	428	2.91	0.88	2.91	0.88
Group 2 pupils are religious and parents are non-religious	92	3.06	0.94	3.06	0.94
Group 5 both pupils and parents are indifferent	460	3.08	0.88	3.08	0.88
Group 4 both pupils and parents are religious	564			3.14	0.92
significance (Scheffé procedure)		0.12		0.13	

Note: Sub-groups for alpha = .05.

The multi-religious model is viewed positively by all the groups in our typology. There are two groups below the average of 3.35 who both have the same mean-value of 3.24: the group of non-religious pupils in the second and first generation. The largest group, pupils and parents who describe themselves as religious, view the multi-religious model more positively (3.43); on a similar scale there is the group of religiously indifferent pupils and parents (3.45). The group which is the most positive toward the multi-religious model are the 'new-religious' pupils, who describe themselves as religious, although their parents are non-religious. For them, the information-based concepts sound most attractive. There is a significant difference between this and the first two groups.

Table 10.5 Religious types and the multi-model

	N	mean 1	sd	mean 2	sd
Group 1 both parents and pupils are non-religious	428	3.24	0.80		
Group 3 pupils are non-religious and parents are religious	185	3.24	0.88		
Group 4 both parents and pupils are religious	564	3.43	0.93	3.43	0.93
Group 5 both pupils and parents are indifferent	460	3.45	0.85	3.45	0.85
Group 2 pupils are religious and parents are non-religious	92			3.50	0.91
significance (Scheffé procedure)		0.14		0.94	

Note: Sub-groups for alpha = .05.

Conclusion

At the outset we asked what kind of religious education would be provided if pupils themselves were to make the decision. In the introduction, we referred to the social changes which render the tradition of mono-religious education simply no longer plausible for all people. Whatever model of religious education we may have in mind and however we evaluate the results obtained on the basis of this model, the results certainly determine the starting point of our teaching. We can, of course, set ourselves objectives at this initial stage. But these objectives are not arbitrary. The tradition of mono-religious work was culturally embedded in western societies until the nineteenth and the first half of the twentieth century. The process of differentiation and multiculturalization is in progress and includes the religious sector. Under the changed conditions of the times, the mono-religious model of the past cannot simply be revived, as this notion was evaluated too negatively by the pupils. Moreover, we must ask ourselves whether it is at all desirable to revive this notion, even if it were possible.

Theologically, a conception of inter-religiousness could be developed, which both values people's religious self-determination and makes allowances for the necessity of dialogue. In any event, in a comparison between the two, the inter-religious model seemed more worthwhile than the multi-religious model, from a theological viewpoint. We have seen, however, that the respondents rate the multi-religious model most highly. What can be said of the advantages of the multi-religious model, which is the favourite model among the pupils? Pupils inevitably have to know more about the different religions because they live in a multi-religious and globalized society. Knowledge is the basis of education which is geared toward understanding. Knowledge of the major religion of the western world is also necessary, because history cannot be understood without Christianity. The main task of the school is providing knowledge and insight. Insight is more than knowledge because it includes the question 'What does the content mean for me and for others?' Religions can be an important indicator in providing orientation for life, perhaps for a better life. To that end, and from a theological point of view, one should not only be acquainted with the different religions, but should also allow oneself to be affected by their messages. This approach is inherent in religion as religion. If the multi-religious model is to be understood as a reductive conception, however, criticism is justified.

It is very clear that the non-denominational and information-based approach appears to be most attractive to adolescents. One may look around in the religious world and marvel, but one need not commit oneself. Perhaps plurality is experienced so naturally today that one takes it as given and sees no reason to make an issue of that variety in itself. Of course, that is also the concern of the inter-religious model, which is in second position. At least there is no doubt that adolescents judge the mono-religious model negatively without reservation. This approach will, however, be at home to a much lesser extent in the school classroom; it belongs, rather, in the sphere of a church community as part of the catechism or religious instruction. Overall, it should perhaps be observed that personal interest in religion is waning. It appears that among the school population a change of religious outlook is on the way which will have consequences right down to the organization of classes. Religion finds itself in a state of flux, but in what direction this will lead remains an open question.

References

Baal, J. van (1971), *Symbols of Communication: An Introduction to the Anthropological Study of Religion* (Assen, van Gorcum).

Beek, J. van (1982), *Spiegel van de Mens: Religie en Antropologie* (Assen, van Gorcum).

Bruner, J. (1992), *Acts of Meaning* (Cambridge, Mass., Harvard University Press).

Camps, A. (1984), *Partners in Dialogue: Christianity and Other World Religions* (New York, Orbis Books).

Dunne, J. S. (1977), *Search for God in Time and Memory* (New York, University of Notre Dame Press).

Edwards, R. B. (1972), *Reason and Religion* (New York, Thomson Learning).

Eliade, M. (1969), *The Quest: History and Meaning in Religion* (Chicago, Ill., University of Chicago Press).

Habermas, J. (1982), *Theorie des kommunikativen Handelns*, Bd. I–II (Frankfurt, Suhrkamp).

Hick, J. (1982), *God Has Many Names: Britain's New Religious Pluralism* (Louisville, Ky., Westminster John Knox Press).

Knitter, P. (1985), *No Other Name? A Critical Survey of Christian Attitudes toward the World Religions* (New York, Orbis Books).

Krüger, J. S. (1989), *Metatheism: Early Buddhism and Traditional Christian Theism* (Pretoria, UNISA Press).

Likert, R. (1932), 'A technique for the measurement of attitudes', *Archives of Psychology*, 140, 1–55.

Mostert, J. P. (1989), 'Reflections on the future of religion', in G. Pillay (ed.), *The Future of Religion* (Pretoria, UNISA Press), pp. 121–34.

Rahner, K. (1975), *Schriften zur Theologie Bd. 12* (Einsiedeln, Benzinger).

Rahner, K. (1978), *Schriften zur Theologie Bd. 13* (Einsiedeln, Benzinger).

Selman, R. L. (1984), *The Growth of Interpersonal Understanding: Developmental and Clinical Analyses* (New York, Academic Press).

Ven, J. A. van der and Ziebertz, H.-G. (eds) (1994), *Religiöser Pluralismus und Interreligiöses Lernen (Religious Pluralism and Inter-religious Learning)* (Weinheim/Kampen, DSV/Kok).

Ven, J. A. van der and Ziebertz, H.-G. (1995), 'Jugendliche in multikulturellem und multireligiösem kontext', *Religionspädagogische Beiträge*, 35, 151–67.

Waldenfels, H. (1987), 'Ist der christliche Glaube der einzig wahre?', *Stimmen der Zeit*, 112, 463–75.

Ziebertz, H.-G. (1993), 'Religious pluralism and religious education', *Journal of Empirical Theology*, 6, 82–9.

Ziebertz, H.-G. (1996), 'Religion in religious education', *Panorama: International Journal of Comparative Religious Education and Values*, 8, 135–45.

Ziebertz, H.-G. (2002), 'Interreligiöses Lernen', in F. Schweitzer, R. Englert, U. Schwab and H.-G. Ziebertz (eds), *Entwürfe Einer Pluralitätsfähigen Religionspädagogik* (Freiburg, Gütersloh), pp. 121–43.

Ziebertz, H.-G., Kalbheim, B. and Riegel, U. (2003), *Religiöse Signaturen Heute* (Freiburg, Gütersloh).

11

Faith in God and Christian religious practice among adolescents in Norway

ERLING BIRKEDAL

Summary

This chapter presents a research project concerned with faith in God and experience of Christian religious practice among 13- to 15-year-olds in an urban part of Norway. The focus is on the interaction between their faith in God and their experience of church-related religion within the home and the local community. Quantitative data were provided by a questionnaire survey of 306 pupils, and qualitative data were provided by 30 in-depth interviews. The quantitative data demonstrated that relatively few adolescents (about one in seven) have experience of church-related religion, apart from religious education in schools. The qualitative data have been employed to illustrate three styles of faith among adolescents: conventional faith (a faith in accordance with what the Church teaches), enquiring faith (critical, but related to conventional faith) and movement away from conventional faith (which may also mean an alternative kind of faith).

Introduction

There are a considerable number of activities taking place in the field of communicating Christian knowledge and Christian faith to children and young people. Such activities are going on in various institutions (such as the family, kindergartens, schools and churches), as well as in the mass media. Many religious educationalists within the churches have traditionally been concerned with the transmission of knowledge, and with the nature of the context for communication with children and young people. There has not been the same degree of systematic research to find out how children and young people themselves experience the Christian religion and Christian religious practice. The motivation for this research project was, therefore, to obtain more information about the receiving side of this communication process. Further, the aim is to gain insights which can contribute to improving the communication between the young people and those who are imparting religious knowledge. There is, then, a religious education motivation for the research.

The main focus is on faith in God and experience of Christian religious practice. This does not, however, mean that it is assumed that young people's faith in God, or their religious concepts, in a broad sense, are entirely tied up with imparted knowledge or experience of such a practice. Such a direct connection, or correspondence, between the contents of people's religiousness and the religious expressions and the religious behaviour which is exercised under the Church's direction, would be narrowing down the religious field. I consider that religiousness, as such, and to a certain extent faith in God, exist relatively independently of institutionalized religion. But an institution (like the Church) can give direction and content to this faith. Or, to put it differently, some people can associate themselves with a faith such as the Church presents, but this does not exclude others from having a different form of faith in God. In this connection what interests us is to look at the interaction between the faith that the adolescents actually possess and the experiences they have of Christian religious practice.

This approach is formulated through two questions. The first question is: How does the interaction function between, on the one hand, young people's faith in God and, on the other hand, their experiences of church-related religion, from both the family and the local neighbourhood? The second question is: What pedagogical challenges will this interaction actualize for church-related educational practice? The first question provides the starting point for analysis and interpretation of empirical methods, while the second question provides a further basis for discussion on this topic. The theoretical understanding and perspective underlying the methodology and the analysis stems from the work of Berger and Luckmann's sociology of knowledge (1991).

There are two main issues of concern for the current research. The first issue concerns what the young people say about their own belief in God, attitudes and religious opinions. Concerning faith in God, this research examines the degree of confidence of faith, contents, practice and involvement attached to this faith in God. The second issue concerns the encounters the young people have had, and are having, with church-related religion and religious practice. This includes practices like saying evening prayers, using grace at mealtimes, reading the Bible at home, attending Sunday school, taking part in Christian children's groups and going to church services. Here we are concerned with the religious practices that are supported or exercised by the Church. The interaction between faith in God and experience with church-related religion is viewed from three different aspects: cognitive, emotional and social.

Method

This project is based on original data collected from adolescents in the central eastern part of Norway (Oslo and the neighbouring districts of the capital). The empirical data were collected over a period of about two and a half years during the mid-1990s, and have been described by Birkedal (2001).

First, there was a quantitative survey (questionnaire) administered to 306 13-year-olds (described as the preliminary survey). This sample comprises all pupils in certain selected forms from a number of different schools. Based on this questionnaire survey there was a qualitative study of 30 pupils, using interviews (the main survey) and two follow-up questionnaires over the next two years. The 30 interviewees were chosen on the basis of their different church-related experiences and faith in God.

A number of different types of analyses have been used, as appropriate to each phase of the data collection. The aim of the interviews was to obtain as complete an understanding as possible of the individual young people. This resulted in some of the young people being analysed and presented in greater depth.

Results

Quantitative analysis

The analysis of the answers to the preliminary questionnaire presents an overview of the respondents. For example, 53% never say evening prayers, while 12% seldom say evening prayers, 23% sometimes say evening prayers and 7% often say evening prayers. These findings are reflected in the percentages who never attend church (55%), occasionally attend church (41%) and often attend church (4%). A total of 13% have attended Sunday school to a greater or lesser extent, while 20% have attended a children's choir. Admittedly, this is a relatively superficial analysis of the adolescents' experience with church-related religion. However, as an introductory survey it provides an overview of the variation we find in this group of adolescents. Further data from the quantitative survey are displayed in Table 11.1.

Table 11.1 1994 questionnaire

Item	Disagree %	Unsure %	Agree %
I believe in God	60	27	13
I am a Christian	71	21	8
Jesus was a good man and a great person	6	41	53
Jesus died for my sins and is my saviour	35	49	16
Jesus shows us that God is love	17	56	27
There is no certainty that Jesus ever lived	19	35	46

Overall the data show that relatively few (one in seven) of the adolescents have experiences with church-related religion and church-related religious practice, apart from religious education in school. Church-related religious practice in the family, like saying evening prayers, using grace at mealtimes and reading the Bible, seems to be less widespread among these adolescents than has been found in previous surveys in Norway (Winsnes, 1981). A confident faith in God is also less widespread among these 13-year-olds than has been found among the Norwegian population generally (Lund, 1999). One in eight say that they believe in God, by ticking off the top two values on a five-point scale about degree of confidence in faith in God.

The questionnaire clearly shows that faith in God among the 13-year-olds is more than a conventional faith maintained by the Church. In this analysis of the adolescents three forms of faith are found. First, there is conventional faith (a faith in accordance with what the Church teaches). Second, there is enquiring faith (critical, but related to conventional faith). Third, there is movement away from conventional faith (which may also mean an alternative kind of faith).

In the following analysis the discussion examines the interaction, or the interplay, between faith in God and experiences, according to the following approaches. First, experience with church-related religion from childhood, in relation to faith in God at the age of 13, is discussed. Second, the maintenance or loss of faith in God during the ages of 13 to 15, seen from a socialization perspective and from an individual perspective respectively, is discussed.

To put some 'flesh and blood' on the questionnaire analyses and reflections we will get to know three individuals in more depth from the data collected during the interviews: Berit, Cecilie and Arne represent each of the three groups mentioned above. Berit provides an example of conventional faith (in accordance with what the Church teaches). Cecilie provides an example of enquiring faith (critical, but related to conventional faith). Arne provides an example of a movement away from conventional faith (which may also mean an alternative kind of faith).

Berit: conventional faith

Berit grew up in a Christian family and often went to church services during childhood. In adolescence, she experienced tensions between the faith she had been taught and her personal faith.

As a 13-year-old Berit says that she does not believe in all parts of the Bible. She finds problematic those parts that seem, to her, to oppose a scientific view of the world: 'I don't believe in Adam and Eve and all that . . . I don't really know, all this is difficult.' She cannot accept Bible stories which she feels to be 'incredibly illogical', examples being Jesus' miracles, resurrection from the dead and the feeding of the five thousand. This conflict does not, however, lead to a rejection of her faith in God: 'I believe in God, but not in the rest of Christianity.'

Although Berit has grown up within a believing fellowship, which she attended with her parents, she does not feel completely at home in the church congregation:

> When I was little, then we always went to church down here, and my parents go quite often, or sometimes sort of, even now, but whether I

belong there . . . not really. Because I sort of, I don't really like it there in a way, it's nothing really special, I think.

Berit feels that it is difficult to take a stand on issues of faith and religion in front of her friends: 'There are many people of my age who don't know whether they believe in God, and I think there are very few who dare tell anyone if they are Christian.'

As a 14-year-old, Berit recognizes that her faith in God has become more secure. She feels that she has changed, and states that the reason for this is that she is maturing: 'I have thought a lot about what I believe as I have become older and more mature.' Her religious practice has also been rekindled. Now she participates in church confirmation classes and finds this to be both positive and interesting. Now she 'sometimes' goes to a church youth club, while at 13 she said that she attended a church youth club 'extremely seldom'.

As a 15-year-old, Berit changes her self-definition. She is now secure in her faith in God. She is also almost sure she would describe herself as 'religious' and 'Christian'. When asked to explain the reason for this change, she refers to her experience of a friend who was ill, which made her pray and think about God: 'One of my closest friends was in a coma and might have died. It made me pray *a lot* more, and think about God more than I usually do.' This experience with illness has clearly made a strong impression on her and influenced her behaviour. She also found close fellowship with her friends in this challenging situation, and they also prayed together.

Berit is one of those who have had experience of Christian practice from childhood, like evening prayers and participation in Sunday school. When we view all the respondents together (n = 306), we see a definite positive correlation between such experience and faith in God. Among those who have such experiences, there are significantly more who show faith in God than among those who do not have such experiences. At the same time, we see that among those who say that they have a confident faith in God, there are also many who do not have such experience of Christian practice from childhood. So faith in God may not be explained only through contact with Christian religious practice during childhood. A combination of, for instance, experience of evening prayers and participation in Sunday school can have a real impact on the development of faith in God.

Berit's story demonstrates that relationships with friends and the social environment are important at this age. The relationship between a young person's own faith in God and a close friend's faith in God is confirmed when we look at the overall responses from the young people interviewed (n = 30), at the ages of 13 and 15 respectively. We see that, even in the small sample of the young people interviewed, there is a harmonization from 13 to 15 years of age. There is more correlation between one's own faith and one's best friend's faith at the age of 15 than there is at the age of 13.

A verification of the importance of the social environment can also be found by looking at moving house and at how long the young person has been living at the same place. Those who have a strong degree of faith in God have lived up to one year or more than three years at the same place. This seems to indicate that the adolescents either 'bring their faith with them', or that they have acquired their faith in a stable environment. Changing friends and environment at this age, however, seems to make young people vulnerable with regards to maintaining faith in God.

There is one further reflection on the relationship between the adolescents' faith and the parents' faith. The analysis shows that experiences of religious practice within the family, and having parents who themselves have faith in God, may have a basic relevance for the adolescent's own faith in God. But the correlation is greater between non-believing parents and non-believing children, than between believing parents and believing children. Unbelief in God seems, so to speak, to be inherited more easily than belief in God.

Cecilie: enquiring faith

As a 13-year-old, Cecilie is a girl who has a strong faith in God, but she is not at home in the church. She has little experience of Christian religious practice from her family. From Cecilie's own words about faith in God and about confirmation classes we find that her image of God is not a conventional one. For her, God is no more than 'someone to talk to. I might as well have been praying to Odin or Thor (or other gods).' God is 'a kind of mind I can talk to, just like I'm talking to myself in a way, but to another person'.

As a 14-year-old, Cecilie says that she quite definitely believes in God. She has a concept of God which corresponds to what she said above, but now she elaborates on what God means to her more fully: 'God gives security. He/she is a supreme power I may pray to, thank, seek comfort from, be mad with, hate and love. God gives a wholeness to my soul.' She defines here more precisely the substance of her faith in God:

> My God cannot be compared with the God who is in the Bible. That is perhaps why I don't like what we learn at confirmation classes. Things lose their soul when someone gives it a particular meaning, solution, reason, and so on. My God is mine, but also everybody else's. He is the God of the one who believes in him. He never punishes, only supports me. Always wants the best for me whatever I do. But also reminds me what is right or wrong. Then it's up to me to be independent and choose.

This experience of a faith in God, which is experienced as an alternative to a church-related faith, contrasts with her experiences with confirmation classes. She experiences confirmation classes as boring. Toward the end of her confirmation classes she says: 'I haven't learnt a shit! I've actually got a more sceptical attitude to Christianity than before I started!!'

Clearly Cecilie has an emotionally rooted faith in God. Her faith is important and meaningful to her. Her faith in God is a central factor of her personality and creates security. But 'the faith is loose', to quote a Norwegian book-title (Engedal and Sveinall, 2000). She does not relate to the faith which the Church teaches.

Cecilie is not the only one having a strained relationship with what the Church teaches. I noticed two different attitudes to the Church among adolescents. They may be opposing views, but at the same time they supplement each other. According to one view, the Church is seen as static and unchangeable. The cathedral is there and has 'always' been there. It is something frightening and old-fashioned, something not for young modern people. According to the other view, the Church represents something secure and stable. In this particular church building, mother and father were christened and got married. Here my great-grandparents or grandparents are buried. Here I was christened and here I am going to be confirmed. In this view their feelings are linked to the particular church building, the geographical place.

Cecilie's sayings also remind us that we no longer have only Christianity in our society. We also have 'other religions and world-views', and so-called neo-religious currents and movements (even though many of these are not necessarily all that new).

Cecilie is one of those who maintain a faith in God, as 'her own kind of faith in God', independent of a church-related fellowship, and seemingly without any other spiritual fellowship either. This may be understood on the grounds of, among other things, the fact that faith in God is important for her and constitutes a personal security. Such a theory is also confirmed by considering the responses of the pupils interviewed (n = 30). When we see a change of faith in God (13–15 years), we see that those adolescents who experience faith in God as a personal security factor are the ones who are more likely to maintain their faith when they are 15 years of age.

Arne: movement away from conventional faith

As a 13-year-old Arne has a faith in God. At this stage in life Arne assumes that he will get confirmed into the Church. He gives his faith as his reason: 'I believe in God, even though I don't go to church all that often, only for Christmas, but I intend to go on being a Christian.' Arne had great confidence in his teacher at primary school, but he had little experience with Christian practice. When asked about his religious faith, Arne refers to what he had been taught at school (or what he has interpreted this teaching to be about): 'He is probably the one who has created everything, then . . . I think, and controls most things. . . . The Bible probably says that you go to hell if you are bad . . . and stuff like that.' His arguments are not presented as if they represent a personal conviction.

It is, therefore, difficult for Arne to maintain his faith into adolescence. Now, at the beginning of secondary school, Arne struggles with intellectual problems concerning his faith in Jesus: 'No, I haven't really quite understood what all that. . . . He died for what people did or for what he did sort of . . . I can't really see that he has done anything wrong, actually. Sort of don't really quite understand it.' Arne shows great confidence, generally, in what the Church represents and in what the representatives of the Church are imparting: 'What they say is probably for the most part correct, I assume.'

As a 14-year-old Arne seems a bit embarrassed when confronted with the question about God, and now says that: 'I'm not very concerned with what to believe in. I don't think about it.' As his reason for this relatively radical change, his own comment is: 'To believe in God, I have to see or experience something with God first. I haven't done so yet . . . I have never seen the faintest trace of God.' He is a rationalist and seeks evidence of God's existence. The concepts of God he has brought with him from childhood are not credible any more when confronting the world which he now experiences.

Arne has a cognitively acquired faith in God. During childhood he had learned about God, and at the age of 13 he had a conventional faith and displayed confidence in significant adults who shared such a faith. Now, however, he has no one with whom he can establish a conversation about faith in his adolescence. In his 'age of doubt' he finds no place for his childlike faith in God, and so he must give this up.

Conclusion

This analysis has distinguished between three forms of faith, characterized as conventional faith, enquiring faith and movement away from conventional faith, possibly toward an alternative kind of faith. We see that there is a difference between those with a conventional faith in God and those with an unconventional faith in God, as to what is significant for maintaining their faith in early adolescence. Conventional Christian faith in God is usually formed and maintained within a Christian faith community. Personal relationships, not least to others of the same age-group, and a sense of acceptance are important for a continued participation in such communities. Those who maintain a conventional faith in God, without any considerable participation in faith communities, are persons who seem to be independent and who have a cognitive approach to and rooting for their faith. For those who have an unconventional faith in God, the relationship to the Church or to organized faith communities will have little or no relevance. On the contrary, it may seem irritating. For these young people, the emotional verification and the experience of God's presence is important, and they usually emphasize that they 'believe in their own way'.

More than anything else, the data demonstrate that individuals have their own unique life and faith history. In order to understand what happens to faith during the period between the ages of 13 and 15, we have to consider the connection between, on the one hand, the new experiences obtained during adolescence itself and, on the other hand, the personal experiences obtained earlier from childhood. Maintaining faith in God in early adolescence seems to correlate with the extent to which new experiences are able to legitimate their faith or make it relevant to them. The basis for faith to be relevant is not, however, the same for every person. Adolescents will feel faith is relevant only when there is contact between, on the one hand, their personal conditions and the rooting of their faith in God from childhood and, on the other hand, the experiences which they have in early adolescence. For adolescents who have acquired faith through knowledge and intellectual reflection (cognitive aspect), a lack of conversation and reflection about faith will presumably be a decisive factor for their faith. For those whose faith is at the centre of their personality, where their faith implies a psychological security (emotional aspect), new affirmations of security in their faith in God will contribute to the maintenance of their faith. Where adolescents have acquired their faith in God in social fellowship with other believers (social aspect), the maintaining of such a fellowship, and contact with other believers, is important for the maintenance of their faith. Those who have the greatest potential for maintaining their faith seem to be those who have their faith in God rooted in the cognitive, in the emotional and in the social, and who also receive a variety of experiences from church-related practice which stimulate and affirm all three aspects.

Pedagogical challenges

Starting with the theoretical perspective and the interpretation of the empirical research, immediate challenges arise for the Church's educational practice. I arrange the pedagogical challenges into three groups. The first concern is that the teacher must necessarily relate to the adolescents where they actually are. Teachers must get to know the context of education. This implies, for instance, that we cannot look at young people of a certain age as a homogeneous group, neither with regard to faith in God nor with regard to their experiences. Differentiation and individualization become the keywords here.

The second main concern is that teachers should arrange for a kind of communication and education which can give Christian faith in God such a legitimacy that it is felt to be relevant, and can be integrated as part of the adolescents' set of world-views. It is important for this not to be a one-way communication. We should listen to each adolescent's experience in life, and arrange for interpretation and understanding in the light of Christian faith in God. Here teachers and the young people are on the same level, and can seek meaning and understanding together. The Church as 'mediator' in the adolescents' 'faith negotiations' and 'existentialist hermeneutics' gives the keywords here.

Third, there is a challenge to the Church, and to other institutions, to consider their pedagogical activity as socialization. There is only a small chance of adolescents getting an experience of religion and religious practice, because the fellowship of believers is largely invisible to most adolescents. This is a problem and a challenge. It implies rather difficult conditions for imparting the faith to a wide group of children and young people. The challenge is to arrange visible faith environments, and for each adolescent to have access to people who are able to communicate what it may mean to have a faith in God. Model-learning (and apprenticeship, modelled on the crafts) and contextual education are the keywords here.

The educational challenges can be gathered together under two categories: longitudinal perspective and a wide perspective. A longitudinal perspective means that teachers are challenged to communicate with each person, based on that person's earlier experiences, considered from those aspects of faith in which the person is rooted (meeting the person, so to speak, 'on their own ground'). A wide perspective means that teachers are challenged to arrange a wide variety of experiences for adolescents, so that their faith can be rooted in all the three aspects mentioned, cognitive, emotional and social. I describe this kind of thinking as 'educational practice based on experiences'. It is important to talk *with* young people, not just *to* them, from a dialogue perspective, in order for the faith to create meaning and relevance. It is important to arrange for adolescents to be able to deal with their religious emotions, to help them integrate their religious experience with their personality. It is also important to establish good relationships during the socialization process which takes place in education. In church-related contexts such a pedagogical theory makes no clear-cut distinction between education and welfare work; the pedagogical practice may, in some cases, be termed a 'welfare educational practice'. In summary, I formulate the pedagogical ideal as an educational welfare practice based on experiences, where individuals are seen in their right context, and where the cognitive, the emotional and the social aspects of church religion will all be activated.

References

Berger, P. L. and Luckmann, T. (1991), *The Social Construction of Reality: A Treatise in the Sociology of Knowledge* (London, Penguin).

Birkedal, E. (2001), *'Noen ganger tror jeg på Gud, men ...' En undersøkelse av gudstro og erfaring med religiøs praksis i tidlig ungdomsalder* (Trondheim, Tapir Akademisk Forlag).

Engedal, L. G. and Sveinall, A. T. (2000), *Troen er løs* (Trondheim, Trondheim Egede Institutt, Tapir Akademisk Forlag).

Lund, M. (1999), *Undersøkelse om Religion* (Bergen, NSD-rapport), p. 115.

Winsnes, O. G. (1981), *Familie og Religiøs sosialisering* (Trondheim, Universitetet i Trondheim, Religionsvitenskapelig Institutt).

12

Adolescent attitudes to 'the other': citizenship and religious education in England

JUDITH EVERINGTON

Summary

This chapter draws on data from a life-history study of trainee secondary religious education teachers and from three subsequent cohorts of trainees. All trainees undertook the same one-year, postgraduate initial teacher-education course. The study, which began in 1997, has identified a number of themes which appear to be common for all four cohorts. The chapter will consider themes which have emerged under the following broad headings: ideals and aspirations, difficulties and dilemmas, negative perceptions of and attitude toward religion, pupils' view that minority ethnic communities 'have nothing to do with them' and pupils' view that minority ethnic communities are a threat to 'British people'. Each of these themes is illustrated by the voices of the trainee teachers.

Introduction

'But what advantage can there be in bringing in citizenship when we already have religious education, and personal and social education, and there isn't even enough room on the timetable to do these things properly?' (trainee religious education teacher, 2001)

From August 2002, secondary schools in England were required to teach a new national curriculum subject entitled 'citizenship'. At the beginning of an initial teacher-training session on the introduction of citizenship and its relationship to religious education, one trainee posed the above question. This chapter has been written in answer to her question and as a contribution to the current debate about whether citizenship should be seen as a threat to, or as an opportunity for, religious education. While some religious educators have viewed the new subject as a competitor for time and curriculum content (Saint Gabriel's Trust, 2000: 67–9), it will be argued here that citizenship education is needed, not only by pupils, but also by teachers of religious education. At the same time, those responsible for meeting the new requirements and for teaching the new subject have much to learn from the experiences and insights of teachers of religious education.

These arguments will be developed through an examination of the ideals and aspirations of beginning religious education teachers, and through the difficulties and dilemmas that these teachers experience in attempting to pursue these ideals in the secondary school classroom. It will be suggested that many of these teachers' ideals and many of the aims that they are required to pursue are similar to, or identical with, those promoted in citizenship. Yet beginning teachers often find that their attempts to pursue these ideals and aims are frustrated. Among the obstacles that beginning teachers encounter are the attitudes and values of the pupils and of school managers, and lack of time. The introduction of citizenship brings with it opportunities to tackle these problems and to meet some long-standing needs. However, a recognition of the problems that religious education teachers face and a commitment to addressing these is also crucial to the success of citizenship.

As a first step in the exploration of this mutually beneficial 'partnership', it is important to clarify what citizenship means in the context of the national curriculum for England and to highlight those areas of shared interest and concern.

Citizenship in the national curriculum for England
The legal requirements for citizenship at secondary level (11–18 years) are set out in 'programmes of study' which state the knowledge, skills and understanding to be taught at Key Stage 3 (11–14 years) and Key Stage 4 (14–16 years). Overviews of the contents of the programmes include the statement that pupils will study 'the legal, political, religious, social, constitutional and economic systems that influence their lives and communities', and that they will 'learn about fairness, social justice, respect for diversity at school,

local, national and global level, and through taking part in community activities'. The programmes themselves require pupils to know about and understand 'the diversity of national, regional, religious and ethnic identities in the United Kingdom and the need for mutual respect and understanding'. They must also be 'taught to use their imagination to consider other people's experiences and be able to think about, express and explain views that are not their own' (Department for Education and Employment and Qualifications and Curriculum Authority, 1999: 14–15).

To assist schools in the planning and delivery of citizenship, the Qualifications and Curriculum Authority (QCA) has produced a guidance booklet (Qualifications and Curriculum Authority, 2000). This includes the 'general teaching requirement' that citizenship 'should be part of a school's celebration of the diversity of its population; it should include consideration of local issues (such as particular manifestations of racism and its removal) as well as national ones . . . In addition, schools will need strategies to ensure that citizenship reflects and values all social and ethnic groups, for example by providing opportunities for pupils to consider their identities, those of others and cultural attributes' (Qualifications and Curriculum Authority, 2000: 5).

Schools are advised that the implementation of the programmes of study requires a whole-school approach. Although there will be some citizenship-dedicated lessons, each subject will make a contribution through its content and through the teaching and learning approaches employed. In the recommended 'concepts approach' it is suggested that key concepts, including equality and diversity, should be used to identify headings that link aspects of knowledge and understanding, the discussion of current issues and the skill of participation and action required in the programmes of study. These include 'human rights (including anti-racism)' and 'respect and tolerance (including conflict resolution)' (Qualifications and Curriculum Authority, 2000: 20). In the 'enquiry approach' it is suggested that pupils address questions such as 'Why is it important to be tolerant and to resolve conflict fairly?', 'Who should people care about?', and 'How have the diverse national, regional, religious and ethnic identities in the United Kingdom come about?' (Qualifications and Curriculum Authority, 2000: 21). One of the proposed advantages of this approach is that it 'offers opportunities to make connections between local and global action in ways that are challenging and relevant to pupils' lives and communities'.

In the programmes of study for and guidance on citizenship there are numerous references to the contributions of the various national curriculum subjects. However, there are no references to religious education in the former, and only three brief references to religious education in the latter. In this *Initial Guidance for Schools*, it is suggested that religious education will make its contribution through the examination of the 'diversity of cultures and religions' in the United Kingdom (Qualifications and Curriculum Authority, 2000: 13), and that religious education teachers will make links to citizenship through their exploration of 'the religious and moral beliefs, values and practices, which underpin social and cultural concerns, policies and developments' (Qualifications and Curriculum Authority, 2000: 14).

The low profile given to religious education suggests that the government does not see, or wish to promote, a close relationship between citizenship and religious education. So, despite the assurances of the Qualifications and Curriculum Authority's principal manager for citizenship and religious education that religious education has an important contribution to make (Keast, 2000), the message relayed to schools is that religious education has less of a role and less to offer than other subjects. This 'message' is unhelpful to religious educators, who are made to feel defensive about their position and reluctant to consider the potential benefits of offloading some of their responsibilities on to other shoulders. It is also unhelpful to those responsible for finding effective ways of delivering the citizenship curriculum and for advising on teaching problems and possibilities. It is unhelpful in this case because it obscures the fact that a sizeable piece of the ground that has been staked out for the new subject has already been well trodden in religious education, and that many of its pitfalls have already been encountered by religious education teachers.

Aims of religious education in relation to citizenship

Religious education has long been concerned with the knowledge, attitudes and skills associated with citizenship. Although space does not permit a detailed justification of this claim, we might note that since the 1970s religious education has been operating with aims which reflect three major concerns (Everington, 2000). These appear in the government's Model Syllabuses for Religious Education (School Curriculum and Assessment Authority, 1994) and the legally binding local agreed syllabuses for religious education. They can be summarized as: a concern to provide a knowledge and understanding of the 'principal' religions represented in the United Kingdom; a concern to promote understanding of and respect for people whose cultures and beliefs are different from one's own, and to promote a positive attitude toward living in a plural society; and a concern to promote the personal, moral and spiritual development of individual pupils. The first two of these concerns are clearly related to the requirements and recommendations for citizenship. When we consider that the third is generally understood to involve the exploration of human experiences which raise fundamental questions about, for example, identity, equality, justice, human rights, relationships and living in communities (see Baumfield, Bowness, Cush and Miller, 1994; Grimmitt, 1987), the relationship to citizenship becomes equally clear.

I have argued elsewhere that it is not possible for religious educators to pursue all of these concerns and to manage the tensions between them effectively (Everington, 2000). There has long been a need to be realistic about what a single subject, allocated minimal time in the school week, can achieve. This is an argument to which I will return later in this discussion. However, at this point it must be acknowledged that the existence of a close correspondence between the aims of religious education and those of citizenship does not, in itself, provide evidence of religious education teachers' commitment to and experience of educating for citizenship. In order to provide this evidence, I will move on to examine data which suggest that people entering the religious education profession are motivated by ideals which are very much in tune with the aims of citizenship, and that they have been, and are, grappling with the possibilities and problems of achieving such aims.

Religious education teachers and citizenship
In the religious education literature, there is a great deal of comment on the 'dreams', aims and aspirations of religious education teachers, and on the difficulties that they experience in attempting to pursue these. While much of this comment relates, directly or

indirectly, to those aspects of citizenship outlined above, it relies, for the most part, on the personal experiences, anecdotes and impressions of the commentator. Very few empirical studies have been undertaken (Sikes and Everington, 2001). In this chapter, an attempt will be made to draw together the empirical evidence that does exist. In order to broaden the limited view provided by quantitative studies and by research which ignores the teachers' perspective or is only indirectly concerned with the situation of religious education, reference will be made to the findings of a life-history study of beginning religious education teachers and to data associated with this study.

Method

In 1997, a group of trainee secondary religious education teachers, undergoing a one-year, postgraduate initial teacher-education course, were invited to participate in a life-history study. The study, which followed the trainees through the course and into their first year in a teaching post, aimed to examine the experience of becoming a religious education teacher through the professional and personal lives of 17 people (Everington and Sikes, 2001; Sikes and Everington, 2001). Trainees were asked to participate in a series of individual, semi-structured interviews and to provide written reflections on their experience of becoming religious education teachers. At the beginning and end of the course they wrote down what they wanted to achieve as teachers of religious education and what they saw as the major challenges to achieving their goals. After their first school placement they produced a 2,000-word reflection on their experiences, which included an analysis of pupils' attitudes toward and responses to religious education, and an account of how the trainee teachers responded and would wish in the future to respond to these.

In order to provide contextual material for the study, trainees who took the course in the following three years were asked to complete the same written exercises as the life-history group. Material provided by these trainees has been analysed in relation to material from the life-history group. This has enabled us to identify a number of 'themes', reflecting experiences which appear to be common to all four cohorts. All told, a total of 68 trainees participated in the project, 17 enrolling in 1997, 17 in 1998, 15 in 1999 and 19 in 2000.

Although it is not possible to generalize from the findings of the study and associated data, they provide a means of identifying issues which can be discussed in relation to the findings of quantitative research and larger-scale studies, and the views and recommendations of commentators from within and outside the religious education profession. Quotations and extracts from our data also provide a means of illustrating the ideals, aspirations, difficulties and dilemmas of religious education teachers which, although referred to in some other studies, are rarely presented through the teachers' own accounts.

Results

Ideals and aspirations

One of the themes that we identified in our analysis of trainees' aims and motivations to teach was a commitment to aims associated with citizenship education, and we are not alone in recognizing such a commitment. In the past six years, two quantitative studies of religious education teachers' aims and motivations have been undertaken. Astley, Francis, Burton and Wilcox (1997: 183) found that when teachers were asked to rate various learning outcomes in terms of their importance as aims of religious education, 'respecting other people's right to hold beliefs different from their own' and 'becoming more tolerant of other religions and world-views' were selected as two of the four most important aims of the subject. Nationwide research, conducted for the Religious Education Teacher Recruitment Initiative project, found that in both 1999–2000 and 2000–1 trainees' responses to an open-ended question about motivation to teach religious education included five 'categories' related to the nature and aims of the subject. Of these, the most popular was 'religious education is a subject highly relevant to life'. In second place was 'belief in the need for cultural education and for tolerance'. Analysis of the 2000–1 data revealed an increase in the number of respondents who were motivated by such a belief (Religious Education Teacher Recruitment Initiative, 2000, 2001).

In our life-history study we also found that the trainees' reasons for entering the profession and their aspirations as teachers of religious education were strongly related to that aspect of citizenship education that has to do with the reduction of prejudice and the promotion of intercultural understanding and respect. The following quotations, from course application forms and written responses provided at the beginning of the course, indicate the nature of their statements:

> I would like to provide an objective view of the six main religions, ensuring children had enough of each not to be prejudiced against a person of another. (Claire)

> I want to teach the six main world religions because people do not know anything/enough about them and that is where prejudice starts. (Caroline)

> I would like to teach a religious education that develops objectivism, tolerance and understanding of others' beliefs. That develops the person to live at ease in a society made up of many different facets. (Clive)

> It will be important to establish in pupils' minds the importance of a multi-faith understanding so as to further a more harmonious society. (James)

> I strongly believe that good religious education is vital in order that cultural differences are better accepted. (Rebecca)

During interviews conducted in the first weeks of the course, a number of trainees chose to talk about their commitment to the reduction of prejudice and the promotion of intercultural understanding and respect. Close reading of the transcripts, together with data provided before and at the beginning of the course, indicated that within this theme there were some significant differences in the trainees' primary concerns.

Some trainees were concerned primarily with contributing to the development of a harmonious multicultural society by providing the knowledge and understanding to enable pupils to manage their working and social relationships with people of 'other cultures', or by encouraging pupils to view people of differing backgrounds as 'neighbours' who, despite their obvious differences, have the same fundamental needs, concerns and values. For others the primary concern was to combat negative attitudes toward and promote respect for religion, religious traditions and the beliefs and practices of religious people. Proposed strategies for achieving this included encouraging pupils to recognize the existence of conflicting 'truth claims' and to develop the skills and attitudes to respectfully agree or disagree with these. Other trainees appeared to be primarily concerned with the development of the individual child, by providing pupils with the self-confidence, awareness and skills to question negative stereotypes and think for themselves, or by enabling the development of 'healthy' individuals by encouraging attitudes of respect and tolerance.

We found that for those trainees who expressed a commitment to these aims initially, commitment increased during the course and, for some, it became stronger during the first year in post. However, this strengthening of commitment was not an indicator of success. Rather, when they began teaching, many of the trainees found it very difficult to pursue their ideals and realize their ambitions. Their accounts and reflections suggest that the difficulties and obstacles that they encountered were not simply the result of their inexperience, lack of skills or trainee status.

Difficulties and dilemmas

A dominant and recurring theme in the difficulties reported by the life-history group and by subsequent cohorts of trainees was pupils' negative attitudes and views, and a lack of time to address these effectively. In recently published guidance for beginning teachers of religious education, Hughes (2000) identifies pupils' 'secularity' and negative attitudes toward religion as major challenges. He suggests that pupils absorb, from the media, the norms of the peer group and the 'cultural air that they breathe', the view that religion is not significant and (quoting the findings of empirical research) that 'to be irreligious is normal' (Kay and Francis, 1996: 144). Hughes proposes that pupils express their 'secularity' in two ways, as 'antagonism and anger toward religion' and as 'apathy about religion' (Hughes, 2000: 74). In our life-history study, and in the accounts and reflections of later cohorts of trainees, we found evidence to support Cooling's analysis. However, our data suggested three distinct, but related, categories of pupils' negativity toward and resistance to religious education:

- negative perceptions of and attitudes toward religion, religious beliefs and practices, and 'religious people';
- a view that the beliefs, values, practices and lifestyles of minority ethnic communities in the United Kingdom have 'nothing to do with them';
- a view that minority ethnic communities in the United Kingdom are 'aliens', a threat to 'British people' and not worthy of study or even respect.

Each of these categories of pupils' attitudes and views has implications for the relationship between religious education and citizenship education.

Negative perceptions of and attitude toward religion

In the life-history group, and in each of the following cohorts, there were trainees who identified negativity toward religion as a major obstacle in their attempts to achieve their aims. A quotation from one of the life-history interviews illustrates the nature of the problem:

> The classes I've seen, all the kids have said, 'I don't believe in religion', and you say, 'Why don't you believe in it?', 'It's a load of rubbish', and they can't have any reason for it, very few of them have any logical thought, no one's actually had the knowledge or experience to say, 'I don't believe it because I think this or that'. (Rebecca, philosophy graduate and agnostic, working in an all-white, working-class school)

In addition to recognizing an antagonism toward religion per se, many of the trainees recounted struggles with pupils' negative perceptions of, and attitudes toward, religious beliefs and practices and 'religious people'. For example, in 2001, Fiona (a theology graduate and committed Christian) reflected on her experience of teaching in a suburban, monocultural school no more than three miles from the centre of the city's Muslim community. She commented: 'The pupils' attitude [to Islam] was like the 18th-century adventurers discovering the Fiji cannibals. It took a great deal of explaining for the children to accept Muslims as everyday people and to differentiate between Islam and all the other "weird religions".'

While Rebecca and Fiona were reflecting on experiences of teaching in monocultural schools, some of the trainees placed in multi-ethnic schools reported similar attitudes. In 1998, Nikki (an anthropology graduate and practising Jew) noted that: 'Whereas perhaps in some circumstances "multicultural" might indicate a certain level of acceptance [of multi-faith religious education] amongst these pupils, I would argue that this acceptance does not exist. Instead, the "other" is seen as odd.'

Perceptions and attitudes very similar to those reported by the trainees have been identified in the small number of qualitative studies to have addressed English pupils' attitudes toward religion(s). Thus, in their studies of 10- and 11-year-olds' views of Judaism and Jews, Short and Carrington (1995) found these views to be riddled with misconceptions and found that some were of a kind likely to fuel hostility. These included the belief that Jews worship 'silly gods' or 'a wall', and that 'you have to put blood on the door so that angels [which kill baby boys] don't come' (Short and Carrington, 1995: 164). As the studies were carried out in schools where there was no sustained study of Judaism, the researchers concluded that their misconceptions derived from sources outside the formal education system.

In Norcross's study (1989) of children's perceptions of Muslims, the research was carried out *after* a unit of religious education work had been completed. Although the teachers had been at pains to provide an accurate and 'objective' account of Muslim beliefs and practices, the children's responses indicated that what they had actually learned was that: 'Muslims miss out on life because they take religion too seriously; they dress in rather ridiculous fashion; some of their practices are silly and they are forced to do hard things' (1989: 88). Norcross (1989) attributed this negative learning outcome to the pupils' attempts to make sense of unfamiliar ideas by drawing on their subconscious socio-cultural conditioning. As heirs of Enlightenment philosophy and values, they had viewed individual autonomy as paramount, spiritual and religious values as irrational and inconsequential, and the culture of non-western peoples as inferior. On the basis of her findings, Norcross proposed that a necessary preparation for the study of any religion is 'cultural education'; that is, an awakening in children's awareness of their own cultural conditioning, of the nature of secularism and of the relativity of all cultural expressions.

Support for this kind of preparatory work is to be found in the writings of a number of religious educators, including Bigger (2000) and Wright (1993). In outlining his view of 'religious education for citizenship', Wright argues that religious education should take as its starting point the child's own perspective and that it is 'imperative that classroom activities give children the time and space to begin to reflect on, interpret and understand the nature of the belief-system with which they are already operating'. Only when this kind of work has been undertaken will they be able to move on to contextualizing or understanding their traditions in relation to other religious and non-religious belief-systems; to broadening their understanding of self, society and the universe; and to reinterpreting and rearticulating their own traditions in the light of their developing awareness of other possibilities and claims (Wright, 1993: 94).

Writing on the relationship between citizenship and education, the Qualifications and Curriculum Authority's principal manager for these two subjects has suggested that:

> Issues and dilemmas of values in citizenship . . . are inseparable from the beliefs that underpin them. The more that ethos, responsibility, community and character are emphasised, the greater the need for education about our beliefs, about ourselves, society, life and the world – what these are, where they come from and the influence they have. (Keast, 2000)

Two points can be made in relation to the findings and recommendations above. First, although there would seem to be considerable support for the view that pupils need to be helped to recognize and examine the nature and implications of their own beliefs, values and attitudes before, as well as during, their encounter with the beliefs, values and attitudes of other people, religious educators need to reflect seriously on how realistic it is for them to take sole responsibility for this kind of work. Pupils' 'self-exploration' is, and should remain, a major concern of religious education. However, for teachers who are rarely allocated more than 45–55 minutes a week, and must devote time to the very careful presentation and examination of six religions, the view that time should be devoted to an examination of 'where our beliefs about ourselves and our society come from' poses a very real dilemma. In many cases it is simply impossible, given the time restraints within which they work.

Schools have been advised, however, that the implementation of the programmes of study for citizenship will require them to provide opportunities for pupils to consider their identities and cultural attributes, and to study the political and social systems that influence their lives. It would seem that the introduction of the new subject offers an opportunity for religious education teachers to share an aspect of their work by asking for some of the citizenship-dedicated lessons to be devoted to an examination of 'cultural conditioning', and for other subject teachers to play a role in enabling pupils to examine the nature and impact of secularism.

Second, the kinds of 'real classroom' challenges faced by our trainee religious education teachers and identified in other religious education-related studies need to be made available to and considered by those involved in managing and teaching citizenship. Without an opportunity to recognize the nature of the challenge, to anticipate problems and to consider a range of strategies for dealing with these, there is a danger that attempts to achieve some of the aims of citizenship will founder on the same rocks that religious educators have begun to circumnavigate.

Pupils' view that minority ethnic communities 'have nothing to do with them'

While many trainees identified negative attitudes toward religious beliefs, practices and people as a major obstacle, others had found some degree of willingness to explore religious beliefs and traditions that pupils identified as 'their own', but a total lack of interest in, and resistance to, studying those of 'others'.

In his examination of the 'story of religious education' from 1944 to 1994, Copley (1997: 187) notes that a 'particularly disturbing aspect of the English-Welsh Christian-folk religion identity has been that religions other than Christianity have remained socially suspect among some people. They have been perceived as foreign, another time-honoured British method for dismissing them.' Empirical research has provided evidence of this perception amongst school pupils. Thus, in their study of inter-ethnic relations in nine multi-ethnic secondary schools, Verma, Zec and Skinner (1994) found that, although some students saw multi-faith religious education as enabling them to learn about others' lifestyles:

> Others saw it as confined to teaching about 'other religions' and as failing to impart broader cultural knowledge. Still others (a minority) actually resented what they saw as religious education's over-preoccupation with pluralism. (Verma, Zec and Skinner, 1994: 78)

> As a year 8 girl interviewed in the research project put it, 'We don't learn about each other in religious education. Religious education deals only with foreigners; with foreign religions.' (Skinner, 1993: 68)

Barnard (2000) conducted a study of 15-year-old 'white' boys in her own 'secular, white majority' boys' school. She found that pupils who were generally keen to stress their *lack* of religious identity were very ready to label themselves 'Christian' when they felt a need to draw a distinction between themselves and the small number of Muslim and Sikh members in their class. According to Barnard (2000: 3), they used this 'label' as a means of explaining their reluctance to learn about 'other' religions ('I don't really want to know about Sikhs. I feel like I've got no interest or connection'), and to complain about the multi-faith syllabus ('It seems like 95% of us are Christian, yet we learn 95% about other religions.') Barnard (2000: 3) proceeded to argue as follows:

> When Christianity is taught as a discrete religion, the 'I'm not religious' attitude surfaces. It is when Christianity is taught in conjunction with other religions that the 'I am a Christian' attitude comes to the fore . . . This affiliation to Christianity is something of a knee-jerk reaction, possibly out of fear, lack of understanding or feeling threatened by other religions . . . Belonging is an aspect of religious education that requires further investigation.

In the reflections of our life-history group, and subsequent cohorts of trainees, we also found evidence of a resistance to studying 'foreign religions' (see Everington and Sikes, 2001). From the latest cohort to provide data, we gained some interesting interpretations of and proposed solutions to this 'difficulty'.

Thus, in 2000 James (a Christian, and a theology graduate teaching in a monocultural, rural, middle-class school) reported that pupils attending his lessons on Sikhism had started to ask questions:

'Do we have to work on this, Sir?' or 'Why can't we stick to looking at Christianity, Sir?' My conclusion was that this happened when the pupils were looking at something that was out of their experience or they were in completely unknown territory that they couldn't relate to, like how Sikhs worship.

James had attempted to 'deal' with this attitude in two ways. He had invited a Sikh trainee teacher to talk about her personal beliefs and to answer pupils' questions, which 'brought home to the pupils that they were looking at a living religion that affects many people's lives'. He had followed this up by stressing 'the advantages of living in a multicultural society, that life would be boring if we were all the same, and that variety is something to be celebrated'.

In the same year, Freda (a black, religious studies graduate and agnostic, teaching in a monocultural, rural, working-class school) noted that when she attempted to move from fairly successful discussions of the pupils' own beliefs and experiences to 'giving more factual information' she encountered the following reactions:

> a lot of negative attitudes toward, not only that religion, but also certain races of people. For instance, with year eight [13–14 years] I was doing, 'What is God like?' When I moved away from their own cultural context to Hindu ideas of what God is like, there were comments like, 'What do we care?' There appeared to be a total lack of interest in other religious ideas about God.

This lack of interest was attributed by Freda to the areas in which the pupils lived:

> The area in which pupils live, and the school that the pupils go to, is predominantly white. There is possibly not the opportunity to mix with people from different ethnic backgrounds, in or out of school. So, because their world is predominantly white, they probably see their future world as being predominantly white, hence they see no need to learn about other cultures, races, or religions. It seems that if the information they are to receive is not part of their 'here and now world' they will quite easily switch off.

Placed in a multi-ethnic school in a large town, Lucy (a Christian theology graduate) reflected that pupils' negative attitudes included:

the attitude that if something was not part of the pupils' own life, they should not have to study it. I think that this is a fundamental and probably universal problem: why bother to make an effort to understand other people, if you don't absolutely have to?

Lucy felt that the resolution of this issue is of such importance for successful religious education that it is worth spending time explaining to pupils why studying something that is not always an integral part of their lives can be very valuable. Unfortunately, in her own teaching she did not feel able to deal with this attitude when it arose: issues of class management took precedence over spending time with an individual pupil whose question was not directly relevant to the lesson.

In summary, the findings, interpretations, and recommendations outlined in this section suggest that:

- pupils need to feel that the learning in which they engage is 'useful' to them;
- their definition of 'useful learning' is heavily influenced by their understanding of who they are, and of the 'world' that they live in and intend to live in;
- many do not view people of 'other religions and cultures' as occupying the same 'world' as themselves and so do not see the point of learning about them. Some resent the expectation that they will see themselves as members of the same 'world'; some feel threatened by this expectation and driven to retaliate.

This summary indicates that promoters of citizenship have much to gain from an awareness and appreciation of religious education teachers' attempts to promote understanding of, and respect for, cultural diversity. In particular, it highlights the importance of paying close attention to those aspects of the new subject that have to do with 'identity'. While policy-makers are concerned to promote in pupils a recognition of and respect for pluralism, and a sense of identity as members of a plural society and the European Community, the evidence provided by religious educators suggests that many English young people have a long way to go before they will be able to view themselves in these terms.

However, this evidence would also seem to provide support for some of the strategies proposed for teaching citizenship. The emphasis on making connections between the local, national and global should make it possible for teachers to affirm pupils' 'personal' sense of identity, before helping them to view themselves in wider contexts and in other roles. Considering how the diverse national, regional, religious and ethnic identities in the United Kingdom have come about should provide some answers to the question, 'What's it got to do with me?' The emphasis on getting pupils involved in community events, and with people from social and ethnic groups different from their own, is a strategy that religious education teachers have already found helpful.

If undertaken with care and sensitivity, this kind of citizenship work can only be of benefit to teachers of religious education. Ideally, it should help pupils to appreciate the value of learning in religious education and rescue teachers from the dilemma of deciding whether to spend their limited time on teaching or on justifying their subject.

Pupils' view that minority ethnic communities are a threat to 'British people'

While many trainee teachers identified a lack of interest in and/or unwillingness to learn about 'the other', some also encountered overt racism. One example of this is provided by a member of the life-history group. In one of her interviews, Rebecca recounted her struggles to teach religious education to pupils who were open about, and assertive in their expression of, racist attitudes. She had responded to these attitudes in two ways, though in each case she found herself on the horns of a dilemma. Her first response was to acknowledge to herself that these attitudes were wrong, but to let the pupils' comments go unchallenged. She did so because she believed in, and had impressed upon the pupils, the importance of thinking for themselves and presenting their own points of view, as long as these were backed up by reasons:

> If someone has actually got a genuine reason not to want to do it [that is, study the beliefs and practices of minority ethnic communities], if someone is racist for example, then much as you can think it's wrong yourself, if they think it's right, you have a problem. You can't really turn around and say to them, 'You are wrong', because if it's an informed opinion, for example, 'I don't think people should come to

live in Britain if they're not British', sort of attitude, rather than 'I don't like you because you're black', then you can see their reasons behind it. I don't agree with those reasons at all, but they've actually got reasons, in that they say, 'They shouldn't be on our social welfare and benefits' or 'They're not fitting into our way of life.' Because they've actually thought about it, you don't have that many grounds to stand on, other than the fact that you've got the law behind you.

Rebecca's strategy for dealing with this kind of attitude was to present religions and religious people in as positive a light as possible and to argue for the benefits of a multicultural, multi-faith society. However, her pupils had countered these arguments by drawing attention to media reports of religious 'fanaticism' and the injustices and cruelty suffered by women within their faith communities. Her attempts to persuade pupils that this was not the religion at fault, but a cultural interpretation of it, appeared to backfire, as the pupils responded negatively: 'But it's their religion that's made them like that, and okay, even if I at least agree with this religion, I don't want to be associated with those people who are doing all these things.'

Rebecca felt that not only had she failed to convince her pupils of the need for respect, but that she was failing to convince herself. She had found herself struggling with a tension between her responsibility to condemn her pupils' 'reasoned' racist arguments as wrong, and her responsibility to promote respect for religious beliefs which appeared to her to be equally wrong:

You say racism is wrong, sexism is wrong, you have all the laws that say it's wrong and then the more you see religion in practice in certain countries, you think *this* is really wrong. I remember I read something about Hinduism and I thought, how can I possibly stand up there and teach kids not to be sexist or racist, when I'm trying to teach objectively that this religion is just as valid as any other religion, when really what's happening is that the laws aren't equal. I remember doing Islam in my A level (at school), we had to do a case study on one country, and the women were getting treated absolutely appallingly. And you think, if this is what their religion is doing, then why am I standing at the front teaching that this is to be respected, because I thought it's not. It really bothered me for a while, because I thought maybe I should be teaching people that it's blatantly wrong.

Rebecca's experiences highlight several issues of relevance to our consideration of the relationship between religious and citizenship education. In the first place, her reflections throw into sharp relief the tension that exists between the ideal of enabling young people to be critical thinkers, with the ability to make up their own minds about the 'truth' of the beliefs that they encounter and the legitimacy or 'rightness' of the practices that they observe, and the ideal of fostering understanding of, and respect for, 'people whose cultures and beliefs are different from one's own' and 'a positive attitude toward living in a plural society'. In religious education increasing attention is being paid to the value of critical evaluation, and there are many teachers who would wish to encourage pupils to look critically at beliefs and practices that are associated with, or drawn directly from, ethnic minority communities in the United Kingdom. However, many are dissuaded from doing so because they are aware that the *will* to be fair and to give 'the other' a chance to make a case for the legitimacy, worthiness or 'respectability' of their traditions does not exist. What does exist, in many cases, is a set of beliefs and attendant emotions that serve to block any attempt to encourage understanding, let alone respect. Gaine (1988: 86) puts it as follows:

> Teaching about cultures . . . does not necessarily do anything to racist attitudes, since many pupils simply do not want to know or are applying (perhaps unconcious) filtering mechanisms. They do not listen to the distinctions between Sikhs and Muslims . . . because they are not interested; they do not want to know because the most important thing to them is that these people . . . are responsible for all the unemployment, bad housing, and so on . . . Because many people believe that they are responsible, this has to be tackled first.

If Gaine is correct, the question posed is *how* these matters can be 'tackled first' and *where* in the school curriculum this is to be done. Lacking an understanding of how to tackle racism in the classroom, and as a visitor to the school, Rebecca was in no position to introduce anti-racist education. However, there were two members of the life-history group who came to recognize the need for this kind of work during their first years in post (in multi-ethnic schools), and possessed sufficient awareness and authority to 'do something about it'.

Claire was so dismayed at the attitudes of her pupils and their parents that she introduced into the religious education syllabus for 14- to 15-year-olds a unit of work on racism. This involved 'studying empathy and prejudice; why people are prejudiced and how we can overcome this; leading into racism, what it is, what we should do about it and a study of Martin Luther King'. Gill's concern had also grown during her first year in post and she had introduced a unit for 13- to 14-year-olds on 'Prejudice and discrimination, focusing on racism'. On reflection, however, Gill felt that 'it is pretty impossible to change these attitudes only through religious education lessons. It seems that in many cases, pupils' views are developed at home during their younger years and that these views are "ingrained".'

In their determination to 'do something' about their pupils' racist attitudes in their religious education syllabuses and lessons, Claire and Gill were following in the footsteps of the many generations of religious education teachers who have taken responsibility for Anti-Racist Education (ARE) in their schools. Studies of the history of ARE in the United Kingdom have shown that cross-curricular initiatives and compulsory courses on 'racism' have appeared and disappeared (see for example Tomlinson, 1992). However, as I have demonstrated elsewhere, 'racism' has remained a constant feature of religious education syllabuses since the 1960s (Everington, 1992), and this situation has been recognized in two empirical studies. Gaine (1988: 49–50) notes that in schools in 'white areas' the topic of 'prejudice' is more likely to be placed in religious education than in any other area of the curriculum. Skinner (1993: 67–8) notes that in multi-ethnic schools 'it is in religious education lessons that pupils are most likely to learn about others' cultures and religions as well as to discuss matters such as . . . countering prejudice'.

While both researchers recognize the value of examining prejudice and racism in religious education, both argue against a reliance on the religious education syllabus and religious education teacher to deal with these matters. Gaine (1988: 50) makes the following comment:

> One shortcoming of the placing of 'race' and 'prejudice' in the religious education slot, is simply the question of time. Very few secondary schools allow more than an hour a week for religious education in years

1–3 and most would be nearer half an hour . . . To go into any kind of factual detail would therefore require many consecutive weeks, and one look at religious education clearly indicates the demands already made upon these slots. It is likely . . . that when racism is approached in this area of the curriculum it is under heavy constraints to be brief, and, more subtly, to be centred on discussions, opinion, and thus founded upon different sorts of suppositions from 'worthwhile' activities elsewhere in the curriculum.

Thus, there would seem to be agreement amongst religious education teachers and researchers that if racism is to be combated in schools it must be addressed beyond, as well as within, religious education lessons. With the introduction of citizenship, schools will be required to provide pupils with opportunities to explore the concepts of human rights and anti-racism, and to consider particular manifestations of racism and its removal at a local and national level (Qualifications and Curriculum Authority, 2000: 5). If account is taken of the kinds of findings and recommendations outlined above, and if schools take seriously the importance of a cross-curricular approach, there is some hope that religious educators will be able to spend their time building on, rather than laying the foundations for, the kind of work that they want and need to do. Ideally, teachers like Rebecca should begin to find it easier to introduce opportunities for critical evaluation of religious beliefs and practices, without feeling that they are simply reinforcing racist attitudes.

Yet, it would be unwise to think in terms of a simple 'division of labour', with citizenship education taking responsibility for telling pupils what to think and do in relation to racism, and religious educators moving on from this. It is clear that Rebecca's dilemma, between enabling young people to be critical thinkers and encouraging an understanding of, and respect for, the plural society and cultural diversity, is a dilemma for both religious and citizenship education. In their discussion of the 'tensions in the citizenship ideal' Jones and Jones (1992) draw attention to three 'understandings of the purpose of citizenship education', which bear a strong resemblance to the three major concerns of religious education outlined at the beginning of this chapter and to the differing 'primary concerns' of our life-history trainees. Jones and Jones (1992: 19) continue to argue as follows:

The purpose of education is the individual development of the child. The purpose of education is to fit the individual for community life in the state of which he or she is a member. The purpose of education is to render the individual sensitive to societies beyond his or her own country, including the global community.

Recognizing that all of these pedagogical objectives are sincerely and justifiably held, the authors question whether they are, or can be, compatible, or whether simultaneous pursuit of these aims 'generates unbearable educational, not to mention political, tensions'. They conclude that there is no easy way of resolving the tensions or of simplifying the complexities:

> If an individual is to be a citizen in any meaningful sense, he or she must learn to understand and cope with them. The individual . . . must be taught about these complexities. The problem of identifying, clarifying and perhaps resolving the contradictions is a very practical and urgent matter for the teaching profession. (Jones and Jones, 1992: 27)

It may be that religious and citizenship educators need to work together to devise the kinds of strategies that will enable pupils *and* teachers to reconcile the demands made by their differing roles, rights and responsibilities.

Conclusion

This chapter was introduced with the question, 'What advantage can there be in bringing in citizenship when we already have religious education, and personal and social education, and there isn't even enough room on the timetable to do these things properly?' In answer to this question, I have recognized the very real commitment that religious education teachers have to working for a harmonious multicultural society and to 'empowering' young people to rise above views and attitudes that can only limit their horizons and potential. At the same time, I have urged these teachers to be realistic about what they can achieve. I have argued that there is a very significant overlap between religious and citizenship education and that, because of this, the opportunity that citizenship offers for sharing responsibilities and for finding more time for what 'really matters' should be welcomed. It has *not* been my intention to encourage religious education teachers to accept their subject's inadequate time allocation, or to hand over the most important elements of their work so that they can concentrate on teaching facts. The struggle to secure the status and time enjoyed by national curriculum subjects must continue, but while this is going on religious education teachers have much to gain from allowing others to do some of the groundwork that is needed if their efforts to promote the spiritual, moral and social development of pupils are to bear fruit.

For those with responsibility for implementing and managing citizenship education, I have attempted to outline the potential benefits of learning about and from the experiences of religious education teachers. I have drawn attention to difficulties, dilemmas and negative experiences that need to be recognized and addressed if many of the aims of citizenship are to stand any chance of being achieved. I have also drawn attention to the positive contribution that religious education can make to the development and dissemination of effective teaching strategies.

Although many of the experiences and findings referred to in this chapter are negative, the intention has been to support the vision of an education which makes a positive difference to the way in which people view and treat each other, and to counter some of the cynicism, hostility and destructive anxiety that both religious and citizenship education can provoke. Only time will tell if this faith is justified.

References

Astley, J., Francis, L. J., Burton, L. and Wilcox, C. (1997), 'Distinguishing between aims and methods in RE: a study among secondary RE teachers', *British Journal of Religious Education*, 19, 171–85.

Baumfield, V., Bowness, C., Cush, D. and Miller, J. (1994), *A Third Perspective: Religious Education in the Basic Curriculum: A Contribution* (London, AREIAC).

Barnard, S. (2000), 'An investigation into the reasons behind the poor attitudes to RE of white, secular majority, year 10 boys', MA field study, University of Warwick.

Bigger, S. (2000), 'Religious education, spirituality and anti-racism', in M. Leicester, C. Modgil and S. Modgil (eds), *Spiritual and Religious Education: Education, Culture and Values*, volume 5 (London, Falmer Press), pp. 15–25.

Cooling, T. (2000), 'Pupil learning', in A. Wright and A.-M. Brandom (eds), *Learning to Teach Religious Education in the Secondary School* (London, RoutledgeFalmer), pp. 71–87.

Copley, T. (1997), *Teaching Religion: Fifty Years of Religious Education* (Exeter, University of Exeter Press).

Department for Education and Employment and Qualifications and Curriculum Authority (1999), *Citizenship: The National Curriculum for England, Key Stages 3–4* (London, Department for Education and Employment and Qualifications and Curriculum Authority).

Everington, J. (1992), 'The role of religious education in combating racism and promoting inter-cultural harmony', unpublished M.Ed. dissertation, University of Birmingham.

Everington, J. (2000), 'Mission impossible: religious education in the 1990s', in M. Leicester, C. Modgil and S. Modgil (eds), *Spiritual and Religious Education: Education, Culture and Values* (London, Falmer Press), pp. 183–97.

Everington, J. and Sikes, P. (2001), 'I want to change the world: the beginning RE teacher, the reduction of prejudice and the pursuit of intercultural understanding and respect', in H.-G. Heimbrock, C. Th. Scheilke and P. Schreiner (eds), *Towards Religious Competence: Diversity as a Challenge for Education in Europe* (Munster, LIT Verlag), pp. 180–99.

Gaine, C. (1988), *No Problem Here: A Practical Approach to Education and 'Race' in White Schools* (London, Hutchinson).

Grimmitt, M. (1987), *Religious Education and Human Development* (Great Wakering, McCrimmon).

Jones, E. B. and Jones, N. (1992), *Education for Citizenship: Ideals and Perspectives for Cross-Curricular Study* (London, Kogan Page).

Kay, W. K. and Francis, L. J. (1996), *Drift from the Churches* (Cardiff, University of Wales Press).

Keast, J. (2000), 'Citizenship, PSHE and RE', *RE Today*, 17, 32.

Norcross, P. (1989), 'The effects of cultural conditioning on multi-faith education in the monocultural primary school', *British Journal of Religious Education*, 11, 87–91.

Qualifications and Curriculum Authority (2000), *Citizenship at*

Key Stages 3 and 4: Initial Guidance for Schools (London, Qualifications and Curriculum Authority).

Religious Education Teacher Recruitment Initiative (2000), *Report on the Religious Education Teacher Recruitment Initiative Motivation Questionnaire 1999–2000* (Abingdon, Culham College Institute).

Religious Education Teacher Recruitment Initiative (2001), *Report on the Religious Education Teacher Recruitment Initiative Motivation Questionnaire 2000–2001* (Abingdon, Culham College Institute).

Saint Gabriel's Trust (2000), *RE – Essence and Development* (Abingdon, Culham College Institute).

School Curriculum and Assessment Authority (1994), *Model Syllabuses for Religious Education: Models 1 & 2* (London, School Curriculum and Assessment Authority).

Short, G. and Carrington, B. (1995), 'Learning about Judaism: a contribution to the debate on multi-faith religious education', *British Journal of Religious Education*, 17, 157–67.

Sikes, P. and Everington, J. (2001), 'Becoming an RE teacher: a life history approach', *British Journal of Religious Education*, 24, 8–19.

Skinner, G. (1993), 'Religious education: equal but different?', in P. D. Pumfrey and G. K. Verma (eds), *The Foundation Subjects and Religious Education in Secondary Schools* (London, Falmer Press), pp. 57–72.

Tomlinson, S. (1992), 'Citizenship and minorities', in E. B. Jones and N. Jones (eds), *Education for Citizenship: Ideals and Perspectives for Cross-Curricular Study* (London, Kogan Page), pp. 35–51.

Verma, G., Zec, P. and Skinner, G. (1994), *The Ethnic Crucible: Harmony and Hostility in Multi-Ethnic Schools* (London, Falmer Press).

Wright, A. (1993), *Religious Education in the Secondary School* (London, David Fulton).

Name index

Addad, M. 22, 34
Adorno, T. W. 168, 181
Alexander, D. 40, 52
Alheit, P. 157–8
Allen, O. 95, 106
Altemeyer, B. 141, 158
Amos, A. 95, 106
Archer, S. L. 171, 183
Argyle, M. 22, 36, 98, 104
Arnold, M. 115
Astley, J. 4, 19, 35, 39–40, 42, 52,
    92, 163, 241, 257
Augst, K. 139, 158

Baacke, D. 157–8
Baal, J. van 209, 220
Bacal, A. 166, 182
Bainbridge, R. M. 113, 125
Balding, J. 70, 91
Ballard, R. 164, 182–3
Bar-Lev, M. 9, 12, 185, 187,
    190–1, 195, 202
Barbour, I. G. 40, 52–3
Barker, D. 44, 52
Barker, E. 40, 52
Barker, M. 70, 93
Barnard, S. 248, 257
Barr, J. 49, 52
Barrett, P. 27, 34, 97, 105
Barth, F. 166, 182
Baumfield, V. 239, 257
Beaudoin, T. 144–7, 158
Beck, U. 151, 158, 163
Beek, J. van 209, 220
Beit-Hallahmi, B. 98, 104
Belavich, T. G. 143, 163
Bem, S. L. 74–5, 91–2
Ben Ari, R. 202
Ben-Shlomo, Y. 89, 91
Bentler, P. M. 32, 36

Berger, P. L. 151, 158, 223, 234
Bibby, R. W. 71–2, 74, 91
Biehl, P. 157, 161
Bigger, S. 246, 257
Birkedal, E. 10, 222, 224, 234
Bladé, J. 97, 104
Blasberg-Kuhnke, M. 157–8
Bolger, J. 22, 35
Bonaiuto, P. 97, 105
Bourdieu, P. 157–8, 160
Bowness, C. 239, 257
Brannen, J. 97, 106
Breeze, E. 96, 106
Bremer, H. 150, 163
Brentano, F. C. 168, 182
Bross, L. S. 32, 37
Brown, A. S. 57–8, 68
Brown, C. G. 90–1
Brown, L. B. 19, 22, 34–5, 75, 92
Brown, M. 165, 182
Bruner, J. 209, 220
Burton, L. 20–1, 31, 35, 241, 257
Butter, E. M. 143, 163
Byrd, R. C. 18, 34

Cairns, J. M. 33–4
Calvin, J. 17
Camps, A. 210, 220
Canals, J. 97, 104
Carr, D. 169, 182
Carrington, B. 245, 259
Chamberlain, K. 32, 38
Charlton, A. 95, 105
Chater, M. F. T. 115, 125
Coe, G. A. 19, 34
Cole, B. 143, 163
Coleman, S. 32, 34
Cooling, M. 112
Cooling, T. 112, 125, 243, 258
Copley, T. 247, 258

Subject index